Arthur Fairbanks

The First Philosophers of Greece

An edition and translation of the remaining fragments of the pre-Sokratic

philosophers, together with a translation of the more important accounts of their

opinions contained in the early epitomes of their works

Arthur Fairbanks

The First Philosophers of Greece
An edition and translation of the remaining fragments of the pre-Sokratic philosophers,
together with a translation of the more important accounts of their opinions contained in the
early epitomes of their works

ISBN/EAN: 9783337075941

Printed in Europe, USA, Canada, Australia, Japan

Cover: Foto ©Thomas Meinert / pixelio.de

More available books at **www.hansebooks.com**

THE

FIRST PHILOSOPHERS
OF GREECE

AN EDITION AND TRANSLATION OF THE
REMAINING FRAGMENTS OF THE PRE-SOKRATIC
PHILOSOPHERS, TOGETHER WITH A TRANSLATION OF THE
MORE IMPORTANT ACCOUNTS OF THEIR OPINIONS
CONTAINED IN THE EARLY EPITOMES
OF THEIR WORKS

BY

ARTHUR FAIRBANKS

NEW YORK
CHARLES SCRIBNER'S SONS
1898

PREFACE

THE Hegelian School, and in particular Zeller, have shown us the place of the earlier thinkers in the history of Greek thought, and the importance of a knowledge of their work for all who wish to understand Plato and Aristotle. Since Zeller's monumental work, several writers (e.g. Benn, *Greek Philosophers*, vol. i. London 1883 ; Tannery, *Science hellène*, Paris 1887 ; Burnet, *Early Greek Philosophy*, London 1892) have traced for us the history of this development, but the student who desires to go behind these accounts and examine the evidence for himself still finds the material difficult of access. This material consists of numerous short fragments preserved by later writers, and of accounts of the opinions of these thinkers given mainly by Aristotle and by the Greek doxographists (i.e. students of early thought who made epitomes of the opinions of the masters). The Greek text of the doxographists is now accessible to students in the admirable critical edition of H. Diels (Berlin 1879). The Greek text of the fragments has been published in numerous short monographs, most of which are not readily accessible to the student to-day; it is contained with a vast deal of other matter in Mullach's *Fragmenta Graecorum Philosophorum* (Paris 1883–1888, vol. i.–iii.), but the text is in many places so carelessly constructed that it does not serve the purposes of the scholar.

In the present work it has been my plan to prepare for the student a Greek text of the fragments of these early philosophers which shall represent as accurately as possible the results of recent scholarship, and to add such critical notes as may be necessary to enable the scholar to see on what basis the text rests. From this text I have prepared a translation of the fragments into English, and along with this a translation of the important passages bearing on these early thinkers in Plato and Aristotle, and in the Greek doxographists as collected by Diels, in order that the student of early Greek thought might have before him in compact form practically all the materials on which the history of this thought is to be based. It has been difficult, especially in the case of Herakleitos and the Pythagoreans, to draw the line between material to be inserted, and that to be omitted; but, in order to keep the volume within moderate limits, my principle has been to insert only the passages from Plato and Aristotle and from the doxographists.

The Greek text of Herakleitos is based on the edition of Bywater; that of Xenophanes on the edition of the Greek lyric poets by Hiller-Bergk; that of Parmenides on the edition of Karsten; and that of Empedokles on the edition of Stein. I have not hesitated, however, to differ from these authorities in minor details, indicating in the notes the basis for the text which I have given.

For a brief discussion of the relative value of the sources of these fragments the student is referred to the Appendix.

My thanks are due to several friends for their kind assistance, in particular to Professor C. L. Brownson and Professor G. D. Lord, who have read much of the book in proof, and have given me many valuable suggestions. Nor can I pass over without mention the debt which all workers in this field owe to Hermann Diels. It is my great regret that his edition of Parmenides' *Lehrgedicht* failed to reach me until most of the present work was already printed. Nevertheless there is scarcely a page of the whole book which is not based on the foundation which he has laid.

ARTHUR FAIRBANKS.

YALE UNIVERSITY:
  November 1897.

CONTENTS

Dox. = Diels, *Doxographi Graeci*, Berlin 1879.

Aet. = *Aetii de placitis reliquiae.*

Hipp. *Phil.* = *Hippolyti philosophumena.*

Epi. = *Epiphanii varia excerpta.*

Herm. = *Hermiae irrisio gentilium philosophorum.*

} Included in
  Diels, *Dox.*

Simp. *Phys.* = *Simplicii in Aristotelis physicorum libros quattuor priores* edidit H. Diels, Berlin 1882.

Simp. *Cael.* = Simplicius, *Commentary on Aristotle's De caelo.*

For other abbreviations, see list of authors in the Index of sources.

THE

FIRST PHILOSOPHERS OF GREECE

— ✦ —

I.

THALES.

ACCORDING to Aristotle the founder of the Ionic physical philosophy, and therefore the founder of Greek philosophy, was Thales of Miletos. According to Diogenes Laertios, Thales was born in the first year of the thirty-fifth Olympiad (640 B.C.), and his death occurred in the fifty-eighth Olympiad (548–545 B.C.). He attained note as a scientific thinker and was regarded as the founder of Greek philosophy because he discarded mythical explanations of things, and asserted that a physical element, water, was the first principle of all things. There are various stories of his travels, and in connection with accounts of his travels in Egypt he is credited with introducing into Greece the knowledge of geometry. Tradition also claims that he was a statesman, and as a practical thinker he is classed as one of the seven wise men. A work entitled ' Nautical Astronomy ' was ascribed to him, but it was recognised as spurious even in antiquity.

Literature : F. Decker, *De Thalete Milesio*, Diss. Halle, 1865 ; Krische, *Forsch. auf d. Gebiet d. alt. Phil.* i. pp. 34–42 ; V. also *Acta Phil.* iv. Lips. 1875, pp. 328–330 ; *Revue Philos.* Mar. 1880 ; *Archiv f. d. Geschichte d. Phil.* ii. 165, 515.

(a) Passages relating to Thales in Plato and in Aristotle.

Plato, *de Legg*. x. 899 B. And as for all the stars and the moon and the years and the months and all the seasons, can we hold any other opinion about them than this same one—that inasmuch as soul or souls appear to be the cause of all these things, and good souls the cause of every excellence, we are to call them gods, whether they order the whole heavens as living beings in bodies, or whether they accomplish this in some other form and manner ? Is there any one who acknowledges this, and yet holds that all things are not full of gods ?

Arist. *Met.* i. 3 ; 983 b 6. Most of the early students of philosophy thought that first principles in the form of matter, and only these, are the sources of all things ; for that of which all things consist, the antecedent from which they have sprung, and into which they are finally resolved (in so far as being underlies them and is changed with their changes), this they say is the element and first principle of things. 983 b 18. As to the quantity and form of this first principle, there is a difference of opinion ; but Thales, the founder of this sort of philosophy, says that it is water (accordingly he declares that the earth rests on water), getting the idea, I suppose, because he saw that the nourishment of all beings is moist, and that warmth itself is generated from moisture and persists in it (for that from which all things spring is the first principle of them) ; and getting the idea also from the fact that the germs of all beings are of a moist nature, while water is the first principle of the nature of what is moist. And there are some who think that the ancients, and they who lived long before the present generation, and the first students of the gods, had a similar idea in regard to nature ; for in their poems Okeanos and Tethys were

the parents of generation, and that by which the gods
swore was water,—the poets themselves called it Styx;
for that which is most ancient is most highly esteemed,
and that which is most highly esteemed is an object to
swear by.   Whether there is any such ancient and early
opinion concerning nature would be an obscure question; but Thales is said to have expressed this opinion
in regard to the first cause.

Arist. *de Coelo* ii. 13; 294 a 28.   Some say that
the earth rests on water.   We have ascertained that the
oldest statement of this character is the one accredited
to Thales the Milesian, to the effect that it rests on water,
floating like a piece of wood or something else of that sort.[1]

Arist. *de Anima* i. 2;   405 a 19.   And Thales,
according to what is related of him, seems to have
regarded the soul as something endowed with the
power of motion, if indeed he said that the loadstone
has a soul because it moves iron.   i. 5; 411 a 7.   Some
say that soul is diffused throughout the whole universe; and it may have been this which led Thales to
think that all things are full of gods.

> Simpl. in Arist. *de Anima* 8 r 32, 16.[2]—Thales posits
> water as the element, but it is the element of
> bodies, and he thinks that the soul is not a body
> at all.   31, 21 D.—And in speaking thus of Thales
> he adds with a degree of reproach that he assigned
> a soul to the magnetic stone as the power which
> moves the iron, that he might prove soul to be a
> moving power in it; but he did not assert that this
> soul was water, although water had been designated
> as the element, since he said that water is the ele-
> ment of substances, but he supposed soul to be un-
> substantial form.   20 r 73, 22.   For Thales, also,
> I suppose, thought all things to be full of gods, the
> gods being blended with them; and this is strange.

---

[1] Cf. Herm. *I. G. P.* 10 (*Dox.* 653).

[2] In references to Simpl. in Arist. *de Anima* and *Physica*, the first
numbers give folio and line, the second, page (and line) in the edition
published by the Berlin Academy.

(b) Passages relating to Thales in the Doxographists.

(Theophrastos, *Dox.* 475) Simpl. *Phys.* 6 r; 23, 21. Of those who say that the first principle [ἀρχή] is one and movable, to whom Aristotle applies the distinctive name of physicists, some say that it is limited; as, for instance, Thales of Miletos, son of Examyes, and Hippo who seems also to have lost belief in the gods. These say that the first principle is water, and they are led to this result by things that appear to sense; for warmth lives in moisture and dead things wither up and all germs are moist and all nutriment is moist. Now it is natural that things should be nourished by that from which each has come; and water is the first principle of moist nature . . .; accordingly they assume that water is the first principle of all things, and they assert that the earth rests on water. Thales is the first to have set on foot the investigation of nature by the Greeks; although so many others preceded him, in Theophrastos's opinion he so far surpassed them as to cause them to be forgotten. It is said that he left nothing in writing except a book entitled 'Nautical Astronomy.'

Hipp. i.; *Dox.* 555. It is said that Thales of Miletos, one of the seven wise men, was the first to undertake the study of physical philosophy. He said that the beginning (the first principle) and the end of all things is water. All things acquire firmness as this solidifies, and again as it is melted their existence is threatened; to this are due earthquakes and whirlwinds and movements of the stars. And all things are movable and in a fluid state, the character of the compound being determined by the nature of the principle from which it springs. This principle is god, and it has neither beginning nor end.

Thales was the first of the Greeks to devote himself to the study and investigation of the stars, and was the originator of this branch of science ; on one occasion he was looking up at the heavens, and was just saying he was intent on studying what was overhead, when he fell into a well ; whereupon a maidservant named Thratta laughed at him and said : In his zeal for things in the sky he does not see what is at his feet.[1] And he lived in the time of Kroesos.

Plut. *Strom.* 1 ; *Dox.* 579.[2] He says that Thales was the earliest thinker to regard water as the first principle of all things. For from this all things come, and to it they all return.

Act. *Plac.* i. 2 ; *Dox.* 275. Thales of Miletos regards the first principle and the elements as the same thing. But there is a very great difference between them, for elements are composite, but we claim that first principles are neither composite nor the result of processes. So we call earth, water, air, fire, elements ; and we call them first principles for the reason that there is nothing antecedent to them from which they are sprung, since this would not be a first principle, but rather that from which it is derived. Now there is something anterior to earth and water from which they are derived, namely the matter that is formless and invisible, and the form which we call entelechy, and privation. So Thales was in error when he called water an element and a first principle. i. 3 ; 276. Thales the Milesian declared that the first principle of things is water. [This man seems to have been the first philosopher, and the Ionic school derived its name from him ; for there were very many successive leaders in philosophy. And Thales was a student of philosophy in

[1] Cf. Plato, *Theaet.* 174 a ; Diog. Laer. i. 34.
[2] Epiphan. iii. 1 ; *Dox.* 589 ; Herm. *I. G. P.* 10 ; *Dox.* 653.

Egypt, but he came to Miletos in his old age.] For he
says that all things come from water and all are resolved
into water. The first basis for this conclusion is the
fact that the seed of all animals is their first principle
and it is moist; thus it is natural to conclude that all
things come from water as their first principle. Secondly,
the fact that all plants are nourished by moisture and
bear fruit, and unless they get moisture they wither
away. Thirdly, the fact that the very fire of the sun
and the stars is fed by the exhalations from the waters,
and so is the universe itself. 7; 301. Thales said that
the mind in the universe is god, and the all is endowed
with soul and is full of spirits; and its divine moving
power pervades the elementary water. 8; 307. Thales
et al. say that spirits are psychical beings; and that
heroes are souls separated from bodies, good heroes are
good souls, bad heroes are bad souls. 8; 307. The
followers of Thales et al. assert that matter is turned
about, varying, changing, and in a fluid state, the
whole in every part of the whole. 12; 310. Thales
and his successors declared that the first cause is immovable. 16; 314. The followers of Thales and Pythagoras hold that bodies can receive impressions and can
be divided even to infinity; and so can all figures, lines,
surfaces, solids, matter, place, and time. 18; 315. The
physicists, followers of Thales, all recognise that the
void is really a void. 21; 321. Thales: Necessity is
most powerful, for it controls everything.

Aet. ii. 1; *Dox.* 327. Thales and his successors hold
that the universe is one. 12; 340. Thales et al. hold
that the sphere of the entire heaven is divided into five
circles which they call zones; and of these the first is
called the arctic zone, and is always visible, the next is
the summer solstice, the next is the equinoctial, the next
the winter solstice, and the next the antarctic, which is
invisible. And the ecliptic in the three middle ones is

called the zodiac and is projected to touch the three middle ones. All these are cut by the meridian at a right angle from the north to the opposite quarter. 13; 341. The stars consist of earth, but are on fire. 20; 349. The sun consists of earth. 24; 353. The eclipses of the sun take place when the moon passes across it in direct line, since the moon is earthy in character; and it seems to the eye to be laid on the disk of the sun. 28; 358. The moon is lighted from the sun. 29; 360. Thales et al. agree with the mathematicians that the monthly phases of the moon show that it travels along with the sun and is lighted by it, and eclipses show that it comes into the shadow of the earth, the earth coming between the two heavenly bodies and blocking the light of the moon.

Aet. iii. 9–10; 376. The earth is one and spherical in form. 11; 377. It is in the midst of the universe. 15; 379. Thales and Demokritos find in water the cause of earthquakes.

Aet. iv. 1; 384. Thales thinks that the Etesian winds blowing against Egypt raise the mass of the Nile, because its outflow is beaten back by the swelling of the sea which lies over against its mouth. 2; 386. Thales was the first to declare that the soul is by nature always moving or self-moving.

Aet. v. 26; 438. Plants are living animals; this is evident from the fact that they wave their branches and keep them extended, and they yield to attack and relax them freely again, so that weights also draw them down.

(Philodemos) Cic. de Nat. Deor. i. 10; Dox. 531. For Thales of Miletos, who first studied these matters, said that water is the first principle of things, while god is the mind which formed all things from water. If gods exist without sense and mind, why should god be connected with water, if mind itself can exist without a body?

II.

ANAXIMANDROS.

ANAXIMANDROS of Miletos was a companion or pupil of Thales. According to Apollodoros he was born in the second or third year of the forty-second Olympiad (611–610 B.C.). Of his life little is known; Zeller infers from the statement of Aelian (*V. H.* iii. 17) to the effect that he led the Milesian colony into Apollonia, that he was a man of influence in Miletos. He was a student of geography and astronomy; and various inventions, such as the sundial, are attributed to him. His book, which was referred to as the first philosophical treatise in Greece, may not have received the title '$\pi\epsilon\rho\grave{\iota}$ $\phi\acute{\upsilon}\sigma\epsilon\omega\varsigma$' until after his death. It soon became rare, and Simplicius does not seem to have had access to it.

> Literature : Schleiermacher, *Abh. d. Berl. Akad.* 1815 ; *Op. Phil.* ii. 171; Krische, *Forschungen*, pp. 42– 52 ; Teichmüller, *Studien*, pp. 1–70, 545–588; Büsgen, *Das ἄπειρον Anax.* Wiesbaden 1867; Lütze, *Das ἄπειρον Anax.* Leipz. 1878 ; J. Neu- hauser, *De Anax. Miles.* Bonn 1879, and in more complete form, Bonn 1883 ; Tannery, *Rev. Phil.* v. (1882) ; Natorp, *Phil. Monatshefte*, 1884 ; Tannery, *Archiv f. d. Gesch. d. Philos.* viii. 448 ff. ; Diels, *ibid.* x. (1897) 228 ff.

(a) FRAGMENTS OF ANAXIMANDROS.

1. Arist. *Phys.* iii. 4; 203 b 13 ff. The words $\grave{\alpha}\theta\acute{\alpha}\nu\alpha\tau\sigma\nu$ $\gamma\grave{\alpha}\rho$ $\kappa\alpha\grave{\iota}$ $\grave{\alpha}\nu\acute{\omega}\lambda\epsilon\theta\rho\sigma\nu$ and by some the words $\pi\epsilon\rho\iota\acute{\epsilon}\chi\epsilon\iota\nu$

ἄπαντα καὶ πάντα κυβερνᾶν are thought to come from Anaximandros.

2. In Simpl. *Phys.* 6 r (24, 19); *Dox.* 476, it is generally agreed that the following phrase is from Anaximandros: κατὰ τὸ χρεών· διδόναι γὰρ αὐτὰ ἀλλήλοις τίσιν καὶ δίκην τῆς ἀδικίας.[1]

Translation.—1. 'Immortal and indestructible,' 'surrounds all and directs all.' 2. '(To that they return when they are destroyed) of necessity; for he says that they suffer punishment and give satisfaction to one another for injustice.'

(b) Passages relating to Anaximandros in Aristotle.

Arist. *Phys.* i. 4; 187 a 12. For some who hold that the real, the underlying substance, is a unity, either one of the three [elements] or something else that is denser than fire and more rarefied than air, teach that other things are generated by condensation and rarefaction. . . . 20. And others believe that existing opposites are separated from the unity, as Anaximandros says, and those also who say that unity and multiplicity exist, as Empedokles and Anaxagoras; for these separate other things from the mixture [μῖγμα].[2]

Phys. iii. 4; 203 b 7. There is no beginning of the infinite, for in that case it would have an end. But it is without beginning and indestructible, as being a sort of first principle; for it is necessary that whatever comes into existence should have an end, and there is a conclusion of all destruction. Wherefore as we say, there is no first principle of this [*i.e.* the infinite], but it itself

---

[1] The fragment is discussed at length by Ziegler, *Archiv f. d. Gesch. d. Philos.* i. (1883) p. 16 ff.

[2] Cf. Theophrastos (*Dox.* 478) under Anaxagoras, *infra*.

seems to be the first principle of all other things and to
surround all and to direct all, as they say who think that
there are no other causes besides the infinite (such as
mind, or friendship), but that it itself is divine; for it
is immortal and indestructible, as Anaximandros and
most of the physicists say.

> Simpl. *Phys.* 32 r; 150, 20.   There is another
> method, according to which they do not attribute
> change to matter itself, nor do they suppose that
> generation takes place by a transformation of the
> underlying substance, but by separation; for the
> opposites existing in the substance which is infinite
> matter are separated, according to Anaximandros,
> who was the earliest thinker to call the underlying
> substance the first principle.   And the opposites
> are heat and cold, dry and moist, and the rest.

Phys. iii. 5 ; 204 b 22.   But it is not possible that
infinite matter is one and simple ; either, as some say,
that it is something different from the elements, from
which they are generated, or that it is absolutely one.
For there are some who make the infinite of this
character, but they do not consider it to be air or water,
in order that other things may not be blotted out by
the infinite ; for these are mutually antagonistic to one
another, inasmuch as air is cold, water is moist, and fire
hot ; if one of these were infinite, the rest would be at
once blotted out ; but now they say that the infinite is
something different from these things, namely, that from
which they come.

Phys. iii. 8 ; 208 a 8.   In order that generation
may actually occur, it is not necessary to prove that the
infinite should actually be matter that sense can perceive ; for it is possible that destruction of one thing is
generation of another, provided the all is limited.

De Coelo iii. 5 ; 303 b 11.   For some say that there
is only one underlying substance ; and of these some

say that it is water, some that it is air, some that it is
fire, and some that it is more rarefied than water and
denser than air ; and these last say that being infinite
it surrounds all the heavens.

Meteor. 2 ; 355 a 21. It is natural that this
very thing should be unintelligible to those who say
that at first when the earth was moist and the universe
including the earth was warmed by the sun, then air was
formed and the whole heavens were dried, and this produced the winds and made the heavens revolve.[1]

Metaph. xii. 2 ; 1069 b 18. So not only is it very
properly admitted that all things are generated from
not-being, but also that they all come from being :—
potentially from being, actually from not-being ; and this
is the unity of Anaxagoras (for this is better than to say
that all things exist together [ὁμοῦ πάντα]), and it is the
mixture [μῖγμα] of Empedokles and Anaximandros.

> Plut. *Symp.* viii. 730 E. Wherefore they (the Syrians)
> reverence the fish as of the same origin and the
> same family as man, holding a more reasonable
> philosophy than that of Anaximandros ; for he
> declares, not that fishes and men were generated
> at the same time, but that at first men were gene-
> rated in the form of fishes, and that growing up as
> sharks do till they were able to help themselves,
> they then came forth on the dry ground.

(c) Passages relating to Anaximandros in the Doxographists.

(Theophrastos, *Dox.* 477) Simpl. *Phys.* 6 r ; 24, 26.
Among those who say that the first principle is one
and movable and infinite, is Anaximandros of Miletos,
son of Praxiades, pupil and successor of Thales. He
said that the first principle and element of all things
is infinite, and he was the first to apply this word to

---

[1] Cf. Theophrastos, *Dox.* 494, *infra*, p. 12.

the first principle ; and he says that it is neither water
nor any other one of the things called elements, but
the infinite is something of a different nature, from
which came all the heavens and the worlds in them ;
and from what source things arise, to that they
return of necessity when they are destroyed ; for he
says that they suffer punishment and give satisfaction [1]
to one another for injustice according to the order of
time, putting it in rather poetical language.   Evidently when he sees the four elements changing into
one another, he does not deem it right to make any one
of these the underlying substance, but something else
besides them.   And he does not think that things come
into being by change in the nature of the element,
but by the separation of the opposites which the eternal
motion causes.   On this account Aristotle compares him
with Anaxagoras.

Simpl. *Phys.* 6 v; 27, 23 ; *Dox.* 478.   The translation is given under Anaxagoras, *infra*.

Alex. in *Meteor.* 91 r (vol. i. 268 Id.), *Dox.* 494.   Some
of the physicists say that the sea is what is left of
the first moisture ; [2] for when the region about the earth
was moist, the upper part of the moisture was evaporated by the sun, and from it came the winds and the
revolutions of the sun and moon, since these made their
revolutions by reason of the vapours and exhalations,
and revolved in those regions where they found an
abundance of them.   What is left of this moisture in
the hollow places is the sea ; so it diminishes in
quantity, being evaporated gradually by the sun, and
finally it will be completely dried up.   Theophrastos
says that Anaximandros and Diogenes were of this
opinion.

[1] *Archiv f. d. Geschichte d. Phil.* i. p. 16 sqq.
[2] Aet. iii. 16 ; *Dox.* 381.

Hipp. *Phil.* 6; *Dox.* 559. Anaximandros was a pupil of Thales. He was a Milesian, són of Praxiades. He said that the first principle of things is of the nature of the infinite, and from this the heavens and the worlds in them arise. And this (first principle) is eternal and does not grow old, and it surrounds all the worlds. He says of time that in it generation and being and destruction are determined. He said that the first principle and the element of beings is the infinite, a word which he was the earliest to apply to the first principle. Besides this, motion is eternal, and as a result of it the heavens arise. The earth is a heavenly body, controlled by no other power, and keeping its position because it is the same distance from all things; the form of it is curved, cylindrical like a stone column;[1] it has two faces, one of these is the ground beneath our feet, and the other is opposite to it. The stars are a circle[2] of fire, separated from the fire about the world, and surrounded by air. There are certain breathing-holes like the holes of a flute through which we see the stars; so that when the holes are stopped up, there are eclipses. The moon is sometimes full and sometimes in other phases as these holes are stopped up or open. The circle of the sun is twenty-seven times that of the moon, and the sun is higher than the moon, but the circles of the fixed stars are lower.[3] Animals come into being through vapours raised by the sun. Man, however, came into being from another animal, namely the fish, for at first he was like a fish. Winds are due to a separation of the lightest vapours and the motion of the masses of these vapours; and moisture comes from

---

[1] Aet. iii. 10; *Dox.* 376. Cf. Plut. *Strom.* 2; *Dox.* 579.

[2] κύκλος, the circle or wheel in which the stars are set, and in which they revolve. The circle of the moon is farther from the earth, and last comes the circle of the sun.

[3] Cf. Aet. ii. 15-25, *infra.*

the vapour raised by the sun [1] from them; [2] and
lightning occurs when a wind falls upon clouds and
separates them.   Anaximandros was born in the third
year of the forty-second Olympiad.

Plut. *Strom.* 2 ; *Dox.* 579.   Anaximandros, the companion of Thales, says that the infinite is the sole cause
of all generation and destruction, and from it the
heavens were separated, and similarly all the worlds,
which are infinite in number.   And he declared that
destruction and, far earlier, generation have taken
place since an indefinite time, since all things are in-
volved in a cycle.   He says that the earth is a cylinder
in form, and that its depth is one-third of its breadth.
And he says that at the beginning of this world
something [τι Diels] productive of heat and cold from
the eternal being was separated therefrom, and a sort of
sphere of this flame surrounded the air about the earth,
as bark surrounds a tree ; then this sphere was broken
into parts and defined into distinct circles, and thus
arose the sun and the moon and the stars.   Farther he
says that at the beginning man was generated from all
sorts of animals, since all the rest can quickly get food
for themselves, but man alone requires careful feeding
for a long time ; such a being at the beginning could
not have preserved his existence.   Such is the teaching
of Anaximandros.

Herm. *I. G. P.* 10 ; *Dox.* 653.   His compatriot Anaximandros says that the first principle is older than
water and is eternal motion ; in this all things come
into being, and all things perish.

Aet. *Plac.* i. 3 ; *Dox.* 277.   Anaximandros of Miletos,
son of Praxiades, says that the first principle of things
is the infinite ; for from this all things come, and all

---

[1] Aet. iii. 6 ; *Dox.* 374.   [2] Cf. Aet. iii. 3 ; *Dox.* 367.

things perish and return to this.[1] Accordingly, an
infinite number of worlds have been generated and
have perished again and returned to their source. So
he calls it infinite, in order that the generation which
takes place may not lessen it. But he fails to say what
the infinite is, whether it is air or water or earth or
some other thing. He fails to show what matter is,
and simply calls it the active cause. For the infinite is
nothing else but matter; and matter cannot be energy,
unless an active agent is its substance. 7; 302. Anaximandros declared that the infinite heavens are gods.

Aet. ii. 1; Dox. 327. Anaximandros (et al.):
Infinite worlds exist in the infinite in every cycle;
Dox. 329, and these worlds are equally distant from
each other. 4; 331. The world is perishable. 11;
340. Anaximandros: The heavens arise from a
mixture of heat and cold. 13; 342. The stars are
wheel-shaped masses of air, full of fire, breathing
out flames from pores in different parts. 15; 345.
Anaximandros et al.: The sun has the highest position of all, the moon is next in order, and beneath it
are the fixed stars and the planets. 16; 345. The
stars are carried on by the circles and the spheres in
which each one moves. 20; 348. The circle of the sun
is twenty-eight times as large as the earth, like a chariot
wheel, having a hollow centre and this full of fire,
shining in every part, and sending out fire through a
narrow opening like the air from a flute. 21; 351.
The sun is equal in size to the earth, but the circle from
which it sends forth its exhalations, and by which it is
borne through the heavens, is twenty-seven times as
large as the earth. 24; 354. An eclipse takes place
when the outlet for the fiery exhalations is closed. 25;
355. The circle of the moon is nineteen times as large

[1] Epiphan. iii. 2; Dox. 589.

as the earth, and like the circle of the sun is full of fire ;
and eclipses are due to the revolutions of the wheel ; for
it is like a chariot wheel, hollow inside, and the centre
of it is full of fire, but there is only one exit for the fire.
28 ; 358.   The moon shines by its own light.   29 ; 359.
The moon is eclipsed when the hole in the wheel is
stopped.

Aet. iii. 3 ; *Dox.* 367. Anaximandros said that
lightning is due to wind ; for when it is surrounded and
pressed together by a thick cloud and so driven out
by reason of its lightness and rarefaction, then the breaking makes a noise, while the separation makes a rift of
brightness in the darkness of the cloud.

Aet. iv. 3 ; *Dox.* 387.   Anaximandros et al. : The
soul is like air in its nature.

Aet. v. 19 ; *Dox.* 430. Anaximandros said that the
first animals were generated in the moisture, and were
covered with a prickly skin ; and as they grew older,
they became drier, and after the skin broke off from
them, they lived for a little while.

Cic. *de Nat. Deor.* i. 10 ; *Dox.* 531.   It was the
opinion of Anaximandros that gods have a beginning,
at long intervals rising and setting, and that they are
the innumerable worlds.   But who of us can think of
god except as immortal ?

III.

ANAXIMENES.

ANAXIMENES of Miletos, son of Eurystratos, was the pupil or companion of Anaximandros. According to Apollodoros, quoted by Diogenes, he was born in the sixty-third Olympiad (528–524 B.C.). Diels[1] has, however, made it seem probable that this date refers to his prime of life, rather than to his birth. Of his life nothing is known.

> Literature: Krische, *Forschungen*, i. 52–57; Teichmüller, *Studien*, 71–104; *Revue Phil.* 1883, p. 6 ff.; *Archiv f. d. Geschichte d. Phil.* i. pp. 315 ff. and pp. 582 ff.

(a) FRAGMENT ACCREDITED TO ANAXIMENES.

Collection des anciens alchimistes grecs, Livre i., Paris 1887, p. 83, ll. 7–10, Olympiodoros. μίαν δὲ κινουμένην ἄπειρον ἀρχὴν πάντων τῶν ὄντων ἐδόξαζεν Ἀναξιμένης τὸν ἀέρα. λέγει γὰρ οὕτως· ἐγγύς ἐστιν ὁ ἀὴρ τοῦ ἀσωμάτου· καὶ ὅτι κατ' ἔκροιαν τούτου γινόμεθα, ἀνάγκη αὐτὸν καὶ ἄπειρον εἶναι καὶ πλούσιον διὰ τὸ μηδέποτε ἐκλείπειν.

Translation—Anaximenes arrived at the conclusion that air is the one, movable, infinite, first principle of all things. For he speaks as follows: Air is the nearest to an immaterial thing; for since we are generated in

[1] *Rhein. Mus.* xxxi. 27.

the flow of air, it is necessary that it should be infinite and abundant, because it is never exhausted.[1]

(*b*) PASSAGES RELATING TO ANAXIMENES IN ARISTOTLE, &c.

Arist. *Meteor.* ii. 1; 354 a 28.   Most of the earlier students of the heavenly bodies believed that the sun did not go underneath the earth, but rather around the earth and this region, and that it disappeared from view and produced night, because the earth was so high toward the north.

> Simpl. *de Coelo* 273 b 45; Schol. Arist. 514 a 33.   He regarded the first principle as unlimited, but not as undefined, for he called it air, thinking that air had a sufficient adaptability to change.
>
> Simpl. *Phys.* 32 r 149, 32.   Of this one writer alone, Theophrastos, in his account of the Physicists, uses the words μάνωσις and πύκνωσις of texture.   The rest, of course, spoke of μανότης and πυκνότης.
>
> Simpl. *Phys.* 257v.   Some say that the universe always existed, not that it has always been the same, but rather that it successively changes its character in certain periods of time; as, for instance, Anaximenes and Herakleitos and Diogenes.

Arist. *de Coelo* ii. 13; 294 b 13.   Anaximenes and Anaxagoras and Demokritos say that the breadth of the earth is the reason why it remains where it is.

Arist. *Meteor.* ii. 7; 365 (a 17), b 6.   Anaximenes says that the earth was wet, and when it dried it broke apart, and that earthquakes are due to the breaking and falling of hills; accordingly earthquakes occur in droughts, and in rainy seasons also; they occur in drought, as has been said, because the earth dries and breaks apart, and it also crumbles when it is wet through with waters.

Arist. *Metaph.* i. 3; 984 a 5.   Anaximenes regarded air as the first principle.

---

[1] For a discussion of the above fragment, v. *Archiv f. d. Geschichte d. Phil.* i. 315.

Plut. *Prim. Frig.* vii. 3, p. 947. According to Anaximenes, the early philosopher, we should not neglect either cold or heat in *being* but should regard them as common experiences of matter which are incident to its changes. He says that the compressed and the condensed state of matter is cold, while the rarefied and relaxed (a word he himself uses) state of it is heat. Whence he says it is not strange that men breathe hot and cold out of the mouth; for the breath is cooled as it is compressed and condensed by the lips, but when the mouth is relaxed, it comes out warm by reason of its rarefaction.

(c) Passages relating to Anaximenes in the Doxographists.

Theophrastos; Simpl. *Phys.* 6r 24, 26; *Dox.* 476. Anaximenes of Miletos, son of Eurystratos, a companion of Anaximandros, agrees with him that the essential nature of things is one and infinite, but he regards it as not indeterminate but rather determinate, and calls it air; the air differs in rarity and in density as the nature of things is different; when very attenuated it becomes fire, when more condensed wind, and then cloud, and when still more condensed water and earth and stone, and all other things are composed of these; and he regards motion as eternal, and by this changes are produced.[1]

Hipp. *Philos.* 7; *Dox.* 560. Anaximenes, himself a Milesian, son of Eurystratos, said that infinite air is the first principle,[2] from which arise the things that have come and are coming into existence, and the things that will be, and gods and divine beings, while other things are produced from these. And the form of air is as follows:— When it is of a very even consistency, it is imperceptible to vision, but it becomes evident as the result of cold or

[1] Cf. Arist. *Phys.* i. 4; and *de Coelo* iii. 5.
[2] V. Epiph. *adv. Haer.* iii. 3; *Dox.* 589.

c 2

heat or moisture, or when it is moved.   It is always in
motion; for things would not change as they do unless
it were in motion.   It has a different appearance when
it is made more dense or thinner ; when it is expanded
into a thinner state it becomes fire, and again winds are
condensed air, and air becomes cloud by compression,
and water when it is compressed farther, and earth and
finally stones as it is more condensed.   So that generation is controlled by the opposites, heat and cold.   And
the broad earth is supported on air ;[1] similarly the sun
and the moon and all the rest of the stars, being fiery
bodies,[2] are supported on the air by their breadth.[3]   And
stars are made of earth, since exhalations arise from
this, and these being attenuated become fire, and of this
fire when it is raised to the heaven the stars are constituted.   There are also bodies of an earthy nature [4] in
the place occupied by the stars, and carried along with
them in their motion.   He says that the stars do not
move under the earth, as others have supposed, but
around the earth,[5] just as a cap is moved about the head.
And the sun is hidden not by going underneath the
earth, but because it is covered by some of the higher
parts of the earth, and because of its greater distance
from us.   The stars do not give forth heat because they
are so far away.   Winds are produced when the air that
has been attenuated is set in motion ; and when it comes
together and is yet farther condensed, clouds are produced,
and so it changes into water.   And hail is formed when
the water descending from the clouds is frozen ; and
snow, when these being yet more filled with moisture
become frozen ;[6] and lightning, when clouds are separated
by violence of the winds ; for when they are separated,

---

[1] Aet. iii. 15; *Dox.* 380.   [2] Aet. ii. 13 ; 342; ii. 20; 348; ii. 25 ; 356.

[3] Aet. ii. 22 ; 352.   [4] Aet. ii. 13 ; 342.

[5] Aet. ii. 16 ; 346.   [6] Aet. iii. 4 ; 370.

the flash is bright and like fire.[1] And a rainbow is produced when the sun's rays fall on compressed air ;[2] and
earthquakes are produced when the earth is changed yet
more by heating and cooling.[3] Such are the opinions
of Anaximenes. And he flourished about the first year
of the fifty-eighth Olympiad.

Plut. *Strom.* 3 ; *Dox.* 579. Anaximenes says that air
is the first principle of all things, and that it is infinite in
quantity but is defined by its qualities; and all things
are generated by a certain condensation or rarefaction of
it. Motion also exists from eternity. And by compression of the air the earth was formed, and it is very broad ;
accordingly he says that this rests on air ; and the sun
and the moon and the rest of the stars were formed from
earth. He declared that the sun is earth because of
its swift motion, and it has the proper amount of heat.

Cic. *de Nat. Deor.* i. 10 ; *Dox.* 531. Afterwards
Anaximenes said that air is god,[4] [and that it arose]
and that it is boundless and infinite and always in
motion ; just as though air without any form could be
god, when it is very necessary that god should be not
only of some form, but of the most beautiful form ; or as
though everything which comes into being were not
thereby subject to death.

Aet. i. 3 ; *Dox.* 278. Anaximenes of Miletos, son of Eurystratos, declared that air is the first principle of things,
for from this all things arise and into this they are all
resolved again. As our soul which is air, he says,
holds us together, so wind [i.e. breath, $\pi\nu\epsilon\hat{\upsilon}\mu\alpha$] and
air encompass the whole world. He uses these words
' air ' and ' wind ' synonymously. He is mistaken in
thinking that animals are composed of simple homo-

---

[1] Aet. iii. 3 ; 368.   [2] Aet. iii. 5 ; 373.
[3] Cf. Aet. iii. 15 ; 379 *infra* and Arist. *Meteor.* ii. 7, *supra.*
[4] Aet. i. 7 ; 302.

geneous air and wind; for it is impossible that one first principle should constitute the substance of things, but an active cause is also necessary; just as silver alone is not enough to become coin, but there is need of an active cause, *i.e.* a coin-maker; [so there is need of copper and wood and other substances].

Aet. ii. 1; 327.   Anaximenes et al.: Infinite worlds exist in the infinite in every cycle. 4; 331.   The world is perishable. 11; 339.   The sky is the revolving vault most distant from the earth. 14; 344.   The stars are fixed like nailheads in the crystalline (vault). 19; 347.   The stars shine for none of these reasons, but solely by the light of the sun. 22; 352.   The sun is broad [like a leaf]. 23; 352.   The stars revolve, being pushed by condensed resisting air.

Aet. iii. 10; 377.   The form of the earth is like a table. 15; 379.   The dryness of the air, due to drought, and its wetness, due to rainstorms, are the causes of earthquakes.

Aet. iv. 3; 387.   Anaximenes et al.: The soul is like air in its nature.

IV.

HERAKLEITOS.

ACCORDING to Apollodoros, Herakleitos son of Blyson flourished in the sixty-ninth Olympiad (504–501 B.C.). An attempt to fix the date from his reference to the expulsion from Ephesos of his friend Hermodoros (Frag. 114) has resulted in a somewhat later date, though it is by no means impossible that Hermodoros was expelled during Persian rule in the city. Beyond the fact that Herakleitos lived in Ephesos we know nothing of his life; of the many stories related about him most can be proved false, and there is no reason for crediting the remainder His philosophic position is clear, however, since he refers to Pythagoras and Xenophanes (Fr. 16–17), and Parmenides (Vss. 46 sqq.) seems to refer to him. His book is said to have been divided into three parts :— (1) Concerning the All ; (2) Political ; (3) Theological Even in antiquity he was surnamed the ' dark ' or the ' obscure.'

Literature : Schleiermacher, *Op. Phil.* ii. 1–146 ; Bernays, *Ges. Abhandl.* i. ; Lassalle, *Die Philosophie Herakleitos des dunklen*, Berl. 1858 ; P. Schuster, ' Heraklit von Ephesos,' in *Act. soc. phil. Lips.* 1873, 111 ; Teichmüller, *Neue Studien zur Gesch. d. Begriffe*, Gotha 1876–1878 ; Bywater, *Heracl. Eph. Reliquiae*, Oxford 1877 ; Gomperz, ' Zu Herakl. Lehre,' *Sitz. d. Wien. Ak.* 1886, p. 977 ff. ; Patin, *Herakl. Einheitslehre*, Leipzig 1886, ' Quellenstudien zu Heraklit,' in *Festschrift f. L. Urlichs*, 1880, *Herakleitische Beispiele*, Progr. Neuburg, 1892–1893 ; E. Pfleiderer, *Die Philosophie des Heraklits im Lichte der Mysterienidee*, Berlin 1886 ; also *Rhein. Mus.* xlii. 153 ff. ; *JBB. f. protest. Theol.* xiv. 177 ff. ; E. Wambier, *Studia Heraclitea*, Diss. Berlin 1891.

(a) Fragments of Herakleitos.

1. οὐκ ἐμεῦ ἀλλὰ τοῦ λόγου ἀκούσαντας ὁμολογέειν σοφόν ἐστι, ἓν πάντα εἶναι.

2. τοῦ δὲ λόγου τοῦδ' ἐόντος αἰεὶ ἀξύνετοι γίνονται ἄνθρωποι καὶ πρόσθεν ἢ ἀκοῦσαι καὶ ἀκούσαντες τὸ πρῶτον. γινομένων γὰρ πάντων κατὰ τὸν λόγον τόνδε ἀπείροισι ἐοίκασι πειρώμενοι καὶ ἐπέων καὶ ἔργων τοιουτέων ὁκοίων ἐγὼ διηγεῦμαι, διαιρέων ἕκαστον κατὰ φύσιν καὶ φράζων ὅκως ἔχει. τοὺς δὲ ἄλλους ἀνθρώπους λανθάνει ὁκόσα ἐγερθέντες ποιέουσι, ὅκωσπερ ὁκόσα εὕδοντες ἐπιλανθάνονται.

3. ἀξύνετοι ἀκούσαντες κωφοῖσι ἐοίκασι· φάτις αὐτοῖσι μαρτυρέει παρεόντας ἀπεῖναι.

4. κακοὶ μάρτυρες ἀνθρώποισι ὀφθαλμοὶ καὶ ὦτα, βαρβάρους ψυχὰς ἐχόντων.

5. οὐ φρονέουσι τοιαῦτα πολλοὶ ὁκόσοισι ἐγκυρέουσι οὐδὲ μαθόντες γινώσκουσι, ἑωυτοῖσι δὲ δοκέουσι.

6. ἀκοῦσαι οὐκ ἐπιστάμενοι οὐδ' εἰπεῖν.

Sources and Critical Notes.

1. Hipp. *Ref. haer.* ix. 9 (cf. Philo, *Leg. all.* iii. 3, p. 88).
λόγου Bernays, δόγματος MS., Bgk.: εἶναι Miller, εἰδέναι MS., Bern. Bgk.

2. Sext. Emp. *adv. math.* vii. 132; (except last clause) Hipp. *Ref. haer.* ix. 9. In part: Arist. *Rhet.* iii. 5, 1407 b 14; Clem. Al. *Strom.* v. 14, p. 716 (= Euseb. *P. E.* xiii. 13, p. 680); Amelius in Euseb. *P. E.* xi. 19, p. 540, (and elsewhere). Cf. Philo, *Quis rer. div. haer.* 43, p. 505; Joh. Sic. in Walz, *Rhett. Gr.* vi. p. 95.
τοῦ δέοντος vulg. except Sext. Emp.: ξετοὶ (for ἀξύνετοι) MS. Hipp.: ἀπείροισι Bern., ἄπειροι εἰσὶν Hipp., ἄπειροι Sext. Emp.

3. Clem. Al. *Strom.* v. 14, p. 718 (Euseb. *P. E.* xiii. 13, p. 681); Theod. *Ther.* i. 13, 49: ἀπιέναι MS. Clem.

4. Sext. Emp. *adv. math.* viii. 126; Stob. *Flor.* iv. 56; cf. Diog. Laer. ix. 7.

5. Clem. Al. *Strom.* ii. 2, p. 432; cf. M. Antoninus, iv. 46.
ὁκόσοις Gataker, ὁκόσοι vulg.: ἐγκυρέουσι Schuster, ἐγκυρσεύουσιν vulg.

6. Clem. Al. *Strom.* ii. 5, p. 442.

TRANSLATION.

1. Not on my authority, but on that of truth, it is wise for you to accept the fact that all things are one.

> Hippolytos quotes this with Fragment 45, to show that Herakleitos taught the underlying unity of all things. On the word λόγος (meaning both discourse and the truth the discourse contains), *v.* Zeller, i. 680, n. 1.

2. This truth, though it always exists, men do not understand, as well before they hear it as when they hear it for the first time. For although all things happen in accordance with this truth, men seem unskilled indeed when they make trial of words and matters such as I am setting forth, in my effort to discriminate each thing according to its nature, and to tell what its state is. But other men fail to notice what they do when awake, in the same manner that they forget what they do when asleep.

> Hippolytos quotes this passage with reference to a universal all-pervading reason.

3. Those who hear without the power to understand are like deaf men ; the proverb holds true of them—' Present, they are absent.'

> Quoted by Clement in illustration of Ev. Luc. xiv. 35.

4. Eyes and ears are bad witnesses for men, since their souls lack understanding.

> Sextus Emp. interprets this as meaning 'rude souls trust the irrational senses.' Cf. Zeller, i. 716, n. 5.

5. Most men do not understand such things as they are wont to meet with ; nor by learning do they come to know them, though they think they do.

6. They know not how to listen, nor how to speak.

> Clement compares this with Eccles. vi. 35.

7. ἐὰν μὴ ἔλπηαι, ἀνέλπιστον οὐκ ἐξευρήσει, ἀνεξε-
ρεύνητον ἐὸν καὶ ἄπορον.

8. χρυσὸν οἱ διζήμενοι γῆν πολλὴν ὀρύσσουσι καὶ
εὑρίσκουσι ὀλίγον.

9. ἀγχιβασίην.

✓   10. φύσις κρύπτεσθαι φιλεῖ.

11. ὁ ἄναξ [οὗ τὸ μαντεῖόν ἐστι τὸ] ἐν Δελφοῖς οὔτε
λέγει οὔτε κρύπτει, ἀλλὰ σημαίνει.

12. σίβυλλα δὲ μαινομένῳ στόματι ἀγέλαστα καὶ
ἀκαλλώπιστα καὶ ἀμύριστα φθεγγομένη χιλίων ἐτέων
ἐξικνέεται τῇ φωνῇ διὰ τὸν θεόν.

13. ὅσων ὄψις ἀκοὴ μάθησις, ταῦτα ἐγὼ προτιμέω.

14. ἀπίστους ἀμφισβητουμένων παρεχόμενοι βε-
βαιωτάς.

15. ὀφθαλμοὶ τῶν ὤτων ἀκριβέστεροι μάρτυρες.

---

7. Clem. Al. *Strom.* ii. 4, p. 437 ; Theod. *Ther.* i. p. 15, 51.

ἔλπησθε Steph., ἔλπηαι Byw. Schus.: ἐξευρήσετε Steph., ἐξευ-
ρήσεις Schus. On punctuation v. Gomperz, *Archiv f. d. G. d.
Phil.* i. 100.

8. Clem. Al. *Strom.* iv. 2, p. 565 ; Theod. *Ther.* i. p. 15, 52.

9. Suidas, under ἀμφισβατεῖν and ἀγχιβατεῖν.

10. Themist. *Or.* v. p. 69 (xii. p. 159). Cf. Philo, *Qu. in gen.* iv. 1
p. 237, *de profug.* 32, p. 573, *de somn.* i. 2, p. 621, *de spec. legg.* 8, p.
344 ; Julian, *Or.* vii. p. 216 c.

11. Plut. *de pyth. orac.* 21, p. 404 ε ; Stob. *Flor.* v. 72, lxxxi. 17 ;
Iambl. *de myst.* iii. 15. Cf. Lucian, *vit. auct.* 14.

τὸ μαντεῖον appears only in Plutarch, and should probably be
omitted.

12. Plut. *de pyth. or.* 6, p. 397 Α. Cf. Clem. Al. *Strom.* i. 15, p.
358 ; Iambl. *de myst.* iii. 8 ; Pseudo-Herakl. *Epist.* viii.

13. Hipp. *Ref. haer.* ix. 9.

MS. ὅσον, corr. Miller.

14. Polyb. iv. 40.

15. Polyb. xii. 27 ; cf. Hdt. i.

7. If you do not hope, you will not find that which is not hoped for; since it is difficult to discover and impossible to attain.

> Clement compares this with Isaias vii. 9. With Gom-
> perz's punctuation: 'Unless you expect the unex-
> pected, you will not find truth; for, &c.'

8. Seekers for gold dig much earth, and find little gold.

9. Controversy.

10. Nature loves to hide.

> 'So we worship the creator of nature, because the
> knowledge of him is difficult.'

11. The Lord [whose is the oracle] at Delphi neither speaks nor conceals, but gives a sign.

12. And the Sibyl with raving mouth, uttering words solemn, unadorned, and unsweetened, reaches with her voice a thousand years because of the god in her.

> Quoted by Plutarch to show that allurements of sense
> are out of place in the holy responses of the god.
> Both this fragment and the preceding seem origi-
> nally to have referred to the nature of Herakleitos's
> teaching; it is obscure, and yet divine.

13. What can be seen, heard, and learned, this I prize.

> Hippolytos contrasts this with Fr. 47, and in this con-
> nection the translation of Schuster, 'Am I to prize
> these (invisible) things above what can be seen,
> heard, learned?' seems the more natural.

14. (For this is characteristic of the present age, when, inasmuch as all lands and seas may be crossed by man, it would no longer be fitting to depend on the witness of poets and mythographers, as our ancestors generally did), 'bringing forth untrustworthy witnesses to confirm disputed points,' in the words of Herakleitos.

15. Eyes are more exact witnesses than ears.

> Cf. Bernays, *Rhein. Mus.* ix. 261 sqq.

16. πολυμαθίη νόον ἔχειν οὐ διδάσκει· Ἡσίοδον γὰρ ἂν ἐδίδαξε καὶ Πυθαγόρην αὖτίς τε Ξενοφάνεα καὶ Ἑκαταῖον.

17. Πυθαγόρης Μνησάρχου ἱστορίην ἤσκησε ἀνθρώπων μάλιστα πάντων· καὶ [ἐκλεξάμενος ταύτας τὰς συγγραφὰς] ἐποίησε ἑωυτοῦ σοφίην, πολυμαθίην, κακοτεχνίην.

18. ὁκόσων λόγους ἤκουσα οὐδεὶς ἀφικνέεται ἐς τοῦτο, ὥστε γινώσκειν ὅτι σοφόν ἐστι πάντων κεχωρισμένον.

19. ἐν τὸ σοφόν, [ἐπίστασθαι γνώμην ἦ κυβερνᾶται πάντα διὰ πάντων]. (65) λέγεσθαι οὐκ ἐθέλει καὶ ἐθέλει Ζηνὸς οὔνομα.

20. κόσμον < τόνδε > τὸν αὐτὸν ἀπάντων οὔτε τις θεῶν οὔτε ἀνθρώπων ἐποίησε, ἀλλ᾽ ἦν αἰεὶ καὶ ἔστι καὶ ἔσται πῦρ ἀείζωον, ἁπτόμενον μέτρα καὶ ἀποσβεννύμενον μέτρα.

---

16. Diog. Laer. ix. 1. First part: Aul. Gell. *N. A.* praef. 12 ; Clem. Al. *Strom.* i. 19, p. 373 : Athen. xiii. p. 610 B : Julian, *Or.* vi. p. 187 D : Proklos in Tim. 31 F.

πολυμαθῆ MSS. Clem. Athen.

17. Diog. Laer. viii. 6.   Cf. Clem. Al. *Strom.* i. 21, p. 396.

Schleiermacher omits ἐκλεξάμενος τ. τ. συγγραφὰς : Vulg. ἐποιήσατο ἑαυτοῦ, the text is from Laurent. ed. Cobet : Casaubon καλοτεχνίην.

18. Stob. *Flor.* iii. 81.

19. Laer. Diog. ix. 1 ; Plut. *de Is.* 77, p. 382 c.   Cf. Kleanthes, *H. Z.* 36 ; Pseudo-Linos, 13, Mul. Byw. 65 ; Clem. Al. *Strom.* v. 14, p. 718 (Euseb. *P. E.* xiii. 13, p. 681) ; Cf. Bernays, *Rhein. Mus.* ix. 256.   The fragments are combined by Gomperz, l. c.

ἤτε οἱ ἐγκυβερνήσει Diog. Laer., τοῦ φρονοῦντος ᾦ κυβερνᾶται τὸ σύμπαν, Plut., γνώμης ἦ . . . πάντα κυβερνᾷς. Kleanth.

20. Clem. Al. *Strom.* v. 14, p. 711 (Euseb. *P. E.* xiii. 13, p. 676). First clause : Plut. *de anim. procr.* 5, p. 1014 A.   Last clause : Sim. in Arist. *de coelo*, p. 132, Kars. ; Olympiod. in Plat. *Phaed.* p. 201, Finc Bywater traces the thought through writers of Stoical school.

μέτρῳ Euseb. ed. Steph. p. 132.

16. Much learning does not teach one to have understanding; else it would have taught Hesiod, and Pythagoras, and again Xenophanes, and Hekataios.

17. Pythagoras, son of Mnesarchos, prosecuted investigations more than any other man, and [selecting these treatises] he made a wisdom of his own—much learning and bad art.

18. No one of all whose discourses I have heard has arrived at this result: the recognition that wisdom is apart from all other things.

> V. Teichmüller, i. 109 ff. on the idea of *katharsis* in Herakleitos.

19. Wisdom is one thing: [to understand the intelligence by which all things are steered through all things]; it is willing and it is unwilling to be called by the name Zeus.

> The first two clauses follow Fr. 16 in Diog. Laer.; the idea in parenthesis often appears in Stoic writers.

20. This order, the same for all things, no one of gods or men has made, but it always was, and is, and ever shall be, an ever-living fire, kindling according to fixed measure, and extinguished according to fixed measure.

> Zeller, i. 645 n. 1, discusses the various interpretations, and prefers to translate the first phrase 'This world, the same for all,' *i.e.* including gods and men.

21. πυρὸς τροπαὶ πρῶτον θάλασσα· θαλάσσης δὲ τὸ μὲν ἥμισυ γῆ, τὸ δὲ ἥμισυ πρηστήρ.

22. πυρὸς ἀνταμείβεται πάντα καὶ πῦρ ἀπάντων, ὥσπερ χρυσοῦ χρήματα καὶ χρημάτων χρυσός.

23. θάλασσα διαχέεται καὶ μετρέεται ἐς τὸν αὐτὸν λόγον ὁκοῖος πρόσθεν ἦν ἢ γενέσθαι †γῆ†.

24. χρησμοσύνη . . . κόρος.

25. ζῇ πῦρ τὸν γῆς θάνατον, καὶ ἀὴρ ζῇ τὸν πυρὸς θάνατον· ὕδωρ ζῇ τὸν ἀέρος θάνατον, γῆ τὸν ὕδατος.

26. πάντα τὸ πῦρ ἐπελθὸν κρινέει καὶ καταλήψεται.

27. τὸ μὴ δῦνόν ποτε πῶς ἄν τις λάθοι ;

28. τὰ δὲ πάντα οἰακίζει κεραυνός.

---

21. Clem. Al. *Strom.* v. 14, p. 712 (Euseb. *P. E.* xiii. 13, p. 676). Cf. Hipp. *Ref. haer.* vi. 17.

πῦρ τροπὰς Eus. D, πυρὸς τροπὰς Eus. F G, ed. Steph.; θάλασσα Eus. F. ; elsewhere θαλάσσης.

22. Plut. *de EI* 8, p. 388 Ε ; cf. Philo, *de incor. mun.* 21, p. 508 ; Diog. Laer. ix. 8; Herakl. *alleg. Hom.* 43 ; Euseb. *P. E.* xiv. 3, p. 720 &c. Probably only the word ἀμείβομαι comes from Herakleitos ; cf. the two forms of Fr. 31 in Plutarch.

23. Clem. Al. *Strom.* v. 14, p. 712 (Euseb. *P. E.* xiii. 13, p. 676).

Euseb. omits γῆ, Schuster reads γῆν : πρόσθεν Eus., πρῶτον Clem.

24. Philo, *Leg. all.* iii. 3, p. 88, *de vict.* 6, p. 242 ; Hipp. *Ref. haer.* ix. 10. Cf. Plut. *de EI* 9, p. 389 C.

25. Maxim. Tyr. xli. 4, p. 489. Cf. M. Antoninus, iv. 46. Plut. *de EI* 18, p. 392 C (Eus. *P. E.* xi. 11, p. 528) and *de prim. frig.* 10, p. 949 Α, gives simply πυρὸς θάνατος ἀέρος γένεσις.

26. Hipp. *Ref. haer.* ix. 10.

27. Clem. Al. *Paedag.* ii. 10, p. 229. τις, τινα Schleierm., τι Gataker.

28. Hipp. *Ref. haer.* ix. 10. Cf. Klean. *H. Z.* 10. Philodem. *de piet.* p. 70, Gomp.

21. The transformations of fire are, first of all, sea ; and of the sea one half is earth, and the other half is lightning flash.

> Zeller, i. 647 n. 1, regards πρηστήρ as identical with κεραυνός of Fr. 28. Burnett, *Early Greek Philosophy*, p. 153 n. 53, suggests fiery stormcloud, Seneca's *igneus turbo*.

22. All things are exchanged for fire, and fire for all things ; as wares are exchanged for gold, and gold for wares.

23. (The earth) is poured out as sea, and measures the same amount as existed before it became earth.

> V. Lassalle, ii. 63 ; Heinze, *Logos*, p. 25 ; Schuster, p. 129 ; Zeller, i. 690 n. 1.

24. Want and satiety.

> Context : Fire is intelligent and the governing cause of all things. Herakleitos calls it want and satiety. In his opinion want is the process of arrangement, and satiety the process of conflagration.

25. Fire lives in the death of earth, and air lives in the death of fire ; water lives in the death of air, and earth in that of water.

> Not accepted by Zeller, i. 676, who regards it as a Stoic version of Fr. 68.

26. Fire coming upon all things will test them, and lay hold of them.

> Burnett suggests that the reference to a judgment (κρινέει) was inserted by Hippolytos to obtain the Christian idea of a judgment.

27. How could one escape the notice of that which never sets ?

> Cf. Schuster, p. 184 ; Zeller, i. 649 n. 2 ; Teichmüller, i. 184.

28. The thunderbolt directs the course of all things.

> Cf. Fr. 19.

29. ἥλιος οὐχ ὑπερβήσεται μέτρα· εἰ δὲ μή, Ἐρινύες μιν δίκης ἐπίκουροι ἐξευρήσουσι.

30. ἠοῦς καὶ ἑσπέρης τέρματα ἡ ἄρκτος, καὶ ἀντίοι τῆς ἄρκτου οὖρος αἰθρίου Διός.

31. εἰ μὴ ἥλιος ἦν, εὐφρόνη ἂν ἦν.

32. νέος ἐφ᾽ ἡμέρῃ ἥλιος.

34.* ὧραι πάντα φέρουσι.

35. διδάσκαλος δὲ πλείστων Ἡσίοδος· τοῦτον ἐπίστανται πλεῖστα εἰδέναι, ὅστις ἡμέρην καὶ εὐφρόνην οὐκ ἐγίνωσκε· ἔστι γὰρ ἕν.

36. ὁ θεὸς ἡμέρη εὐφρόνη, χειμὼν θέρος, πόλεμος εἰρήνη, κόρος λιμός· ἀλλοιοῦται δὲ ὅκωσπερ ὁκόταν συμμιγῇ <θύωμα> θυώμασι· ὀνομάζεται καθ᾽ ἡδονὴν ἑκάστου.

---

29. Plut. *de exil.* 11, p. 604 A; *de Iside* 48, p. 370 D.   Cf. Hipp. *Ref. haer.* vi. 26; Iambl. *Prot.* 21, p. 132.

Pseudo-Herakl. *Ep.* ix. reads πολλαὶ δίκης Ἐρινύες, ἁμαρτημάτων φύλακες: Plut. 370 D reads λανθάνειν φησὶ τῇ πάντων γενέσει καταρώμενον, ἐκ μάχης καὶ ἀντιπαθείας τὴν γένεσιν ἐχόντων: ἥλιον δὲ μὴ ὑπερβήσεσθαι τοὺς προσήκοντος δρους· εἰ δὲ μή, γλώττας [κλῶθας, Hubman] μιν δίκης ἐπικούρους ἐξευρήσειν.

30. Strabo, i. 6, p. 3.   Vulg. adds γὰρ after ἠοῦς.

31. Plut. *Aq. et ign.* 7, p. 957 A.   Cf. Plut. *de fort.* 3, p. 98; Clem. Al. *Prot.* 11, p. 87; *Somn. Scip.* 1, 20.

32. Arist. *Met.* ii. 2, p. 355 a 9; Alexander Aph. in *Met.* l. l. 93 a; Olymp. in *Met.* l. l.; Prokl. in *Tim.* p. 334 B.   Cf. Plotin. *Enn.* ii. 1, p. 97; Plato, *Polit.* vi. p. 498 B (and Schol.); Olymp. in Plat. *Phaed.* p. 201 Finc.

33. Diog. Laer. i. 23 yields no fragment.

34. Plut. *Quaes. Plat.* viii. 4, p. 1007 E.   Cf. Plut. *de def. orac.* 12, p. 416 A; M. Antonin. ix. 3.

35. Hipp. *Ref. haer.* ix. 10.   MSS. εὐφροσύνην, corr. Miller.

36. Hipp. *Ref. haer.* ix. 10 (cf. v. 21).

After λιμός Bergk inserts from Hippolytos τἀναντία ἅπαντα ωὑτὸς νόος.   Bergk adds οἶνος after ὅκωσπερ, Schuster after θυώμασι; Bernays suggests θύωμα after συμμιγῇ, Zeller ἀὴρ, Diels πῦρ. MSS. read συμμιγῇ.

---

* I keep Bywater's numbers, though I omit some of his fragments. Such omissions are referred to in the critical notes.

29. The sun will not overstep his bounds ; if he does, the Erinnyes, allies of justice, will find him out.

30. The limit of the evening and the morning is the Bear ; and opposite the Bear is the boundary of bright Zeus.

> Strabo regards this as a Homeric expression for the fact that the northern circle is the boundary of rising and setting. Zeus *aithrios* means the clear heavens.

31. If there were no sun, it would be night.

32. The sun is new every day.

33. (Herakleitos and Demokritos bear witness that Thales was an astronomer, and predicted eclipses, etc.)

34. The seasons bring all things.

> ' Time is not motion of a simple sort, but, so to speak, motion in an order which has measure and limits and periods.   The sun, guardian of these, ... appoints and announces the seasons, which, according to Herakleitos, bring all things.'

35. Hesiod is the teacher of most men ; they suppose that his knowledge was very extensive, when in fact he did not know night and day, for they are one.

36. God is day and night, winter and summer, war and peace, satiety and hunger ; but he assumes different forms, just as when incense is mingled with incense ; every one gives him the name he pleases.

* D

37. εἰ πάντα τὰ ὄντα καπνὸς γένοιτο, ῥῖνες ἂν διαγνοῖεν.

38. †αἱ ψυχαὶ ὀσμῶνται καθ᾽ "Αιδην.†

39. τὰ ψυχρὰ θέρεται, θερμὸν ψύχεται, ὑγρὸν αὐαίνεται, καρφαλέον νοτίζεται.

40. σκίδνησι καὶ συνάγει, πρόσεισι καὶ ἄπεισι.

41—42. ποταμοῖσι δὶς τοῖσι αὐτοῖσι οὐκ ἂν ἐμβαίης· ἕτερα γὰρ (καὶ ἕτερα) ἐπιρρέει ὕδατα.

43. μέμφεται τῷ Ὁμήρῳ Ἡράκλειτος εἰπόντι· ὡς ἔρις ἔκ τε θεῶν ἔκ τ᾽ ἀνθρώπων ἀπόλοιτο· οἰχήσεσθαι γάρ φησι πάντα.

44. πόλεμος πάντων μὲν πατήρ ἐστι πάντων δὲ βασιλεύς, καὶ τοὺς μὲν θεοὺς ἔδειξε τοὺς δὲ ἀνθρώπους, τοὺς μὲν δούλους ἐποίησε τοὺς δὲ ἐλευθέρους.

---

37. Arist. de sensu 5, p. 443 a 21.

38. Plut. de fac. in orbe lun. 28, p. 943 ε. Patin, Einheitslehre, p. 23, points out that this so-called fragment is probably due to a misunderstanding of the passage in Aristotle (Fr. 37).

39. Schol. Tzetz. ad Exeg. in Iliad. p. 126, Hermann. Cf. Hippokrates, περὶ διαίτης 1, 21 ; Pseudo-Herakl. Epist. v.

40. Plut. de EI 18, p. 392 B.   V. Pseudo-Herakl. Epist. vi.

41. Plut. Quaes. nat. 2, p. 912 A.   First half : Plato, Krat. 402 A ; Arist. Metaph. xiv. 5, p. 1010 a 13 ; Plut. de sera num. vind. 15, p. 559 c ; de EI 18, p. 392 A ; Simplic. in Arist. Phys. 17 p. 77, 32 ; Ibid. f. 308 v.

Plato and Simpl. read ἐς τὸν αὐτὸν ποταμόν. Byw. inserts καὶ ἕτερα ; cf. his fr. 42 infra.

42. Arius Didymus in Euseb. P. E. xv. 20, p. 821. [Cf. Sext. Emp. Pyrrh. hyp. iii. 115.] ποταμοῖσι τοῖσι αὐτοῖσι ἐμβαίνουσιν ἕτερα καὶ ἕτερα ὕδατα ἐπιρρεῖ.

43. Simpl. in Arist. Cat. p. 104 Δ ed. Basil. (Scholl. in Arist. 88 b 28) ; Schol. Ven. ad Il. xviii. 107, and Eustath. p. 1133, 56. Cf. Arist. Eth. Eud. vii. 1, p. 1235 a 26 ; Plutarch de Isid. 48, 370 D ; Numen. in Chalcid. on Tim. 295.

44 Hipp. Ref. haer. ix. 9. First part : Plut. de Iside 48, p. 370 D ; Prok on Tim. 54 A (cf. 24 B) ; Lucian, quomodo hist. consc. 2 ; Icar. 8.

37. If all things should become smoke, then perception would be by the nostrils.

> Arist. 'Some think that odour is a smoky exhalation, . . . and that every one is brought in contact with this in smelling. So Herakleitos says that if all things,' etc. The reference is originally to the conflagration of the universe [ἐκπύρωσις].

38. Souls smell in Hades.

> Plutarch adds the reason : Because they retain a perception of what is fiery.

39. Cool things become warm. the warm grows cool ; the wet dries, the parched becomes wet.

40. It scatters and brings together : it approaches and departs.

> This follows the next fragment, as illustrating change.

41–42. You could not step twice in the same rivers ; for other and yet other waters are ever flowing on.

43. Herakleitos blamed Homer for saying: Would that strife might perish from among gods and men ! For then, said he, all things would pass away.

> Aristotle assigns a different reason : For there could be no harmony without sharps and flats, nor living beings without male and female, which are contraries.

44. War is father of all and king of all ; and some he made gods and some men, some slaves and some free.

45. οὐ ξυνίασι ὅκως διαφερόμενον ἑωυτῷ ὁμολογέει· παλίντροπος ἁρμονίη ὅκωσπερ τόξου καὶ λύρης.

46. τὸ ἀντίξουν συμφέρον. ἐκ τῶν διαφερόντων καλλίστην ἁρμονίαν. πάντα κατ' ἔριν γίνεσθαι.

47. ἁρμονίη ἀφανὴς φανερῆς κρείσσων.

48. μὴ εἰκῆ περὶ τῶν μεγίστων συμβαλώμεθα.

49. χρὴ εὖ μάλα πολλῶν ἵστορας φιλοσόφους ἄνδρας εἶναι.

50. γναφέων ὁδὸς εὐθεῖα καὶ σκολιὴ μία ἐστὶ καὶ ἡ αὐτή.

51. ὄνοι σύρματ' ἂν ἔλοιντο μᾶλλον ἢ χρυσόν.

52. θάλασσα ὕδωρ καθαρώτατον καὶ μιαρώτατον, ἰχθύσι μὲν πότιμον καὶ σωτήριον, ἀνθρώποις δὲ ἄτοπον καὶ ὀλέθριον.

53. Sues coeno, cohortales aves pulvere (vel cinere) lavari.   54. βορβόρῳ χαίρειν.

---

45. Hipp. *Ref. haer.* ix. 9.   Cf. Plato, *Symp.* 187 A, *Soph.* 242 D ; Plut. *de anim. procr.* 27, p. 1026 B.

MSS. ὁμολογέειν, corr. Miller.   Cf. (Bywater 56) Plut. *de tranq.* 15, 473 ; *de Is.* 45, 369 ; Porphyr. *de ant. nym.* 29 ; Simpl. *Phys.* 11 r 50, 11.   These writers give παλίντονος ; παλίντροπος is probably from Parmenides v. 59 ; Plutarch inserts κόσμου.

46. Arist. *Eth. Nic.* viii. 2, p. 1155 b 14.   Cf. Theophr. *Metaph.* 15 ; Arist. *Eth. Eud.* vii. 1 ; 1235 a 13.   These are rather summary phrases than quotations.

47. Plut. *de anim. procr.* 27, p. 1026 c ; Hipp. *Ref. haer.* ix. 9-10.

48. Diog. Laer. ix. 73.

49. Clem. Al. *Strom.* v. 14, p. 733.

50. Hipp. *Ref. haer.* ix. 10.   MSS. γραφέων, corr. Duncker. The MSS. reading may be a participle introducing the quotation, and wrongly included in the excerpt, as Tannery suggests (*Science hellén.* pp. 198 ff.).

51. Arist. *Eth. Nic.* x. 5, p. 1176 a 6.   Cf. Albertus M. *de veget.* vi. 401 (p. 545 Mey.) *R. P.* 40 B : ' Boves ... felices ... cum inveniant orobum ad comendum.'   Bywater, *Journal Philol.* 1880, p. 230.

52. Hipp. *Ref. haer.* ix. 10.   Cf. Sext. Emp. *Pyrrh. hyp.* i. 55.

53. Columella, *de R. R.* viii. 4.   Cf. Galen, *Protrept.* 13, p. 5 ed. Bas.

54. Athen. v. 178 F.   Cf. Clem. Al. *Protrept.* 10, p. 75 ; Sext. Emp. *Pyrrh. hyp.* i. 55 ; Plotin. *Enn.* i. 6, p. 55.

45. Men do not understand how that which draws apart agrees with itself; harmony lies in the bending back, as for instance of the bow and of the lyre.

> V. Bernays, *Rhein. Mus.* vii. p. 94. Reading παλίν-
> τονος from fragment 56, we obtain the meaning
> 'opposite tension' more distinctly.

46. Opposition unites. From what draws apart results the most beautiful harmony. All things take place by strife.

> Quoted by Aristotle as an illustration of the search for
> a deeper principle, more in accordance with nature.

47. Hidden harmony is better than manifest.

48. Let us not make rash conjectures about the greatest things.

49. Men who desire wisdom must be learners of very many things.

50. For woolcarders the straight and the crooked path is one and the same.

51. Asses would rather have refuse than gold.

52. The sea is the purest and the foulest water; it is drinkable and healthful for fishes; but for men it is unfit to drink and hurtful.

> Quoted by Hippolytos as an example of Herakleitos'
> identification of opposites.

53-54. Swine like to wash in the mire; barnyard fowls in the dust.

55. πᾶν ἑρπετὸν πληγῇ νέμεται.

56 = 45.

57. ἀγαθὸν καὶ κακὸν ταὐτόν.

58. οἱ ἰατροὶ τέμνοντες καίοντες πάντη βασανίζοντες κακῶς τοὺς ἀρρωστοῦντας ἐπαιτιῶνται μηδέν' ἄξιον μισθὸν λαμβάνειν παρὰ τῶν ἀρρωστούντων.

59. συνάψειας οὖλα καὶ οὐχὶ οὖλα, συμφερόμενον διαφερόμενον, συνᾷδον διᾷδον· ἐκ πάντων ἓν καὶ ἐξ ἑνὸς πάντα.

60. δίκης οὔνομα οὐκ ἂν ᾔδεσαν, εἰ ταῦτα μὴ ἦν.

61. †τῷ μὲν θεῷ καλὰ πάντα καὶ ἀγαθὰ καὶ δίκαια, ἄνθρωποι δὲ ἃ μὲν ἄδικα ὑπειλήφασιν, ἃ δὲ δίκαια.†

62. εἰδέναι χρὴ τὸν πόλεμον ἐόντα ξυνόν, καὶ δίκην ἔριν· καὶ γινόμενα πάντα κατ' ἔριν καὶ †χρεώμενα†.

63. ἔστι γὰρ εἱμαρμένα πάντως. . . .

---

55. Arist. *de mundo* 6, p. 401 a 8 (Apuleius, *de mundo* 36 ; Stob. *Ecl.* i. 2, p. 86). From Cod. Flor. of Apuleius Goldbacher obtains the following (*Zeit. f. d. Oester. Gymn.* 1876, p. 496) : Ζεὺς ἅπαντα εὐεργετεῖ ὁμῶς ὡς ἄν τινα μέρη σώματος αὐτοῦ.

56. V. 45.

57. Arist. *Top.* viii. 5, p. 159 b 30 ; *Phys.* i. 2, p. 185 b 20 ; Hipp. *Ref. haer.* ix. 10 ; Simpl. in *Phys.* 11 v. 50, 11 ; 18 v. 82, 23.

58. Hipp. *Ref. haer.* ix. 10. Cf. Xen. *Mem.* i. 2, 54 ; Plato, *Gorg.* 521 F, *Polit.* 293 B ; Simpl. in Epict. 13, p. 83 D, and 27 p. 178 A.

   Vulg. μηδὲν, Sauppe μηδένα: vulg. μισθῶν, Wordsworth μισθὸν. Bywater objects to βασανίζοντες and omits the phrases τοὺς ἀρρωστοῦντας and παρὰ τῶν ἀρρωστούντων.

59. Arist. *de mundo* 5, p. 396 b 12 (Apuleius, *de mundo* 20 ; Stob. *Ecl.* i. 34, p. 690).

   Stob. *VA* συλλάψει εἰς, Arist. *Q* συνάψας, *OR* συνάψιες : Arist. *P*, Stob. and Apul. ὅλα : Zeller omits καί.

60. Clem. Al. *Strom.* iv. 3, p. 568. Cf. Pseudo-Herakl. *Epist.* vii.

61. Schol. B in *Il.* iv. 4, p. 120 Bk. Cf. Hippokr. *de diaeta* i. 11 *RP.* 37 c ; Bernays, Herakl. 22. Probably a Stoic deduction from Herakleitos, and therefore to be omitted here.

62. Orig. *cont. Cels.* vi. 42, p. 312. Cf. Plut. *de soll. anim.* 7, p. 964 ; Laer. Diog. ix. 8.

   Vulg. εἰ δὲ, Schleierm. εἰδέναι: vulg. ἐρεῖν, Schl. ἔριν.

[63. Stob. *Ecl.* i. 6, p. 178. Vulg. εἱμαρμένη, A εἱμαρμένα.

55. Every beast is tended by blows.

> Cf. Zeller, i. p. 724: 'Every creature feeds on earth.'

(56. Identical with 45.)

57. Good and bad are the same.

58. (Good and bad are one; at any rate, as Hera-kleitos says) physicians, who cut and burn and in every way torment the sick, complain that they do not receive any adequate recompense from them.

59. Thou shouldst unite things whole and things not whole, that which tends to unite and that which tends to separate, the harmonious and the discordant; from all things arises the one, and from the one all things.

60. They would not have known the name of justice, were it not for these things.

> According to the context in Clement 'these things' refers to injustice.

61. (God, ordering things as they ought to be, perfects all things in the harmony of the whole, as Herakleitos says that) for god all things are fair and good and just, but men suppose that some are unjust and others just.

> Cf. Hippocr. de Diaeta (Bernays, Herakl. 22; RP 37 c) Accordingly the arrangements (laws) which men have made are never constant, either when they are right, or when they are not right; but the arrangements the gods have made are always right, both those which are right and those which are not right; so great is the difference between them.

62. Men should know that war is general and that justice is strife; all things arise and [pass away] through strife.

63. For they are absolutely destined. . .

64. θάνατός ἐστι ὁκόσα ἐγερθέντες ὁρεόμεν, ὁκόσα δὲ εὕδοντες ὕπνος.

65. v. 19.

66. τοῦ βίου οὔνομα βίος, ἔργον δὲ θάνατος.

67. θεοὶ θνητοί, ἄνθρωποι ἀθάνατοι, ζῶντες τὸν ἐκείνων θάνατον τὸν δὲ ἐκείνων βίον τεθνεῶτες.

68. ψυχῆσι γὰρ θάνατος ὕδωρ γενέσθαι, ὕδατι δὲ θάνατος γῆν γενέσθαι· ἐκ γῆς δὲ ὕδωρ γίνεται, ἐξ ὕδατος δὲ ψυχή.

69. ὁδὸς ἄνω κάτω μία καὶ ὡυτή.

70. ξυνὸν ἀρχὴ καὶ πέρας.

71. ψυχῆς πείρατα οὐκ ἂν ἐξεύροιο πᾶσαν ἐπιπορευόμενος ὁδόν.

---

64. Clem. Al. *Strom.* iii. 3, p. 520.   Cf. *Strom.* v. 14, p. 712; Philo, *de Joseph.* 22, p. 59.

66. Schol. in *Il.* i. 49; Cramer, *A. P.* iii. p. 122; *Etym. Mag.* under βίος; Tzetz. Ex. in *Il.* p. 101; Eust. in *Il.* i. 49, p. 41.   Cf. Hippokr. *de diaeta* 21 οὔνομα τρόφη, ἔργον δὲ οὐχί.

67. Hipp. *Ref. haer.* ix. 10; Herakl. *Alleg. Hom.* 24, p. 51; Maxim. Tyr. x. 4, p. 107, xli. 4, p. 489; Lucian, *Vit. auct.* 14; Porph. *de ant. nymph.* 10; Clem. Al. *Paed.* iii. 1, p. 251; Philo, *Leg. alleg.* i. 33, p. 65, and *Qu. in Gen.* iv. 152, p. 360.   Human and divine nature identical: Dio Cass. *Frr.* i.–xxxv. Ch. 30, i. 40 Dind.; Stob. *Ecl.* i. 39, p. 768.

   Hipp. reads ἀθάνατοι θνητοί, θνητοὶ ἀθάνατοι; Clement ἄνθρωποι θεοί, θεοὶ ἄνθρωποι.

68. Philo, *de incorr. mundi* 21, p. 509; Aristides Quint. ii. p. 106 Meib.; Clem. Al. *Strom.* vi. 2, p. 746; Hipp. *Ref. haer.* v. 16; Julian, Or. v. p. 165 D; Prokl. in *Tim.* p. 36 c; Olympiod. in Plat. *Gorg.* p. 357 Jahn; idem, p. 542.

69. Hipp. *Ref. haer.* ix. 10.   Cf. Plato, *Phileb.* 43 A; Kleomed. π. μετεώρων i. p. 75 Bak.; Maximus Tyr. xli. 4, p. 489; Tertull. *adv. Marc.* ii. 28 Diog. Laer. ix. 8; Plotin. *Enn.* iv. 8, p. 468; Iambl. Stob. *Ecl.* i. 41; Hippokr. π. τροφῆς 45; Philo, *de incorr. mun.* 21, p. 508; and *de somn.* i. 24, p. 644; and *de vit. Moys.* i. 6, p. 85; Muson. Stob. *Flor.* cviii. 60; M. Antonin. vi. 17.

70. Porphyr. Schol. B. *Il.* xiv. 200, p. 392 Bek.   Cf. Hippokr. π. τόπων 1, π. διαίτης 1, 19, π. τροφῆς 9.   Philo, *Leg. all.* i. 3, p. 44; Plut. *de EI* 8, p. 388 c.

71. Diog. Laer. ix. 7; Tertull. *de anima* 2.   Cf. Hipp. *Ref. haer.* v. 7.

64. All the things we see when awake are death, and all the things we see when asleep are sleep.

> For various interpretations, v. Teichmüller, i. 97 sq. ; Zeller, i. 715 ; Patin, *Einheitslehre*, 19.

65. v. 19.

66. The name of the bow is life, but its work is death.

> A similar play on words is found in Fr. 101.

67. Gods are mortals, men are immortals, each living in the others' death and dying in the others' life.

> Cf. Sext. Emp. *Pyrrh.* iii. 230, R.P. 38.

68. For to souls it is death to become water, and for water it is death to become earth ; but water is formed from earth, and from water, soul.

> Clement quotes this as borrowed from Orpheus ; and Hippolytos also found it in the poets.

69 Upward, downward, the way is one and the same.

70. Beginning and end are common (to both ways).

71. The limits of the soul you could not discover, though traversing every path.

72. ψυχῇσι τέρψις ὑγρῇσι γενέσθαι.

73. ἀνὴρ ὁκότ' ἂν μεθύσθῃ, ἄγεται ὑπὸ παιδὸς ἀνήβου σφαλλόμενος, οὐκ ἐπαίων ὅκη βαίνει, ὑγρὴν τὴν ψυχὴν ἔχων.

74–76. αὔη ψυχὴ σοφωτάτη καὶ ἀρίστη.

77. ἄνθρωπος, ὅκως ἐν εὐφρόνῃ φάος, ἅπτεται ἀποσβέννυται.

78. ταῦτ' εἶναι ζῶν καὶ τεθνηκός, καὶ τὸ ἐγρηγορὸς καὶ τὸ καθεῦδον, καὶ νέον καὶ γηραιόν· τάδε γὰρ μεταπεσόντα ἐκεῖνά ἐστι κἀκεῖνα πάλιν μεταπεσόντα ταῦτα.

79. αἰὼν παῖς ἐστι παίζων πεσσεύων· παιδὸς ἡ βασιληίη.

72. Numen. Porphyr. *de antro nymph.* 10.

73. Stob. *Flor.* v. 120.   Cf. M. Antonin. iv. 46.

74–76. Plutarch, *Rom.* 28; Aristid. Quint. ii. p. 106; Porphyr. *de antro nymph.* 11; Synesius, *de insomn.* p. 140 A Petav.; Stob. *Flor.* v. 120; Glykas, *Ann.* i. p. 74 B; Eustath. *Il.* xxiii. 261, p. 1299, 17.

> Reading αὐγὴ ξηρὴ ψυχὴ (Bywater 75 and 76); Philo, Euseb. *P. E.* viii. 14, p. 399; and *de prov.* ii. 109, p. 117; Muson. Stob. *Flor.* xvii. 43; Plut. *de esu carn.* i. 6, p. 995 E; and *de def. orac.* 41, p. 432 F; Clem. Al. *Paedag.* ii. 2, p. 184; Galen, π. τῶν τῆς ψυχῆς ἠθῶν 5, i. p. 346 Bas.; Hermeias on Plato, *Phaedr.* 73; Porphyr. ἀφορμ. πρὸς τὰ νοητά 33, 78. 'Ac suspicor illud αὐγὴ irrepsisse pro αὔη; quod aliquis exposuerit illa voce ξηρά, unde orta est illa lectio,' Stephan. *Poes. Phil.* p. 139.

77. Clem. Al. *Strom.* iv. 22, p. 628.

> Bywater emends the text of Clement to read: ἄνθρωπος ὅπως ἐν εὐφρόνῃ φάος ἅπτεται, ὡσαύτως ἀποθανὼν ὄψεις. ζῶν δὲ ἅπτεται τεθνεῶτος εὕδων, ἀποσβεσθεὶς ὄψεις, ἐγρηγορὼς ἅπτεται εὕδοντος, and compares Sext. Emp. *Math.* vii. 130; Seneca, *Epist.* 54.

78. Plut. *Consol. ad Apoll.* 10, p. 106 E; and *de EI* 18, p. 392 D. (Bernays, *Rhein. Mus.* vii. p. 100, thinks that more of the contents of these passages is drawn from Herakleitean sources.)   Clem. Al. *Strom.* iv. 22, p. 628; Sext. Emp. *Pyrrh.* iii. 230; Tzetz. *Chil.* ii. 722.

79. Hipp. *Ref. haer.* ix. 9.   Cf. Clem. Al. *Paed.* i. 5, p. 111; Iambl. Stob. *Ecl.* ii. 1, p. 12; Prokl. in *Tim.* 101 F; Plato, *Legg.* i. 644 D, x. 903 D; Philo, *de vit. Moys.* i. 6, p. 85; Plut. *de EI* 21, p. 393 E; Lucian, *vit. auct.* 14.

72. It is a delight to souls to become wet.

73. Whenever a man gets drunk, he is led about by a beardless boy, stumbling, not knowing whither he goes, for his soul is wet.

74. The dry soul is wisest and best.

Byw. 75. A dry beam is the wisest and best soul; Fr. 76. Where the earth is dry, the soul is wisest and best.

> If Fr. 74 is the genuine form, the corruptions are very early. We cannot, however, regard all three forms as genuine, and it is at least doubtful whether Fr. 75 expresses a Herakleitean idea.
> Zeller and others add to Fr. 74 the rest of the phrase in Plutarch, ' flashing through the body as lightning through the cloud.'

77. Man, like a light in the night, is kindled and put out.

78. Life and death, and waking and sleeping, and youth and old age, are the same ; for the latter change and are the former, and the former change back to the latter.

79. Lifetime is a child playing draughts; the kingdom is a child's.

> Clement understood αἰών to be Zeus ; Hippolytos made it equivalent to αἰώνιος, the eternal (king).

80. ἐδιζησάμην ἐμεωυτόν.

81. ποταμοῖσι τοῖσι αὐτοῖσι ἐμβαίνομέν τε καὶ οὐκ ἐμβαίνομεν, εἰμέν τε καὶ οὐκ εἰμεν.

82. κάματός ἐστι τοῖς αὐτοῖς μοχθεῖν καὶ ἄρχεσθαι.

83. μεταβάλλον ἀναπαύεται.

84. καὶ ὁ κυκεὼν διίσταται μὴ κινεόμενος.

85. νέκυες κοπρίων ἐκβλητότεροι.

86. γενόμενοι ζώειν ἐθέλουσι μόρους τ᾽ ἔχειν· [μᾶλλον δὲ ἀναπαύεσθαι,] καὶ παῖδας καταλείπουσι μόρους γενέσθαι.

90. τοὺς καθεύδοντας ἐργάτας εἶναι [καὶ συνεργοὺς] τῶν ἐν τῷ κόσμῳ γινομένων.

---

80. Plut. adv. Colot. 20, p. 1118 c ; Dio Chrys. Or. 55, p. 282 ; Tatian, Or. ad Graec. ; Diog. Laer. ix. 5 ; Plotin. Enn. iv. 8, p. 468 ; Julian, Or. vi. p. 185 A ; Prokl. on Tim. 106 E ; Suidas s. v. ποστοῦμος. Cf. Clem. Al. Strom. ii. 1, p. 429 ; Plotin. Enn. v. 9, p. 559 ; Hesychius ἐδίζησα.

81. Herakl. Alleg. Hom. 24 ; Seneca, Epist. 58. Cf. Epicharm. Fr. B 40 Lorenz.

82. Plotin. Enn. ix. 8, p. 468 ; Iambl. Stob. Ecl. i. 41, p. 906 ; Aeneas Gaz. Theophrast. p. 9 Barth.   Cf. Hippokr. π. διαίτης i. 15 ; Philo, de cherub. 26, p. 155.

83. Plotin. Enn. iv. 8, p. 468 and p. 473 ; Iambl. Stob. Ecl. i. 41, p. 906 and p. 894 ; Aeneas G. Theophrast. p. 9 and p. 11.

84. Theophrast. π. ἰλίγγων 9, p. 138 Wim. ; Alexand. Aphr. Probl. p. 11 Usen. Cf. M. Antonin. iv. 27.

MSS. Alexander, κυκλεύων and ἴσταται : Theophrast. begins the sentence with μὴ, corr. Bernays.

85. Strabo, xvi. 26, p. 784 ; Plutarch, Qu. conv. iv. 4, p. 669 A ; Pollux, Onom. v. 163 ; Origen, c. Cels. v. 14, p. 247 (quoting Celsus, v. 24, p. 253) ; Julian, Or. vii. p. 226 c.   Cf. Philo, de profug. ii. p. 555 ; Plotin. Enn. v. 1, p. 483 ; Schol. V. ad Il. xxiv. 54 (= Eustath. ad Il. p. 1338, 47) ; Epictet. Diss. ii. 4, 5.

86. Clem. Al. Strom. iii. 3, p. 516.   Mullach assigns the bracketed words to Clement.

87-89. Plut. de orac. def. 11, p. 415 E, and cf. Plac. phil. 24, p. 909 ; Censorin. de D. N. 17 ; Io. Lydus, de mensibus iii. 10, p. 37, ed. Bonn (Crameri A. P. i. p. 324) ; cf. Philo, Qu. in gen. ii. 5, p. 82.   These passages do not yield any definite fragment of Herakleitos.

90. M. Antonin. vi. 42.   Pfleiderer rejects καὶ συνεργούς.

80. I inquired of myself.

> The translation follows the sense in Diogenes; in
> Plutarch it is parallel with the Delphic oracle,
> 'I have sought to know myself.'

81. In the same rivers we step and we do not step;
we are and we are not.

> Cf. Fr. 41.

82. It is weariness to toil at the same things, and to
be subject to them.

83. Changing it finds rest.

84. Even a potion separates into its ingredients
when it is not stirred.

85. Corpses are more fit to be thrown away than
dung.

86. Being born they wish to live and to meet death,
[or rather to find rest,] and they leave behind children
to die.

> **87.** Thirty years make a generation, according to Hera-
> kleitos. **88.** Not without reason does Herakleitos call a
> month a generation. **89.** A man may become a grandfather
> in thirty years.

90. The sleeping are workmen (and fellow-workers)
in what happens in the world.

91. ξυνόν ἐστι πᾶσι τὸ φρονέειν. ξὺν νόῳ λέγοντας ἰσχυρίζεσθαι χρὴ τῷ ξυνῷ πάντων, ὅκωσπερ νόμῳ πόλις καὶ πολὺ ἰσχυροτέρως. τρέφονται γὰρ πάντες οἱ ἀνθρώπειοι νόμοι ὑπὸ ἑνὸς τοῦ θείου· κρατέει γὰρ τοσοῦτον ὁκόσον ἐθέλει καὶ ἐξαρκέει πᾶσι καὶ περιγίνεται.

92. τοῦ λόγου δ' ἐόντος ξυνοῦ, ζώουσι οἱ πολλοὶ ὡς ἰδίην ἔχοντες φρόνησιν.

93. ᾧ μάλιστα διηνεκέως ὁμιλέουσι, τούτῳ διαφέρονται.

94. οὐ δεῖ ὥσπερ καθεύδοντας ποιεῖν καὶ λέγειν.

95. τοῖς ἐγρηγορόσιν ἕνα καὶ κοινὸν κόσμον εἶναι, τῶν δὲ κοιμωμένων ἕκαστον εἰς ἴδιον ἀποστρέφεσθαι.

96. ἦθος ἀνθρώπειον μὲν οὐκ ἔχει γνώμας, θεῖον δὲ ἔχει.

97. ἀνὴρ νήπιος ἤκουσε πρὸς δαίμονος ὅκωσπερ παῖς πρὸς ἀνδρός.

100. μάχεσθαι χρὴ τὸν δῆμον ὑπὲρ τοῦ νόμου ὅκως ὑπὲρ τείχεος.

---

91. Stob. *Flor.* iii. 84.   Cf. Kleanth. *H. Zeus* 24; Hippokr. π. τροφῆς 15; Plut. *de Isid.* 45, p. 369 A; Plotin. *Enn.* vi. 5, p. 668; Empedokles, v. 231 Stn.

92. Sext. Emp. *Math.* vii. 133, where the quotation is apparently longer.   Burnett, 140, n. 35, acutely suggests φρονέειν for λόγου.

93. M. Antonin. iv. 46.

94. M. Antonin. iv. 46.

95. Plut. *de superst.* 3, p. 166 c.   Cf. Hippolyt. *Ref. haer.* vi. 26; Iambl. *Protrept.* 21, p. 132 Arcer.   The form is Plutarch's.

96. Origen, *c. Cels.* vi. 12, p. 291.

97. Origen, *c. Cels.* vi. 12, p. 291.   Cf. M. Antonin. iv. 46 Bern.

δαήμονος E. Petersen, *Hermes*, 1879, xiv. 304.

98. Plato, *Hipp. Maj.* 289 B.   Cf. M. Antonin. iv. 16.

99. *Ibid.* 289 A.   The words of Herakleitos cannot be restored.   Cf. Plotin. *Ennead.* vi. p. 626; Arist. *Top.* iii. 2, 117 b 118.

100. Diog. Laer. ix. 2.

91. Understanding is common to all. It is necessary for those who speak with intelligence to hold fast to the common element of all, as a city holds fast to law, and much more strongly. For all human laws are nourished by one which is divine, and it has power so much as it will; and it suffices for all things and more than suffices.

92. And though reason is common, most people live as though they had an understanding peculiar to themselves.

93. With what they most constantly associate, with this they are at variance.

94. It is not meet to act and speak like men asleep.

Cf. Fr. 2 and 90.

95. They that are awake have one world in common, but of the sleeping each turns aside into a world of his own.

96. For human nature has not wisdom, but divine nature has.

97. Man is called a baby by god, even as a child is by man.

The translation is Burnett's, following the suggestion of Petersen in *Hermes* xiv. 1879, p. 304.

Fr. 98. And does not Herakleitos, whom you bring forward, say this very thing, that the wisest of men will appear as an ape before God, both in wisdom and in beauty and in all other respects? Fr. 99. You are ignorant, sir, of that fine saying of Herakleitos, that the most beautiful of apes is ugly in comparison with beings of another kind, and the most beautiful of earthen pots is ugly in comparison with maidenkind, as Hippias the wise man says.

100. The people ought to fight for their law as for a wall.

101. μόροι μέζονες μέζονας μοίρας λαγχάνουσι.

102. ἀρηιφάτους θεοὶ τιμῶσι καὶ ἄνθρωποι.

103. ὕβριν χρὴ σβεννύειν ἢ πυρκαιήν.

104. ἀνθρώποισι γίνεσθαι ὁκόσα θέλουσι οὐκ ἄμεινον. νοῦσος ὑγίειαν ἐποίησε ἡδὺ καὶ ἀγαθόν, λιμὸς κόρον, κάματος ἀνάπαυσιν.

105. θυμῷ μάχεσθαι χαλεπόν· ὅ τι γὰρ ἂν χρηίζῃ γίνεσθαι, ψυχῆς ὠνέεται.

106. †ἀνθρώποισι πᾶσι μέτεστι γιγνώσκειν ἑαυτοὺς καὶ σωφρονεῖν†.

107. †σωφρονεῖν ἀρετὴ μεγίστη· καὶ σοφίη ἀληθέα λέγειν καὶ ποιεῖν κατὰ φύσιν ἐπαίοντας†.

108-109. ἀμαθίην ἄμεινον κρύπτειν· ἔργον δὲ ἐν ἀνέσει καὶ παρ᾽ οἶνον.

110. νόμος καὶ βουλῇ πείθεσθαι ἑνός.

---

101. Clem. Al. *Strom.* iv. 7, p. 586; Theodor. *Ther.* viii. p. 117, 33. Cf. Hipp. *Ref. haer.* 8.   Theodor. reads μόνοι.

102. Clem. Al. *Strom.* iv. 4, p. 571; Theodor. *Ther.* viii. p. 117, 33.

103. Diog. Laer. ix. 2.   *M* Cobet σβεννύναι, *L* σβεννύην.

104. Stob. *Flor.* iii. 83, 4.   Cf. εὐαρέστησις, Clem. Al. *Strom.* ii. 21, p. 497; Theodor. *Ther.* xi. p. 152, 25.

105. Arist. *Eth. Nik.* ii. 2, p. 1105 a 8; and *Eth. Eud.* ii. 7, p. 1223 b 22; and *Pol.* v. 11, p. 1315 a 29; Plut. *de cohib. ira* 9, p. 457 D; and *Erot.* 11, p. 755 D; Iambl. *Protrep.* p. 140 Arc.; and *Coriol.* 22.

106. Stob. *Flor.* v. 119.   Neither this nor the following fragment can be regarded as genuine.

107. Stob. *Flor.* iii. 84.

108. Plut. *qu. conv.* iii. prooem. p. 644 F; and *de audien.* 12, p. 43 D; and *virt. doc. posse* 2, p. 439 D; Stob. *Flor.* xviii. 32.

109. Stob. *Flor.* iii. 82 κρύπτειν ἀμαθίην κρέσσον ἢ ἐς τὸ μέσον φέρειν. A variation of 108.

110. Clem. Al. *Strom.* v. 14, p. 718 (Euseb. *P. E.* xiii. 13, p. 681).

Euseb. βουλῇ, Clem. βουλή.   καί is suspicious.

101. Greater deaths gain greater portions.

102. Gods and men honour those slain in battle.

103. Wantonness must be quenched more than a conflagration.

104. It is not good for men to have whatever they want. Disease makes health sweet and good; hunger, satiety; toil, rest.

105. It is hard to contend with passion; for whatever it desires to get it buys at the cost of soul.

106. It is the part of all men to know themselves and to be temperate. 107. To be temperate is the greatest virtue; and it is wisdom to speak the truth and to act according to nature with understanding.

108. It is better to conceal stupidity, but it is an effort in time of relaxation and over the wine.

109. It is better to conceal ignorance than to put it forth into the midst.

110. It is law to obey the counsel of one.

E

111. τίς γὰρ αὐτῶν νόος ἢ φρήν ; [δήμων] ἀοιδοῖσι
ἕπονται καὶ διδασκάλῳ χρέωνται ὁμίλῳ, οὐκ εἰδότες ὅτι
πολλοὶ κακοί, ὀλίγοι δὲ ἀγαθοί. αἱρεῦνται γὰρ ἓν ἀντία
πάντων οἱ ἄριστοι, κλέος ἀέναον θνητῶν, οἱ δὲ πολλοὶ
κεκόρηνται ὅκωσπερ κτήνεα.

112. ἐν Πριήνῃ Βίας ἐγένετο ὁ Τευτάμεω οὗ πλέων
λόγος ἢ τῶν ἄλλων.

113. εἷς ἐμοὶ μύριοι, ἐὰν ἄριστοις ᾖ.

114. ἄξιον Ἐφεσίοις ἡβηδὸν ἀπάγξασθαι πᾶσι καὶ
τοῖς ἀνήβοις τὴν πόλιν καταλιπεῖν, οἵτινες Ἑρμόδωρον
ἄνδρα ἑωυτῶν ὀνήιστον ἐξέβαλον, φάντες· ἡμέων μηδὲ
εἷς ὀνήιστος ἔστω, εἰ δὲ μή, ἄλλῃ δὲ καὶ μετ' ἄλλων.

115. κύνες καὶ βαύζουσι ὃν ἂν μὴ γινώσκωσι.

116. ἀπιστίη διαφυγγάνει μὴ γινώσκεσθαι.

117. βλὰξ ἄνθρωπος ἐπὶ παντὶ λόγῳ ἐπτοῆσθαι
φιλέει.

118. δοκεόντων ὁ δοκιμώτατος γινώσκει φυλάσσειν·
καὶ μέντοι καὶ δίκη καταλήψεται ψευδέων τέκτονας καὶ
μάρτυρας.

---

111. Clem. Al. *Strom.* v. 9, p. 682 ; and iv. 7, p. 586; Prokl. on *Alkib.*
p. 255 Creuz, ii. 525 Cous.   Clement omits first clause ; Proklos ends
with ἀγαθοί.

Some MSS. omit αὐτῶν; Prokl. αἰδοῦς ἠπιόων τε καὶ διδασκάλῳ
χρειῶν τε ὁμίλῳ οὐκ.   Clem. καὶ νόμοισι χρέεσθαι ὁμίλῳ εἰδότας.
MSS. p. 682 ἐναντία.   Restored by Bernays, *Heraclit.* i.
p. 34.

112. Diog. Laer. i. 88.

113. Galen, π. διαγνώσεως σφυγμῶν I. ι. iii. p. 53 ed. Bas.; Symmachus,
Epist. ix. 115 (105 Paris 1604) ; Theod. Prod. in *Lazerii Misc.* i. p. 20 ;
and *Tetrastich. in Basil.* i. (fol. κ 2 vers. ed. Bas.) ; Diog. Laer. ix. 16 ;
Cicero, *ad Att.* xvi. 11 ; Cf. Seneca, *Ep.* 7.

114. Strabo, xiv. 25, p. 642 ; Cicero, *Tusc.* v. 105 ; Muson., Stob.
Flor. xl. 9 ; Laer. Diog. ix. 2 ; Iambl. *de vita Pyth.* 30, p. 154 Arc.   Cf.
Lucian *vit. auct.* 14.

115. Plut. *An seni sit ger. resp.* vii. p. 787.

116. Plut. *Coriol.* 38 ; Clem. Al. *Strom.* v. 13, p. 699.   Clem. ἀπιστίη.

117. Plutarch, *de audiendo* 7, p. 41A ; *de aud. poet.*, p. 28D.

118. Clem. Al. *Strom.* v. 1, p. 649.   Bergk φλνάσσειν, Bernays Bywater πλάσσειν.

111. For what sense or understanding have they ? They follow the bards and employ the crowd as their teacher, not knowing that many are bad and few good. For the very best choose one thing before all others, immortal glory among mortals, while the masses eat their fill like cattle.

112. In Priene was born Bias son of Teutamas, who is of more account than the rest.

Diogenes adds the apothegm ' most men are bad.'

113. To me one man is ten thousand if he be the best.

114. The Ephesians deserve to be hanged, every one that is a man grown, and the youth to abandon the city, for they cast out Hermodoros the best man among them, saying :—Let no one among us be best, and if one be best, let him be so elsewhere and among others.

115. Dogs also bark at those they do not know.

116. As the result of incredulity (divine things) miss being known.

Either because men are incredulous, or the things incredible. Cf. Zeller, *Phil. Gr.* i.⁴ 574A 2. Gomperz combined this with fragment 10.

117. The fool is wont to be in a flutter at every word.

118. The most esteemed of those in estimation knows how to be on his guard ; yet truly justice shall overtake forgers of lies and witnesses to them.

If the reference is to Homer, read πλάττειν, ' knows how to create myths.'

119. τὸν Ὅμηρον ἄξιον ἐκ τῶν ἀγώνων ἐκβάλλεσθαι καὶ ῥαπίζεσθαι, καὶ Ἀρχίλοχον ὁμοίως.

121. ἦθος ἀνθρώπῳ δαίμων.

122. ἀνθρώπους μένει τελευτήσαντας ἄσσα οὐκ ἔλπονται οὐδὲ δοκέουσι.

123. ἔνθα †δεόντι† ἐπανίστασθαι καὶ φύλακας γίνεσθαι ἐγερτὶ ζώντων καὶ νεκρῶν.

124. νυκτιπόλοι, μάγοι, βάκχοι, λῆναι, μύσται.

125. τὰ γὰρ νομιζόμενα κατ᾽ ἀνθρώπους μυστήρια ἀνιερωστὶ μυεῦνται.

126 = 130b.

127. εἰ μὴ γὰρ Διονύσῳ πομπὴν ἐποιεῦντο καὶ ὕμνεον ᾆσμα αἰδοίοισι, ἀναιδέστατα εἴργαστ᾽ ἄν· ωὑτὸς δὲ Ἀίδης καὶ Διόνυσος. ὅτεῳ μαίνονται καὶ ληναΐζουσι.

---

119. Diog. Laer. ix. 1. Schleiermacher attributes to H. on the basis of Schol. Ven. A. on *Iliad* xviii. 251 Eustath. 1142, 5; Bywater suggests Herakleides and compares Eust. p. 705, 60, and Achilles Tat. *Isag.* p. 124 n Petav.

120. Seneca, *Ep.* 12 'Unus dies par omni est.' The Greek cannot be restored from Plutarch, *Camill.* 19 φύσιν ἡμέρας ἀπάσης μίαν οὖσαν.

121. Plutarch, *Qu. Plat.* i. 2, 999E ; Alex. Aphrod. *de fato* 6, p. 16 (*de anima* ii. 48, p. 150); Stob. *Flor.* civ. 23. Cf. Pseudo-Herakl. *Ep.* 9.

122. Clem. Al. *Strom.* iv. 22, p. 630 ; *Protrept.* 2, p. 18 (Euseb. *P. E.* ii. 3, p. 66); Theodoret. *Ther.* viii. p. 118, 1. Cf. Themist. (Plut.) in Stob. *Flor.* cxx. 28.

123. Hippolyt. *Ref. haer.* ix. 10 ; the fragment is quoted to show that Herakleitos believes in the resurrection of the flesh, and recognises that god is the cause of this resurrection. Cf. Clem. Al. *Strom.* v. 1, p. 649.

Sauppe suggests ἔνθα θεὸν δεῖ . . . φύλακα, Bernays ἔνθαδε ἐόντας: MSS. ἐγερτιζόντων, corr. Bernays. Schuster suggests δαίμων ἐθέλει ἔνθαδε ἐόντι ἐπιίστασθαι καὶ φυλακὸς κ. τ. λ.

124. Clem. Al. *Protrept.* 2, p. 18 (Euseb. *P. E.* ii. 3, p. 66).

125. Clem. Al. *Protrept.* 2. p. 19 (Euseb. *P.E.* ii. p. 67). Bywater compares Arnobius *adv. nat.* v. 29.

126. (v. 130.)

127. Clem. Al. *Protrept.* 2, p. 30. MSS. ἐποιοῦντο, corr. Lobeck: MSS. εἴργασται, corr. Schleierm. Clem. Al. ὅτεῳ, Plutarch, *de Isid.* 28, p. 362A ὅτε οὖν . . . ληραίνουσιν.

128. Iamblich. *de Myst.* v. 15. The Greek text cannot be restored.

119. (He used to say that) Homer deserved to be cast out of the lists and flogged, and Archilochos likewise.

120. One day is equal to every other.

121. Character is a man's guardian divinity.

122. There awaits men at death what they do not expect or think.

123. Then [it is necessary] that God raise them up, and that they become guardians of the living and the dead.

> Or adopting Sauppe's conjectures in full 'that he become a watchful guardian. . .'

124. Night-walkers, wizards, bacchanals, revellers, sharers in the mysteries.

125. For what are esteemed mysteries among men they celebrate in an unholy way.

127. For if it were not to Dionysos that they made the procession and sang the song with phallic symbols, their deeds would indeed be most shameful; but Hades and Dionysos are the same, to whomever they go mad and share the revel.

128. I distinguish two kinds of sacrifices; those of men altogether purified, which would occur rarely, as Herakleitos says, in the case of a single individual, or of some very few men easily counted; secondly, those that are material and corporeal and composite through change, such as are in harmony with those who are still restrained by the body.

129. ἄκεα.

130. καθαίρονται δὲ αἵματι μιαινόμενοι ὥσπερ ἂν εἴ τις ἐς πηλὸν ἐμβὰς πηλῷ ἀπονίζοιτο. μαίνεσθαι δ' ἂν δοκοίη, εἴ τις αὐτὸν ἀνθρώπων ἐπιφράσαιτο οὕτω ποιέοντα. καὶ τοῖς ἀγάλμασι τουτέοισι εὔχονται, ὁκοῖον εἴ τις τοῖς δόμοισι λεσχηνεύοιτο, οὔ τι γινώσκων θεοὺς οὐδ' ἥρωας οἵτινές εἰσι.

130a. εἰ θεοί εἰσι, ἵνα τί θρηνέετε αὐτούς; εἰ δὲ θρηνέετε αὐτούς, μηκέτι τούτους ἡγέεσθε θεούς.

SPURIOUS FRAGMENTS.

131. πάντα ψυχῶν εἶναι καὶ δαιμόνων πλήρη.

132. τήν τε οἴησιν ἱερὰν νόσον ἔλεγε καὶ τὴν ὄρασιν ψεύδεσθαι.

133. ἐγκαλυπτέος ἕκαστος ὁ ματαίως ἐν δόξῃ γενόμενος.

129. Iamblich. de Myst. i. 11.

130. Greg. Naz. Or. xxv. (xxiii.) 15, p. 466, ed. Par. 1778 πηλῷ πηλὸν καθαιρόντων. Elias Cretensis on the Gregory passage (cod. Vat. Pii II. 6, fol. 90 r) gives first thirteen words (Byw. 130). Cf. Apollonius, Ep. 27. Byw. 126, the last sentence, from Origen, c. Cels. i. 5, p. 6 (quoting Celsus); and in part vii. 62, p. 384, Clem. Al. Prot. 4, p. 44. The whole passage, lacking the last eight words, is published by Neumann, Hermes xv. 1880, p. 605 (cf. also xvi. 159), from fol. 83 a of a MS. entitled Χρησμοὶ θεῶν (containing also works ascribed to Justin Martyr) formerly in the Strassburg library.

This same MS. gives the following fragment, the last clauses of which Neumann joins to the passage as given in the text: δαιμόνων ἀγάλμασιν εὔχονται οὐκ ἀκούουσιν, ὥσπερ ἀκούοιεν, οὐκ ἀποδιδοῦσιν, ὥσπερ οὐκ ἀπαιτοῖεν.

130a. Given by Neumann from the Strassburg MS. just referred to. The saying is attributed to Xenophanes by Aristotle, Rhet. 23; 1400 b 5 and Plutarch, v. infra, p. 78.

131. Diog. Laer. ix. 7.

132. Diog. Laer. ix. 7. Cf. Floril. Monac. 195, p. 282.

133. Apollonius, Ep. 18.

129. (Herakleitos fittingly called religious rites) *cures* (for the soul).

130. They purify themselves by defiling themselves with blood, as if one who had stepped into the mud were to wash it off with mud. If any one of men should observe him doing so, he would think he was insane. And to these images they pray, just as if one were to converse with men's houses, for they know not what gods and heroes are.

130a. If they are gods, why do ye lament them ? And if ye lament them, no longer consider them gods.

> The fragment in the critical notes reads : ' To images of gods they pray, to those who do not hear, as though they might hear; to those who do not answer, as though they might not make request.'

131. All things are full of souls and of divine spirits.

132. He was wont to say that false opinion is a sacred disease, and that vision is deceitful.

133. Each one who has come to be esteemed without due grounds, ought to hide his face.

134. οἴησις προκοπῆς ἐγκοπὴ προκοπῆς.

135. τὴν παιδείαν ἕτερον ἥλιον εἶναι τοῖς πεπαιδευμένοις.

136. ἡ εὔκαιρος χάρις λιμῷ καθάπερ τροφὴ ἁρμόττουσα τὴν τῆς ψυχῆς ἔνδειαν ἰᾶται.

137. συντομωτάτην ὁδὸν ὁ αὐτὸς ἔλεγεν εἰς εὐδοξίαν τὸ γενέσθαι ἀγαθόν.

---

134. *Floril. Monac.* 199, p. 283.   Cf. Philo, ap. Ioan. Dam. *S. P.* 693 E, fr. p. 652 Mang.   Stob. *Flor.* iv. 88 credits it to Bion; Maxim. Conf. *Serm.* 34, p. 624 Combef.

135. *Floril. Monac.* 200, p. 283.

136. Maximus Conf. *Serm.* 8, p. 557.

137. Maximus Conf. *Serm.* 46, p. 646.

138. Schol. ad Eurip. *Hek.* 134, i. p. 254 Dind.

TRANSLATION.

134. False opinion of progress is the stoppage of progress.

135. Their education is a second sun to those that have been educated.

136. As food is timely in famine, so opportune favour heals the need of the soul.

137. The same one was wont to say that the shortest way to glory was to become good.

138 Timaios wrote thus: So Pythagoras does not appear to have discovered the true art of words, nor yet the one accused by Herakleitos, but Herakleitos himself is the one who is the pretender.

PASSAGES IN PLATO AND ARISTOTLE REFERRING TO
HERAKLEITOS.

Plato, *Thecæet.* 160 D.   Homer, and Herakleitos, and
the whole company which say that all things are in
motion and in a state of flux.   Cf. 152 D H.

Kratylos, 401 D.   According to Herakleitos all things
are in motion and nothing abides.   Cf. 402 A, and frag.
41 ; also 412 D, 440 c.

Plato also alludes to fragments 32, 45, 98–99.

Aristotle : *Topica* i. 11, 104 f 21.   All things are in
motion, according to Herakleitos.

Top. viii. 5 ; 155 f 30.   Wherefore those that hold
different opinions, as that good and bad are the same
thing, as Herakleitos says, do not grant that the opposite
cannot coexist with itself; not as though they did not
think this to be the case, but because as followers of
Herakleitos they are obliged to speak as they do.

Phys. i. 2 ; 185 b 19.   But still, if in the argument all
things that exist are one, as a cloak or a himation, it
turns out that they are stating the position of Herakleitos ;
for the same thing will apply to good and bad, and to
good and not-good, so that good and not-good, and man
and horse, will be the same ; and they will not be argu-
ing that all things are one, but that they are nothing,
and that the same thing applies to such and to so much.

Phys. iii. 5 ; 205 a 3.   As Herakleitos says that all
things sometime become fire.

De cœlo i. 10 ; 279 b 16.   And others in their turn
say that sometimes combination is taking place, and at
other times destruction, and that this will always continue, as Empedokles of Agrigentum, and Herakleitos of
Ephesos.

De anima i. 2 ; 405 a 25.   And Herakleitos also
says that the first principle is soul, as it were a

fiery exhalation, of which all other things consist ;
for it is the least corporeal and always in a state of
flux, and the moving is known by the moving; and he
agreed with most thinkers in holding that things are in
motion.

De part anim. i. 5 ; 645 a 17.   And as Herakleitos is
reported to have said to strangers who wanted to meet
him, who stopped when they entered and saw him
getting warm by an oven—for he bade them enter boldly,
since, said he, gods are here—so should one enter upon
the investigation of each of the animals without timidity,
as there is in them all something natural and beautiful.

Met. i. 3 ; 984 a 7.   Hippasos of Metapontum and
Herakleitos of Ephesos call fire the first cause.   Cf.
996 a 9, 1001 a 15.

Met. iii. 3 ; 1005 b 24.   For it is impossible for any
one to postulate that the same thing is and is not, as
some think Herakleitos says.

Met. iii. 5 ; 1010 a 13.   V. Frag. 41–12, *supra.*

Met. iii. 7 ; 1012 a 24.   For the word of Herakleitos,
that all things are and are not, seems to make all things
true.

Met. x. 5 ; 1062 a 32.   For one might ask Herakleitos
himself after this manner and speedily compel him to
agree that it is never possible for opposite statements to
be true about the same things.   Cf. 1063 b 24.

Met. xii. 4 ; 1078 b 12.   For the doctrine of ideas is
held by its supporters because they are convinced by
Herakleitos's words in regard to the truth, viz., that all
things perceived by the senses are always in a state
of flux ; so that if there is to be a science and a knowledge of anything, it is necessary to assume the existence
of other objects in nature besides those that are perceived
by sense, for there can be no science of things in a state
of flux.

Eth. ii. 3 ; 1105 a 8. It is harder to fight against pleasure than against anger, as Herakleitos says.

Eth. vii. 3 ; 1146 b 30. For some believe their opinions no less strongly than what they know by scientific procedure ; and Herakleitos is an example of this.

Eth. viii. 2 ; 1155 b 4. And Herakleitos says that opposition unites, and that the most beautiful harmony results from opposites, and that all things come into being through strife.

Eth. x. 5 ; 1176 a 6. As Herakleitos says, an ass would prefer refuse to gold, for natural food is sweeter to asses than gold.

> Sext. *Emp. adv. Math.* vii. 129. According to Herakleitos we become intelligent when we get this divine reason by breathing it in, and in sleep we are forgetful, but on waking we gain our senses again. For in sleep since the pores of the senses are closed, the mind in us is separated from what is akin to it in what surrounds us, and its connection through pores is only preserved like a sort of root ; and being cut off it loses its former power of memory ; but when we wake it peeps out through the pores of sense as through little doors, and entering into connection with what surrounds us it regains the power of reason.

PASSAGES REFERRING TO HERAKLEITOS IN THE ' DOXOGRAPHISTS.'

Ar. Did. *Epit.* 39, 2 ; *Dox.* 471. Zeno as well as Herakleitos says that the soul is a perceptive exhalation. The latter desiring to make it clear that souls always gain mental faculties by giving forth exhalations, likened them to rivers ; and these are his words : (Fr. 42) 'Other and yet other waters are flowing on upon those who step in the same rivers.'

Sim. in *Phys.* 6r ; *Dox.* 475. (Theophrastos says)

Hippasos of Metapontum and Herakleitos of Ephesos
teach that the one is moved and limited, but they make
fire the first principle and derive all things from fire by
condensation and rarefaction, and again they resolve
them into fire since this one thing is the essential
nature underlying their appearance; for Herakleitos
says that all things are transformations of fire [πυρὸς
ἀμοιβὴν], and he finds a certain order and definite time
in the changes of the universe according to a fated
[εἱμαρμένην] necessity.

Theoph. *de Sens.* 1 ; *Dox.* 499. The followers of
Anaxagoras and Herakleitos say that men perceive by
the presence in themselves of the opposite quality.

Phil. *de Piet.* 14, 25 ; *Dox.* 548. (Chrysippos) in
his third book says that the universe is one of the beings
endowed with sense, fellow-citizen with men and gods,
and that strife and Zeus are the same thing, as Herakleitos says.

Hipp. *Phil.* 44 ; *Dox.* 558. Herakleitos the Ephesian,
a philosopher of the physical school, was always lament-
ing, charging all men with ignorance of the whole of life,
but still he pitied the life of mortals. For he would say
that he himself knew all things, but that other men knew
nothing. His language agrees quite well with that of
Empedokles when he says that strife and love are the
first principles of all things, and that god is intelligent
fire, and that all things enter into a common motion
and do not stand still. And as Empedokles said that
the whole region occupied by man is full of evils, and
that the evils extend from the region about the earth as
far as the moon but do not go farther, inasmuch as all
the region beyond the moon is purer, so also it seemed to
Herakleitos.

Epi. *adv. Haer.* iii. 20 ; *Dox.* 591. Herakleitos the
Ephesian, son of Bleson, said that fire is the source of

all things, and that all things are resolved into fire again.

Galen, *His. Phil.* 62; *Dox.* 626. Herakleitos says that the sun is a burning mass, kindled at its rising, and quenched at its setting.

Herm. *I.G.P.* 13; *Dox.* 654. Perhaps I might yield to the arguments of noble Demokritos and want to laugh with him, unless Herakleitos led me to the opposite view as he said weeping : Fire is the first principle of all things, and it is subject to rarefaction and condensation, the one active, the other passive, the one synthetic, the other analytic. Enough for me, for I am already steeped in such first principles.

Aet. i. 3 ; *Dox.* 283. Herakleitos and Hippasos say that the first principle of all things is fire ; for they say that all things arise from fire and they all end by becoming fire. As this is quenched all things come into the order of the universe ; for first the dense part of it contracting into itself becomes earth, then the earth becoming relaxed by fire is rendered water in its nature, then it is sublimated and becomes air ; and again the universe and all bodies are consumed by fire in the conflagration. [Fire then is the first principle because all things arise from this, and the final principle because all things are resolved into this.]

Aet. i. 5 ; *Dox.* 292. Hippasos of Metapontum and Herakleitos the Ephesian say that the all is one, ever moving and limited, and that fire is its first principle.

Aet. i. 7; *Dox.* 303. Herakleitos says that the periodic fire is eternal, and that destined reason working through opposition is the creator [δημιουργὸν] of things.

Aet. i. 9 ; *Dox.* 307. H. et al. declare that matter is subject to change, variation, and transformation, and that it flows the whole through the whole.

Aet. i. 13 ; *Dox.* 312. H. introduces certain very

small and indivisible particles (or H. seems to some to leave particles, instead of the unity).

Aet. i. 23 ; *Dor.* 320. H. denies rest and fixed position to the whole ; for this is the attribute of dead bodies ; but he assigns eternal motion to what is eternal, perishable motion to what is perishable.

Aet. i. 27 ; *Dor.* 322. H. says that all things happen according to fate and that fate itself is necessity. Indeed he writes 'For it is absolutely destined.' (Frag. 63.)

Aet. i. 23 ; *Dor.* 323. H. declares that reason, pervading the essence of the all, is the essence of fate. And it is itself ethereal matter, seed of the generation of the all, and measure of the allotted period.

Aet. ii. 1 ; *Dor.* 327, Herakleitos et al.   The universe is one.   4 ; *Dor.* 331.   The universe is generated not according to time, but according to thought.   11 ; *Dor.* 340 ; H. et al.   The heaven is of a fiery nature. 13 ; *Dor.* 342. H. and Parmenides.   The stars are compressed bits of fire.   17 ; *Dor.* 346.   H. and Parm. The stars are nurtured by an exhalation from the earth. 20 ; *Dor.* 351.   H. and Hekataios.   The sun is an intelligent burning mass rising out of the sea.   (The same words are assigned to Stoics, Plut. 2, 890 A ; *Dor.* 349.) 21 ; *Dor.* 351.   It is as great ' as the width of a human foot.'   22 ; *Dor.* 352.   It is bowl-shaped, rather gibbous. 24 ; *Dor.* 354. An eclipse takes place by the turning of the bowl-shaped body so that the concave side is upward, and the convex side downward toward our vision. [25 ; *Dor.* 356. The earth is surrounded with mist.] 27 ; *Dor.* 358. (The moon) is bowl-shaped.[1]   28 ; *Dor.* 359. Sun and moon are subject to the same influences.   For these heavenly bodies being bowl-shaped, receive bright rays from the moist exhalation, and give light in appearance [πρὸς τὴν φαντασίαν] ; the sun more

_____
[1] Cf. Galen. *Hist. Phil.* 64 ; *Dor.* 626.

brightly, for it moves in purer æther [ἀήρ], and the moon moves in thicker æther and so it shines more dimly. 29 ; *Dox.* 359. Eclipses of the moon are occasioned by the turning of the bowl-shaped body. 32 ; *Dox.* 364. The great year consists of eighteen thousand sun-years. According to Diogenes and Herakleitos the year consists of three hundred and sixty-five days.

Aet. iii. 3 ; *Dox.* 369. Thunder is occasioned by a gathering of winds and clouds, and the impact of gusts of wind on the clouds ; and lightning by a kindling of the exhalations ; and fiery whirlwinds [πρηστῆρας] by a burning and a quenching of the clouds.

Aet. iv. 3 ; *Dox.* 338. Parmenides and Hippasos and Herakleitos call the soul a fiery substance. 7 ; *Dox.* 392. H. says that souls set free from the body go into the soul of the all, inasmuch as it is akin to them in nature and essence.

Aet. v. 23 ; *Dox.* 434. Herakleitos and the Stoics say that men come to maturity at about fourteen years, with the beginning of sexual life ; for trees come to maturity when they begin to bear fruit. . . And at about the age of fourteen men gain understanding of good and evil, and of instruction as to these matters.

V.

THE ELEATIC SCHOOL: XENOPHANES.

XENOPHANES of Kolophon, son of Dexias (Apollodoros says of Orthomenes), was the founder of the Eleatic School. After a careful review of the evidence, Zeller (*Vorsokr. Phil.* pp. 521–522) concludes that he was born about 580 B.C. ; it is agreed by all writers that he lived to a great age. The stories of his travels and adventures are very numerous. He speaks of the war between the Ionic colonies and the Persians as beginning in his youth. According to Diogenes he sang the founding of Elea in 2,000 hexameter verses. The reference to him by Herakleitos (Fr. 16) indicates the general respect for his philosophy. He composed poetry of all varieties, and is said to have recited his own poems. His philosophic views were embodied in a poem which was early lost, and to which later ages gave the name ' περὶ φύσεως.'

Literature : Brandis, *Comm. Eleat.* 1813 ; Cousin, *Nouv. frag. phil.* 1828, pp. 9–45; Karsten, *Phil. Graec. vet. reliq.* i. 1, 1830 ; Bergk, *Poet. Lyr. Graec.* ii.; F. Kern, *Quaestionum Xenophanearum cap. duo*, Naumb. 1864 ; *Beiträge*, Danzig 1871 ; *Ueber Xenophanes*, Stettin 1874 ; Freudenthal, *Die Theologie des Xenophanes*, 1886 ; and *Archiv f. d. Gesch. d. Phil.* i. 1888, p. 322 sqq.; Thill, *Xénophane de Colophon*, Luxemb. 1890.

On the book *De Xen. Zen. Gorg. Aristotelis*, v. Fülleborn, Halle 1789 ; Bergk, 1848 ; Mullach, 1845 ; Ueberweg, *Philol.* viii. 1853, p. 104 sqq.; xxvi. 1868, p. 709 sqq.; Vermehren, 1861 ; F. Kern, *Symbola crit. ad libellum* π. Ξενοφ. etc. Oldenb. 1867 ; Diels' *Doxogr.* pp. 109–113 ; Zeller, *Geschichte d. Phil. d. Griechen*, i. 499–521.

F

(a) Fragments of Xenophanes.[*]

1 εἷς θεὸς ἔν τε θεοῖσι καὶ ἀνθρώποισι μέγιστος,
   οὔτε δέμας θνητοῖσιν ὁμοίιος οὔτε νόημα.

2 οὖλος ὁρᾷ, οὖλος δὲ νοεῖ, οὖλος δέ τ' ἀκούει.

3 ἀλλ' ἀπάνευθε πόνοιο νόου φρενὶ πάντα κραδαίνει.

4 αἰεὶ δ' ἐν ταὐτῷ μίμνει κινούμενον οὐδέν,
   οὐδὲ μετέρχεσθαί μιν ἐπιπρέπει ἄλλοτε ἄλλῃ.

5 ἀλλὰ βροτοὶ δοκέουσι γεννᾶσθαι θεούς,
   τὴν σφετέραν δ' ἐσθῆτά τ' ἔχειν φωνήν τε δέμας τε.

6 . . . ἀλλ' εἰ χεῖρας ἔχον βόες ἠε λέοντες,
   <ὡς> γράψαι χείρεσσι καὶ ἔργα τελεῖν ἅπερ ἄνδρες,
   καί κε θεῶν ἰδέας ἔγραφον καὶ σώματ' ἐποίουν
   τοιαῦθ', οἷόν περ καὶ αὐτοὶ δέμας εἶχον <ἕκαστοι>
   ἵπποι μέν θ' ἵπποισι, βόες δέ τε βουσὶν ὁμοῖα.

Sources and Critical Notes.

1. Clem. Alex. *Strom.* v. p. 714. Euseb. *Praep. Ev.* xiii. 13, p. 678 D. MS. οὐδε δ', ... οὔτε, corr. Potter.

2. Sext. Emp. *Math.* ix. 144.

3. Simplic. *Phys.* 6 r 23, 20 ; *Dox.* 481.

4. Simplic. *Phys.* 6 r 23, 11 ; *Dox.* 481.

5. Clem. Al. *Strom.* v. p. 714 ; Euseb. *Praep. Ev.* xiii. 13, p. 678 D, following Fr. 1. Theodoret, *Gr. Aff. Curat.* iii. 72, p. 49.

   V. 1 : Theod., Clem. ed. Par. and Ed. Floren., Euseb. *CFGI* read ἀλλ' οἱ βροτοί. Text follows remaining MSS. of Clem. and Euseb. V. 2 : Theod. καὶ ἴσην, Clem. and Euseb. τὴν σφετέραν; Theod. τ' αἴσθησιν, Clem. and Euseb. δ' ἐσθῆτα.

6. Clem. Euseb. and Theod. after preceding fragment. Line 5 stands third in MSS. and earlier texts ; Karsten places it fifth.

   V. 1 : Clem. and Theod. ἀλλ' εἰ τοι χεῖρας εἶχον : Clem. Euseb. λέοντες, Theod. ἐλέφαντες. V. 2 : Euseb. *FG* καί, other MSS. ἠ, corr. Hiller. V. 3 : Euseb. and Theod. καί κε : Eus. *DEFG* δώματ'. V. 4 : MSS. ἴσχον, corr. Karst.: MSS. ὁμοῖον, Meineke ἕκαστοι. V. 5 : Clem. Theod. ὁμοῖοι, Eus. ὔμοιοι, Karst. ὁμοῖα.

---

[*] The text follows in the main the edition of Bergk-Hiller, *Poet. Lyr. Graec.*, Leipzig, 1890.

TRANSLATION.

1. God is one, supreme among gods and men, and not like mortals in body or in mind.[1]

2. The whole [of god] sees, the whole perceives, the whole hears.[2]

3. But without effort he sets in motion all things by mind and thought.

4. It [*i.e.* being] always abides in the same place, not moved at all, nor is it fitting that it should move from one place to another.

5. But mortals suppose that the gods are born (as they themselves are), and that they wear man's clothing and have human voice and body.[3]

6. But if cattle or lions had hands, so as to paint with their hands and produce works of art as men do, they would paint their gods and give them bodies in form like their own—horses like horses, cattle like cattle.[4]

---

[1] Zeller, *Vorsokratische Philosophie*, p. 530, n. 3.

[2] Zeller, 526, n. 1. No author is given in the context; Karsten follows Fabricius in accrediting it to Xenophanes.

[3] Zeller, 524, n. 2. Cf. Arist. *Rhet.* ii. 23 ; 1399 b 6.

[4] Zeller, 525, n. 2. Diog. Laer. iii. 16 ; Cic. *de nat. Deor.* i. 27.

7 πάντα θεοῖς ἀνέθηκαν Ὅμηρός θ' Ἡσίοδός τε
   ὅσσα παρ' ἀνθρώποισιν ὀνείδεα καὶ ψόγος ἐστί,
   καὶ πλεῖστ' ἐφθέγξαντο θεῶν ἀθεμίστια ἔργα,
   κλέπτειν, μοιχεύειν τε καὶ ἀλλήλους ἀπατεύειν.

8 ἐκ γαίης γὰρ πάντα, καὶ εἰς γῆν πάντα τελευτᾷ.

9 πάντες γὰρ γαίης τε καὶ ὕδατος ἐκγενόμεσθα.

10 γῆ καὶ ὕδωρ πάντ' ἐσθ' ὅσα γίνοντ' ἠδὲ φύονται.

11 πηγή δ' ἐστι θάλασσ' ὕδατος, πηγὴ δ' ἀνέμοιο·
    οὔτε γὰρ ἐν νέφεσιν <πνοιαί κ' ἀνέμοιο φύοιντο
    ἐκπνείοντος> ἔσωθεν ἄνευ πόντου μεγάλοιο
    οὔτε ῥοαὶ ποταμῶν οὔτ' αἰθέρος ὄμβριον ὕδωρ
    ἀλλὰ μέγας πόντος γενέτωρ νεφέων ἀνέμων τε
    καὶ ποταμῶν.

12 γαίης μὲν τόδε πεῖρας ἄνω παρὰ ποσσὶν ὁρᾶται
    αἰθέρι προσπλάζον, τὰ κάτω δ' ἐς ἄπειρον ἱκάνει.

13 ἥν τ' Ἶριν καλέουσι, νέφος καὶ τοῦτο πέφυκε
    πορφύρεον καὶ φοινίκεον καὶ χλωρὸν ἰδέσθαι.

---

7. Sext. Emp. *Math.* ix. 193 and i. 289 combined.

  V. 3 : MSS. ὅς, Karst. καὶ.

  8. Sext. Emp. *Math.* x. 313 ; Stob. *Ecl. Phys.* i. p. 294, *Dox.* 284 ;
Schol. Vill. and Schol. Min. to Homer, *Il.* Η 99.

  9. Sext. Emp. *Math.* ix. 361 and x. 313 ; Eustath. *Il.* Η 99, p. 668, 60.

  10. Simplic. *Phys.* 41 r 189, 1, attributes this verse to Anaximenes
on the authority of Porphyry. Joh. Philoponus (*Phys.* i. 188 b 30) attributes it to Xenophanes on the same authority.

  MS. γίνονται, corr. Diels.

  11. Schol. Genev. to Homer, *Il.* I 199, 2.   V. *Sitz. d. berl. Akad.*
June 18, 1891.   I have inserted Diels' emendation in lines 2 and 3.   The
first line also occurs in Stob. *Flor.* ed. Gais. iv. App. p. 6.

  12. Achill. Tat. in *Isagoge ad Aratum* (*Petavii Doctr. Tempor.* iii.
p. 76).   Cf. Aristotle, *de Xenophane*, &c., 2 ; 976 a 32.

  V. 2 : καὶ ῥεῖ προσπλάζον, τὰ κάτω δ' εἰς, Karst. αἰθέρι.

  13. Eustath. *Il.* Λ 24, p. 827, 59 ; Schol. Vill. ad *Il.* Λ 27 and Schol.
Leyd. in Valckenaer, *Diatr. Eurip.* p. 195.

7. Homer and Hesiod attributed to the gods all things which are disreputable and worthy of blame when done by men; and they told of them many lawless deeds, stealing, adultery, and deception of each other.[1]

8. For all things come from earth, and all things end by becoming earth.[2]

9. For we are all sprung from earth and water.[3]

10. All things that come into being and grow are earth and water.

11. The sea is the source of water and the source of wind; for neither would blasts of wind arise in the clouds and blow out from within them, except for the great sea, nor would the streams of rivers nor the rain-water in the sky exist but for the sea; but the great sea is the begetter of clouds and winds and rivers.

12. This upper limit of earth at our feet is visible and †touches the air,† but below it reaches to infinity.[4]

13. She whom men call Iris (rainbow), this also is by nature cloud, violet and red and pale green to behold.

---

[1] Zeller, 525, n. 3.   Cf. Diog. Laer. ix. 18; Sext. Emp. *Pyrrh.* i. 224.
[2] Cf. Stob. *Ecl. Phys.* ii. 282, ἐκ πυρὸς γὰρ τὰ πάντα καὶ εἰς πῦρ τὰ πάντα τελευτᾷ, which Karsten does not assign to Xenophanes.
[3] Zeller, 541, n. 1.   Cf. Sext. Emp. *Pyrrh.* ii. 30.
[4] Cf. Arist. *de Coelo* ii. 13; 294 a 21.

14 καὶ τὸ μὲν οὖν σαφὲς οὔτις ἀνὴρ γένετ' οὐδὲ τις ἔσται
εἰδὼς ἀμφὶ θεῶν τε καὶ ἄσσα λέγω περὶ πάντων·
εἰ γὰρ καὶ τὰ μάλιστα τύχοι τετελεσμένον εἰπών,
αὐτὸς ὅμως οὐκ οἶδε· δοκὸς δ' ἐπὶ πᾶσι τέτυκται.

15 ταῦτα δεδόξασθαι μὲν ἐοικότα τοῖς ἐτύμοισι.

16 οὔτοι ἀπ' ἀρχῆς πάντα θεοὶ θνητοῖς ὑπέδειξαν,
ἀλλὰ χρόνῳ ζητέοντες ἐφευρίσκουσιν ἄμεινον.

17 πὰρ πυρὶ χρὴ τοιαῦτα λέγειν χειμῶνος ἐν ὥρῃ
ἐν κλίνῃ μαλακῇ κατακείμενον, ἔμπλεον ὄντα,
πίνοντα γλυκὺν οἶνον, ὑποτρώγοντ' ἐρεβίνθους·
τίς πόθεν εἰς ἀνδρῶν; πόσα τοι ἔτε' ἐστί, φέριστε;
πηλίκος ἦσθ' ὅθ' ὁ Μῆδος ἀφίκετο;

18 νῦν αὖτ' ἄλλον ἔπειμι λόγον, δείξω δὲ κέλευθον.

    *   *   *   *   *   *

καί ποτέ μιν στυφελιζομένου σκύλακος παριόντα
φασὶν ἐποικτῖραι καὶ τόδε φάσθαι ἔπος·
παῦσαι μηδὲ ῥάπιζ', ἐπεὶ ἦ φίλου ἀνέρος ἐστίν   5
ψυχή, τὴν ἔγνων φθεγξαμένης ἀίων.

---

14. Sext. Emp. *Math.* vii. 49 and 110, and viii. 326. Vv. 1-2: Plut.
aud. poet. 17 E; Laer. Diog. ix. 72. Vv. 3-4: Hipp. *Phil.* 14, *Dox.*
565; Origen, *Philos.* xiv. vol. i. p. 892; Galen, *de diff. puls.* iii. 1, viii.
p. 62. Last half line: Sext. Emp. *Pyrrh.* ii. 18; Proklos in *Tim.*
p. 78, &c.

    V. 1: Sext. Diog. ἴδεν. V. 3: Galen ἢν γὰρ καὶ τὰ μέγιστα τύχῃ
τετελεσμένα, Hipp. τύχῃ.

15. Plut. *Symp.* ix. 746 B. Karst. reads δεδόξασται.

16. Stob. *Flor.* xxix. 41 G, *Ecl. Phys.*, I. 224.

    V. 1: *Flor.* ἐπέδειξαν, *Ecl.* παρέδαξαν. V. 2: *Ecl.* MS. *Flor.*
ἐφευρίσκουσιν, other MSS. ἐφεύρισκον.

17. Athen. ii. p. 54 E. V. 3: Eustath. p. 948, 40.

18. Diog. Laer. viii. 36; Suidas, v. Ξενοφάνης. *Anthol. Graec.* i. 86,
p. 345, ed. Bosch. prefixes two verses which Karsten assigns to Apollodoros on the evidence of Athen. 418 E.

    V. 1: MSS. νῦν οὖν τ', corr. Steph. V. 3: Suidas φησί γ'. V. 5:
Karst. τῆς. Suidas BE φθεγξαμένην.

14. Accordingly there has not been a man, nor will there be, who knows distinctly what I say about the gods or in regard to all things, for even if one chances for the most part to say what is true, still he would not know ; but every one thinks he knows.[1]

15. These things have seemed to me to resemble the truth.

16. In the beginning the gods did not at all reveal all things clearly to mortals, but by searching men in the course of time find them out better.

17. The following are fit topics for conversation for men reclining on a soft couch by the fire in the winter season, when after a meal they are drinking sweet wine and eating a little pulse : Who are you, and what is your family ?   What is your age, my friend ?   How old were you when the Medes invaded this land ?

18. Now, however, I come to another topic, and I will show the way. . . .   They say that once on a time when a hound was badly treated a passer-by pitied him and said, ' Stop beating him, for it is the soul of a dear friend ; I recognised him on hearing his voice.'

[1] Zeller, 549, n. 2. Burnett, ' All are free to guess.'

19 ἀλλ' εἰ μὲν ταχυτῆτι ποδῶν νίκην τις ἄροιτο
   ἢ πενταθλεύων, ἔνθα Διὸς τέμενος
   πὰρ Πίσαο ῥοῆσ' ἐν Ὀλυμπίῃ, εἴτε παλαίων,
   ἢ καὶ πυκτοσύνην ἀλγινόεσσαν ἔχων,
   εἴτε τὸ δεινὸν ἄεθλον, ὃ παγκράτιον καλέουσιν,   5
   ἀστοῖσίν κ' εἴη κυδρότερος προσορᾶν,
   καί κε προεδρίην φανερὴν ἐν ἀγῶσιν ἄροιτο,
   καί κεν σῖτ' εἴη δημοσίων κτεάνων
   ἐκ πόλεως καὶ δῶρον, ὅ οἱ κειμήλιον εἴη·
   εἴτε καὶ ἵπποισιν, ταῦτά χ' ἅπαντα λάχοι,   10
   οὐκ ἐὼν ἄξιος, ὥσπερ ἐγώ· ῥώμης γὰρ ἀμείνων
   ἀνδρῶν ἠδ' ἵππων ἡμετέρη σοφίη.
   ἀλλ' εἰκῆ μάλα τοῦτο νομίζεται· οὐδὲ δίκαιον
   προκρίνειν ῥώμην τῆς ἀγαθῆς σοφίης.
   οὔτε γὰρ εἰ πύκτης ἀγαθὸς λαοῖσι μετείη,   15
   οὔτ' εἰ πενταθλεῖν, οὔτε παλαισμοσύνην,
   οὐδὲ μὲν εἰ ταχυτῆτι ποδῶν, τόπερ ἐστὶ πρότιμον
   ῥώμης ὅσσ' ἀνδρῶν ἔργ' ἐν ἀγῶνι πέλει,
   τούνεκεν ἂν δὴ μᾶλλον ἐν εὐνομίῃ πόλις εἴη·
   σμικρὸν δ' ἄν τι πόλει χάρμα γένοιτ' ἐπὶ τῷ,   20
   εἴ τις ἀεθλεύων νικῷ Πίσαο παρ' ὄχθας·
   οὐ γὰρ πιαίνει ταῦτα μυχοὺς πόλεως.

20 ἁβροσύνας δὲ μαθόντες ἀνωφελέας παρὰ Λυδῶν,
   ὄφρα τυρρανίης ἦσαν ἄνευ στυγερῆς,
   ἤεσαν εἰς ἀγορὴν παναλουργέα φάρε' ἔχοντες,
   οὐ μείους ὥσπερ χίλιοι εἰς ἐπίπαν,
   αὐχαλέοι, χαίτῃσιν ἀγαλλόμενοι εὐπρεπέεσσιν,   5
   ἀσκητοῖς ὀδμὴν χρίμασι δευόμενοι.

---

19. Athen. x. 413 f.

V. 3: Schneidewin ῥοὰς, cf. v. 21. V. 5: MSS. τί, Wakef. τὸ. V. 6: Vulg. πρὸς ἄκρα, Jacobs προσορᾶν from MS. A προσέραν. V. 8: MSS. σιτείη, corr. Turnebus. V. 10: Dindorf connects with the preceding line and reads οὔ κ' ἔοι ἄξιος. V. 15: A λαοῖσιν ἔτ' εἴη, corr. Steph.

20. Athen. xii. p. 526.

V. 1: MSS. ἀφροσύνας, corr. Schneider V. 2: Vulg. ἐπὶ στυγερῆς. corr. Dindorf. V. 4: AB ὥσπερ, PVL ἤπερ. V. 5: Last word: Schneidewin τανᾶῃσιν, Bergk¹ prefers ἀγάλμασί τ'.

19. But if one wins a victory by swiftness of foot, or
in the pentathlon, where the grove of Zeus lies by Pisas'
stream at Olympia, or as a wrestler, or in painful boxing,
5 or in that severe contest called the pancration, he would
be more glorious in the eyes of the citizens, he would win
a front seat at assemblies, and would be entertained
by the city at the public table, and he would receive a
gift which would be a keepsake for him. If he won
10 by means of horses he would get all these things
although he did not deserve them, as I deserve them,
for our wisdom is better than the strength of men or of
horses. This is indeed a very wrong custom, nor is it
right to prefer strength to excellent wisdom. For if there
15 should be in the city a man good at boxing, or in the
pentathlon, or in wrestling, or in swiftness of foot, which
is honoured more than strength (among the contests men
enter into at the games), the city would not on that
account be any better governed. Small joy would it be
20 to any city in this case if a citizen conquers at the games
on the banks of the Pisas, for this does not fill with
wealth its secret chambers.

20. Having learned profitless luxuries from the Ly-
dians, while as yet they had no experience of hateful
tyranny, they proceeded into the market-place, no less
than a thousand in number all told, with purple garments
completely covering them, boastful, proud of their comely
locks, anointed with unguents of rich perfume.

21 νῦν γὰρ δὴ ζάπεδον καθαρὸν καὶ χεῖρες ἁπάντων
καὶ κύλικες· πλεκτοὺς δ' ἀμφιτιθεῖ στεφάνους,
ἄλλος δ' εὐῶδες μύρον ἐν φιάλῃ παρατείνει·
κρατὴρ δ' ἔστηκεν μεστὸς εὐφροσύνης·
ἄλλος δ' οἶνος ἕτοιμος, ὃς οὔποτέ φησι προδώσειν,   5
μείλιχος ἐν κεράμοισ', ἄνθεος ὀσδόμενος·
ἐν δὲ μέσοισ' ἁγνὴν ὀδμὴν λιβανωτὸς ἵησιν,
ψυχρὸν δ' ἔστιν ὕδωρ καὶ γλυκὺ καὶ καθαρόν·
πάρκεινται δ' ἄρτοι ξανθοὶ γεραρή τε τράπεζα
τυροῦ καὶ μέλιτος πίονος ἀχθομένη·   10
βωμὸς δ' ἄνθεσιν ἂν τὸ μέσον πάντῃ πεπύκασται,
μολπῇ δ' ἀμφὶς ἔχει δώματα καὶ θαλίη.
χρὴ δὲ πρῶτον μὲν θεὸν ὑμνεῖν εὔφρονας ἄνδρας
εὐφήμοις μύθοις καὶ καθαροῖσι λόγοις.
σπείσαντας δὲ καὶ εὐξαμένους τὰ δίκαια δύνασθαι   15
πρήσσειν· (ταῦτα γὰρ ὦν ἐστι προχειρότερον·)
οὐχ ὕβρις πίνειν ὁπόσον κεν ἔχων ἀφίκοιο
οἴκαδ' ἄνευ προπόλου, μὴ πάνυ γηραλέος·
ἀνδρῶν δ' αἰνεῖν τοῦτον, ὃς ἐσθλὰ πιὼν ἀναφαίνει,
ὡς οἱ μνημοσύνη καὶ <πόνος> ἀμφ' ἀρετῆς.   20
οὔτι μάχας διέπειν Τιτάνων οὐδὲ Γιγάντων,
οὐδέ τι Κενταύρων, πλάσματα τῶν προτέρων,
ἢ στασίας σφεδανάς· τοῖσ' οὐδὲν χρηστὸν ἔνεστιν·
θεῶν <δὲ> προμηθείην αἰὲν ἔχειν ἀγαθόν.

---

21. Athen. xi. p. 462.

Vv. 4–8 : Eustath. Od. ι 359, p. 1633, 53. V. 2 : MSS. ἀμφιτιθεὶς, corr.
Dindorf. V. 13 : Bergk⁴ reads πορσύνει. V. 4 : Eust. omits δὲ and reads
ἐμφροσύνης. V. 5 : AE οἶνος ἐστὶν ἕτοιμος, Karst. ἄλλῳ δ' οἶνος ἕτοιμος. Text
follows Meineke and Bergk. V. 11 : Vulg. αὐτὸ μέσον, corr. Karst. V. 14 :
MSS. λόγοις, Eichstädt νόοις, Schneid. νόμοις V. 16 : Vulg. puts colon
after πρήσσειν and period at end of line. Meineke puts comma at end of
line, and colon after ὕβρις. Bergk reads ταῦτα γὰρ ὦν ... ὕβρις as paren-
thetical. Schneid. προαιρέτεον. V. 19 : Hermann ἀναφαίνῃ. V. 20 : Vulg.
ἡ μνημοσύνη, καὶ τὸν ὃς, Schneid. οἱ μνημοσύνη καὶ πόνος, Bergk οἱ μνημο-
σύν' ᾖ, καὶ τὸν, ὃς. V. 21 : Bergk διέπει. V. 22 : Hermann οὐδέ τι, Bergk
οὐδ' αὖ : MSS. πλασμάτων, corr. Hermann. V. 23 : MSS. φενδόνας,
Scalig. φλεδόνας, Osann. σφεδανάς. V. 24 : Scalig. adds δὲ : MSS.
ἀγαθήν, corr. Franke et al.

21. For now the floor is clean, the hands of all and
the cups are clean ; one puts on the woven garlands,
another passes around the fragrant ointment in a vase ;
the mixing bowl stands full of good cheer, and more wine,
5 mild and of delicate bouquet, is at hand in jars, which
says it will never fail.   In the midst frankincense
sends forth its sacred fragrance, and there is water, cold,
and sweet, and pure ; the yellow loaves are near at hand,
and the table of honour is loaded with cheese and rich
10 honey.   The altar in the midst is thickly covered with
flowers on every side ; singing and mirth fill the house.
Men making merry should first hymn the god with
propitious stanzas and pure words ; and when they have
poured out libations and prayed for power to do the
15 right (since this lies nearest at hand), then it is no un-
fitting thing to drink as much as will not prevent your
walking home without a slave, if you are not very old.
And one ought to praise that man who, when he has
drunk, unfolds noble things as his memory and his toil
20 for virtue suggest ; but there is nothing praiseworthy in
discussing battles of Titans or of Giants or Centaurs, fic-
tions of former ages, nor in plotting violent revolutions.
But it is good always to pay careful respect to the gods.

22 πέμψας γὰρ κωλῆν ἐρίφου σκέλος ἦραο πῖον
   ταύρου λαρινοῦ, τίμιον ἀνδρὶ λαχεῖν,
   τοῦ κλέος Ἑλλάδα πᾶσαν ἐφίξεται οὐδ' ἀπολήξει
   ἔστ' ἂν ἀοιδάων ᾖ γένος Ἑλλαδικόν.

23 οὐδέ κεν ἐν κύλικι πρότερον κεράσειέ τις οἶνον
   ἐγχέας, ἀλλ' ὕδωρ καὶ καθύπερθε μέθυ.

24 ἤδη δ' ἑπτά τ' ἔασι καὶ ἑξήκοντ' ἐνιαυτοί
   βληστρίζοντες ἐμὴν φροντίδ' ἀν' Ἑλλάδα γῆν·
   ἐκ γενετῆς δὲ τότ' ἦσαν ἐείκοσι πέντε τε πρὸς τοῖς,
   εἴπερ ἐγὼ περὶ τῶνδ' οἶδα λέγειν ἐτύμως.

25 οὐκ ἴση πρόκλησις αὕτη, ἀσεβεῖ πρὸς εὐσεβῆ.

26 ἀνδρὸς γηρέντος πολλὸν ἀφαυρότερος.

27 ἑστᾶσιν δ' ἐλάτης <βάκχοι> πυκινὸν περὶ δῶμα.

28 ἐξ ἀρχῆς καθ' Ὅμηρον ἐπεὶ μεμαθήκασι πάντες.

29 εἰ μὴ χλωρὸν ἔφυσε θεὸς μέλι, πολλὸν ἔφασκον
   γλύσσονα σῦκα πέλεσθαι.

30 <ἁγνὸν> ἐνὶ σπεάτεσσι τεοῖς καταλείβεται ὕδωρ.

31 ὁππόσα δὴ θνητοῖσι πεφήνασιν εἰσοράασθαι.

---

22. Athen. ix. p. 368 E. V. 3: MSS. ἀφίξεται, corr. Karst. V. 4: Meineke κλέος Ἑλλαδικῶν, Bergk ἀοιδοπόλων ᾖ γένος Ἑλλαδικῶν.

23. Athen. xi. p. 782. V. 2: Vulg. ἐγχεύας, corr. Casaub.

24. Diog. Laer. ix. 19.

25. Arist. Rhet. i. 15; p. 377 a 20.

26. Etym. Magn. s.v. Γηρᾶς; attributed to Xenophon.

27. Schol. ad Aristoph. Equit. v. 408. Vulg. ἐλάται, MS. Θ ἐλάτε, V ἐλάτη. Lobeck, Aglaoph. p. 308 i, suggests ἑκστᾶσιν δ' ἐλατῶν πυκινοὶ περὶ δώματα βάκχοι, and compares Eurip. Bacch. 110.

(28). Draco Straton. p. 33, ed. Herm.; Cram. An. Oxon. iii. p. 296 (Herod. περὶ διχρόν. p. 367 Lehrs); Cram. An. Oxon. iv. p. 415 (Choerob. dict. p. 566 Gais.).

(29). Herod. περὶ μον. λέξ. 41, 5. MSS. Ξεινοφῶν, corr. Dind. Cf. Etym. Magn. 235, 4. Etym. Gud. 301, 15.

(30). Herod. Ibid. 30, 30. MSS. καὶ μὴν, corr. Lehrs. Cf. περὶ κλισ. ὀνομ. 772, 33.

31). Herod. περὶ διχρόν. 296, 5.

22. For sending the thigh-bone of a goat, thou didst receive the rich leg of a fatted bull, an honourable present to a man, the fame whereof shall come to all Greece, and shall not cease so long as there is a race of Greek bards.

23. Nor would any one first pour the wine into the cup to mix it, but water first and the wine above it.

24. Already now sixty-seven years my thoughts have been tossed restlessly up and down Greece, but then it was twenty and five years from my birth, if I know how to speak the truth about these things.[1]

25. Nor is this (an oath) an equal demand to make of an impious man as compared with a pious man.

26. Much more feeble than an aged man.

27. Bacchic wands of fir stand about the firmly built house.

28. From the beginning, according to Homer, since all have learned them.[2]

29. If the god had not made light-coloured honey, I should have said that a fig was far sweeter.

30. Holy water trickles down in thy grottoes.

31. As many things as they have made plain for mortals to see !

---

[1] Bergk[4] interprets φροντίδα by *carmen*.

[2] Hiller, *Deut. Litt. Zeitg.*, 1886, Coll. 474-475, suggests ' (Men know the wanderings of Odysseus) from the beginning as Homer tells them, since all have learned them.'

SAYINGS OF XENOPHANES.

Arist. *Rhet.* ii. 23 ; 1399 b 6 (Karsten, *Fr.* 34). Xenophanes asserts that those who say the gods are born are as impious as those who say that they die ; for in both cases it amounts to this, that the gods do not exist at all.

Ibid. 1400 b 5 (K. 35).   When the inhabitants of Elea asked Xenophanes whether they should sacrifice to Leukothea and sing a dirge or not, he advised them not to sing a dirge if they thought her divine, and if they thought her human not to sacrifice to her.[1]

Plutarch, *de vit. pud.* p. 530 F (K. 36). When Lasos, son of Hermiones, called that man a coward who was unwilling to play at dice with him, Xenophanes answered that he was very cowardly and without daring in regard to dishonourable things.

Diog. Laer. ix. 20 (K. 37). When Empedokles said to him (Xenophanes) that the wise man was not to be found, he answered : Naturally, for it would take a wise man to recognise a wise man.

Plut. *de comm. not.* p. 1084 E (K. 38).   Xenophanes, when some one told him that he had seen eels living in hot water, said : Then we will boil them in cold water.

Diog. Laer. ix. 19 (K. 39).   ' Have intercourse with tyrants either as little as possible, or as agreeably as possible.'

Clem. Al. *Strom.* vii. p. 841.   And Greeks suppose the gods to be like men in their passions as well as in their forms ; and accordingly they represent them, each race in forms like their own, in the words of Xenophanes : Ethiopians make their gods black and snub-nosed, Thracians red-haired and with blue eyes ; so also they conceive the spirits of the gods to be like themselves.[2]

[1] Cf. Plutarch, *Amat.* p. 763 D ; *Is. et Os.* p. 379 B.

[2] Cf. Theod. *Graec. Aff. Cur.* iii. p. 49.

A. Gellius, *Noct. Att.* iii. 11 (K. 31).   Some writers have stated that Homer antedated Hesiod, and among these were Philochoros and Xenophanes of Kolophon ; others assert that he was later than Hesiod.

(*b*) PASSAGES RELATING TO XENOPHANES IN PLATO AND ARISTOTLE.

Plato, *Soph.* 242D.   And the Eleatic group of thinkers among us, beginning with Xenophanes and even earlier, set forth in tales how what men call all things is really one.

De Coelo, ii. 13 ; 294 a 21.   On this account some assert that there is no limit to the earth underneath us, saying that it is rooted in infinity, as, for instance, Xenophanes of Kolophon ; in order that they may not have the trouble of seeking the cause.[1]

De mirac. oscult. 38 ; 833 a 16.   The fire at Lipara, Xenophanes says, ceased once for sixteen years, and came back in the seventeenth.   And he says that the lava-stream from Aetna is neither of the nature of fire, nor is it continuous, but it appears at intervals of many years.

Metaph. i. 5 ; 986 b 10.   There are some who have expressed the opinion about the All that it is one in its essential nature, but they have not expressed this opinion after the same manner nor in an orderly or natural way.   986 b 23.   Xenophanes first taught the unity of these things (Parmenides is said to have been his pupil), but he did not make anything clear, nor did he seem to get at the nature of either of these things, but looking up into the broad heavens he said : The unity is god.

[1] Two passages from the *Rhet.* ii. 23 are translated above, p. 78. Extracts from the book ordinarily called *De Xenophane, Zenone, Gorgia,* and ascribed to Aristotle, are in part translated below, p. 80, n. 2 ff., in connection with the fragment of Theophrastos which covers exactly the same ground.

These, as we have said, are to be dismissed from the
present investigation, two of them entirely as being
rather more crude, Xenophanes and Melissos; but Parmenides seems to speak in some places with greater care.[1]

(c) Passages relating to Xenophanes in the 'Doxographists.'

Theophrastos, Fr. 5; Simpl. *Phys.* 5v : 22, 36 ; *Dox.*
480. Theophrastos says that Xenophanes of Kolophon,
teacher of Parmenides, asserted that the first principle
is one, and that being is one and all-embracing, and is
neither limited nor infinite, neither moving nor at
rest. Theophrastos admits, however, that the record
of his opinion is derived from some other source than
the investigation of nature. This all-embracing unity
Xenophanes called god; he shows that god is one because god is the most powerful of all things; for, he
says, if there be a multiplicity of things, it is necessary
that power should exist in them all alike; but the most
powerful and most excellent of all things is god.[2] And
he shows that god must have been without beginning,
since whatever comes into being must come either from
what is like it or from what is unlike it; but, he says,
it is no more natural that like should give birth to like,
than that like should be born from like; but if it had
sprung from what is unlike it, then being would have

---

[1] V. Zeller, *Vorsokr. Phil.* i. 513, n. 1; Diels' *Dox.* p. 110; Teichmüller, *Studien*, p. 607.

[2] Cf. Arist. *Xen. Zen. Gorg.* 977 a 23. It is natural that god should
be one ; for if there were two or more, he would not be the most
powerful and most excellent of all. . . . If, then, there were several
beings, some stronger, some weaker, they would not be gods; for it is
not the nature of god to be ruled. Nor would they have the nature of
god if they were equal, for god ought to be the most powerful; but
that which is equal is neither better nor worse than its equal.

sprung from not-being.[1]   So he showed that god is
without beginning and eternal.   Nor is it either infinite
or subject to limits; for not-being is infinite, as having
neither beginning nor middle nor end; moreover
limits arise through the relation of a multiplicity of
things to each other.[2]   Similarly he denies to it both
motion and rest; for not-being is immovable, since
neither could anything else come into it nor could
it itself come into anything else; motion, on the one
hand, arises among the several parts of the one, for
one thing changes its position with reference to another,
so that when he says that it abides in the same state and
is not moved (Frag. 4.), 'And it always abides in the
same place, not moved at all, nor is it fitting that it
should move from one place to another,' he does not
mean that it abides in a rest that is the antithesis of
motion, but rather in a stillness that is out of the sphere
of both motion and rest.   Nikolaos of Damascus in his
book *On the Gods* mentions him as saying that the first
principle of things is infinite and immovable.[3]   According to Alexander he regards this principle as limited
and spherical.   But that Xenophanes shows it to be
neither limited nor infinite is clear from the very words

[1] Cf. Arist. *X.Z.G.* 977 a 19.   He adds: For even if the stronger were
to come from the weaker, the greater from the less, or the better from the
worse, or on the other hand the worse from the better, still being could
not come from not-being, since this is impossible.   Accordingly god is
eternal.

[2] Cf. Arist. *X.Z.G.* 977 b 6.   The second part reads: But if there
were several parts, these would limit each other.   The one is not like
not-being nor like a multiplicity of parts, since the one has nothing by
which it may be limited.

[3] Arist. *X.Z.G.* 977 b 13.   He adds: Nothing, however, can be moved
into not-being, for not-being does not exist anywhere.   But if there is
change of place among several parts, there would be parts of the one.
Therefore the two or more parts of the one may be moved; but to remain
immovable and fixed is a characteristic of not-being.   The one is
neither movable nor is it fixed; for it is neither like not-being, nor like a
multiplicity of being.

G

quoted,—Alexander says that he regarded it as limited
and spherical because it is homogeneous throughout;
and he holds that it perceives all things, saying (Frag. 3)
'But without effort he sets in motion all things by mind
and thought.' [1]

Theophrast. Fr. 5a ; Galen, in Hipp. *d. n. h.* xv. 35 K. ;
Dox. 481. Several of the commentators have made
false statements about Xenophanes, as for instance
Sabinos, who uses almost these very words : ' I say that
man is not air, as Anaximenes taught, nor water,
as Thales taught, nor earth, as Xenophanes says in
some book;' but no such opinion is found to be expressed by Xenophanes anywhere. And it is clear from
Sabinos's own words that he made a false statement intentionally and did not fall into error through ignorance.
Else he would certainly have mentioned by name the
book in which Xenophanes expressed this opinion. On
the contrary he wrote 'as Xenophanes says in some
book.' Theophrastos would have recorded this opinion
of Xenophanes in his abridgment of the opinions of
the physicists, if it were really true. And if you are
interested in the investigation of these things, you can
read the books of Theophrastos in which he made this
abridgment of the opinions of the physicists.

Hipp. *Philos.* i. 14 ; *Dox.* 565. Xenophanes of
Kolophon, son of Orthomenes, lived to the time of
Cyrus. He was the first to say that all things are incomprehensible, in the following verses : (Frag. 14) 'For
even if one chances for the most part to say what is
true, still he would not know ; but every one thinks he

---

[1] Arist. *X.Z.G.* 977. Since god is a unity, he is homogeneous in all
his parts, and sees and hears and has other sensations in all his parts.
Except for this some parts of god might rule and be ruled by one another,
a thing which is impossible. Being homogeneous throughout he is a
sphere in form; for it could not be spheroidal in places but rather
throughout.

knows.'[1] And he says that nothing comes into being, nor is anything destroyed, nor moved; and that the universe is one and is not subject to change. And he says that god is eternal and one, homogeneous throughout, limited, spherical, with power of sense-perception in all parts. The sun is formed each day from small fiery particles which are gathered together; the earth is infinite, and is not surrounded by air or by sky; an infinite number of suns and moons exist, and all things come from earth. The sea, he said, is salt because so many things flow together and become mixed in it; but Metrodoros assigns as the reason for its saltness that it has filtered through the earth.[2] And Xenophanes believes that once the earth was mingled with the sea, but in the course of time it became freed from moisture; and his proofs are such as these: that shells are found in the midst of the land and among the mountains, that in the quarries of Syracuse the imprints of a fish and of seals had been found, and in Paros the imprint of an anchovy at some depth in the stone, and in Melite shallow impressions of all sorts of sea products. He says that these imprints were made when everything long ago was covered with mud, and then the imprint dried in the mud. Farther he says that all men will be destroyed when the earth sinks into the sea and becomes mud, and that the race will begin anew from the beginning; and this transformation takes place for all worlds.

Plut. *Strom.* 4; *Dox.* 580. Xenophanes of Kolophon, going his own way and differing from all those that had gone before, did not admit either genesis or destruction, but says that the all is always the same. For if it came into being, it could not have existed before this; and not-being could not come into existence

[1] Epiph. *adv. Haer.* iii. 9; *Dox.* 590.
[2] Zeller, *Vorsokr. Phil.* 543, n. 1.

nor could it accomplish anything, nor could anything
come from not-being. And he declares that sensations
are deceptive, and together with them he does away with
the authority of reason itself. And he declares that the
earth is constantly sinking little by little into the sea. He
says that the sun is composed of numerous fiery particles
massed together. And with regard to the gods he
declares that there is no rule of one god over another,
for it is impious that any of the gods should be ruled ;
and none of the gods have need of anything at all, for
a god hears and sees in all his parts and not in some
particular organs.[1]   He declares that the earth is infinite
and is not surrounded on every side by air ; and all
things arise from earth ; and he says that the sun and
the stars arise from clouds.

Galen, *Hist. Phil.* 3 ; *Dox.* 601. Xenophanes of
Kolophon is said to be the chief of this school, which is
ordinarily considered aporetic (skeptical) rather than
dogmatic. 7 ; *Dox.* 604. To the class holding eclectic
views belongs Xenophanes, who has his doubts as to all
things, except that he holds this one dogma : that all
things are one, and that this is god, who is limited,
endowed with reason, and immovable.

Aet. *Plac.* i. 3 ; *Dox.* 284. Xenophanes held that
the first principle of all things is earth, for he wrote
in his book on nature : 'All things come from earth,
and all things end by becoming earth.'[2]

Aet. ii. 4 ; *Dox.* 332. Xenophanes et al.: The
world is without beginning, eternal, imperishable.
13 ; 343. The stars are formed of burning cloud ; these
are extinguished each day, but they are kindled again
at night, like coals ; for their risings and settings are

[1] Zeller, *Vorsokr. Phil.* p. 526, n. 4 ; *Arch. f. d. Gesch. d. Phil.* ii.
1889, pp. 1–5.
[2] Epiph. *adv. Haer.* iii. 9 ; *Dox.* 590.

really kindlings and extinguishings. 18 ; 347. The objects which appear to those on vessels like stars, and which some call Dioscuri, are little clouds which have become luminous by a certain kind of motion. 20 ; 348. The sun is composed of fiery particles collected from the moist exhalation and massed together, or of burning clouds. 24 ; 354. Eclipses occur by extinction of the sun ; and the sun is born anew at its risings. Xenophanes recorded an eclipse of the sun for a whole month, and another eclipse so complete that the day seemed as night. 24 ; 355. Xenophanes held that there are many suns and moons according to the different regions and sections and zones of the earth ; and that at some fitting time the disk of the sun comes into a region of the earth not inhabited by us, and so it suffers eclipse as though it had gone into a hole ; he adds that the sun goes on for an infinite distance, but it seems to turn around by reason of the great distance. 25 ; 356. The moon is a compressed cloud. 28 ; 358. It shines by its own light. 29 ; 360. The moon disappears each month because it is extinguished. 30 ; 362. The sun serves a purpose in the generation of the world and of the animals on it, as well as in sustaining them, and it drags the moon after it.

Aet. iii. 2 ; 367. Comets are groups or motions of burning clouds. 3 ; 368. Lightnings take place when clouds shine in motion. 4 ; 371. The phenomena of the heavens come from the warmth of the sun as the principal cause. For when the moisture is drawn up from the sea, the sweet water separated by reason of its lightness becomes mist and passes into clouds, and falls as rain when compressed, and the winds scatter it ; for he writes expressly (Frag. 11) : ' The sea is the source of water.'

Aet. iv. 9 ; 396. Sensations are deceptive.

Aet. v. 1 ; 415. Xenophanes and Epikouros abolished the prophetic art.

VI.

THE ELEATIC SCHOOL: PARMENIDES.

PARMENIDES, the son of Pyres (or Pyrrhes), of Elea, was born about 515 B.C.; his family was of noble rank and rich, but Parmenides devoted himself to philosophy. He was associated with members of the Pythagorean society, and is himself called a Pythagorean by later writers.   In the formation of his philosophic system however he was most influenced by his aged fellow-townsman, Xenophanes; the doctrines of Xenophanes he developed into a system which was embodied in a poetic work 'On Nature.'   The statement that he made laws for the citizens may have reference to some connection with the Pythagorean society.

> Literature : The fragments of Parmenides have been collected by Peyron, Leipzig 1810 ; Karsten, Amsterdam 1830 ; Brandis, *Comm. Eleat.* Altona 1813 ; Vatke, Berlin 1864 ; Stein, *Symb. philol. Bonn.* Leipzig 1867 ; V. *Revue Phil.* 1883, 5 : 1884, 9. Berger, *Die Zonenlehre d. Parm.* München, 1895.

(*a*) FRAGMENTS OF PARMENIDES.

Ἵπποι ταί με φέρουσιν, ὅσον τ' ἐπὶ θυμὸς ἱκάνοι,
πέμπον, ἐπεί μ' ἐς ὁδὸν βῆσαν πολύφημον ἄγουσαι
δαίμονος ἢ κατὰ πάντ' αὐτὴ φέρει εἰδότα φῶτα.
τῇ φερόμην· τῇ γάρ με πολύφραστοι φέρον ἵπποι
5 ἅρμα τιταίνουσαι· κοῦραι δ' ὁδὸν ἡγεμόνευον.
ἄξων δ' ἐν χνοιῇσιν ‹ἵει› σύριγγος ἀυτὴν

αἰθόμενος (δοιοῖς γὰρ ἐπείγετο δινωτοῖσιν
κύκλοις ἀμφοτέρωθεν), ὅτε σπερχοίατο πέμπειν
Ἡλιάδες κοῦραι, προλιποῦσαι δώματα νυκτός,

Sources and Critical Notes.

1–30. (Followed without break by 53–58) Sext. Emp. *Math.* vii. 111.
Cf. Porphyrius, *de antro nymph.* ch. 22.   28–32. Simpl. *de coelo*
557, 25.   28–30. Laer. Diog. ix. 22.   29–30. Plut. *adv. Colot.* 1114 ᴅ.
Prokl. *Tim.* p. 105 ʙ; Clem. Al. *Strom.* ᴠ. p. 682.

Vv. 6–8 Karsten transfers to a position after v. 10 (order: 5, 9, 10, 6,
7, 8, 11), comma at end of v. 5 and period at end of v. 8.   Stein transfers
vv. 4–8 to a position after v. 21, and changes δαίμονος of v. 3 to δαίμονες
in apposition with Ἡλιάδες κοῦραι.   Order: 3, 9, 10 . . . 20, 21, 4, 5 . . .
7, 8, where a break occurs, and v. 22 begins a new section.

V. 2: SV ζησαν.   V. 3: MSS. πάντα τῇ φέρει, Karst. πάντ' ἀδαῆ
φ., Hermann καὶ πάντ' αὐτῇ, Stein πάντα μάθη.   Diels compares
v. 32 and Verg. *Aen.* vi. 565.   V. 4: C φερομένην, G φέρομαι.
V. 6: Karsten inserts ἵει.   V. 7: G αἰσθόμενος, Stein ἀχθόμενος:
GR ἐπήγετο, C ἐπήγετος   V. 10: MSS. κρατερῶν, except G
κρατεραῖς, corr. Karsten.   V. 12: MSS. καὶ σφᾶς.   V. 14:
CRV δίκην.   V. 17: FG ταῖς.   V. 20: MSS. CGRV ἀρηρότα τῇ,
Hermann ἀρηρότας ᾖ.   V. 25: V ἵπποι: R τε, other MSS. ταί.
V. 26: CR οὗτοι, G οὔτε.   V. 27: Stein τηλοῦ for ἐκτὸς.   V.
28: CR πείθεσθαι.   V. 29: Prokl. εὐφέγγεος, Simpl. εὐκυκλέος:
Plut., Diog., Sext. L ἀτρεκές; text follows Prokl. and other MSS.
of Sext. Stein compares Sextus's explanation ἀμετακίνητον 215 6.
V. 31: Stein suggests τοῦτο.   V. 32: MSS. εἶναι, corr. Karsten.

TRANSLATION.

(Prooemium)   The horses which bear me con-
ducted me as far as desire may go, when they had
brought me speeding along to the far-famed road
of a divinity who herself bears onward through all
5 things the man of understanding.   Along this road
I was borne, along this the horses, wise indeed, bore
me hastening the chariot on, and maidens guided
my course.   The axle in its box, enkindled by the
heat, uttered the sound of a pipe (for it was driven
on by the rolling wheels on either side), when the
maiden daughters of Helios hastened to conduct me

10 εἰς φάος, ὠσάμεναι κρατῶν ἄπο χερσὶ καλύπτρας.
   ἔνθα πύλαι νυκτός τε καὶ ἤματός εἰσι κελεύθων,
   καί σφας ὑπέρθυρον ἀμφὶς ἔχει καὶ λάινος οὐδός,
   αὐταὶ δ' αἰθέριαι πλῆνται μεγάλοισι θυρέτροις.
   τῶν δὲ Δίκη πολύποινος ἔχει κληῖδας ἀμοιβούς.
15 τὴν δὴ παρφάμεναι κοῦραι μαλακοῖσι λόγοισιν
   πεῖσαν ἐπιφραδέως, ὥς σφιν βαλανωτὸν ὀχῆα
   ἀπτερέως ὤσειε πυλέων ἄπο.   ταὶ δὲ θυρέτρων
   χάσμ' ἀχανὲς ποίησαν ἀναπτάμεναι, πολυχάλκους
   ἄξονας ἐν σύριγξιν ἀμοιβαδὸν εἰλίξασαι,
20 γόμφοις καὶ περόνῃσιν ἀρηρότε· τῇ ῥα δι' αὐτῶν
   ἰθὺς ἔχον κοῦραι καθ' ἁμαξιτὸν ἄρμα καὶ ἵππους.
   καί με θεὰ πρόφρων ὑπεδέξατο, χεῖρα δὲ χειρὶ
   δεξιτερὴν ἔλεν, ὧδε δ' ἔπος φάτο καί με προσηύδα·
   ὦ κοῦρ' ἀθανάτοισι συνήορος ἡνιόχοισιν,
25 ἵπποις ταί σε φέρουσιν ἱκάνων ἡμέτερον δῶ,
   χαῖρ', ἐπεὶ οὔτι σε μοῖρα κακὴ προύπεμπε νέεσθαι
   τήνδ' ὁδόν· ἦ γὰρ ἀπ' ἀνθρώπων ἐκτὸς πάτου ἐστίν·
   ἀλλὰ θέμις τε δίκη τε.   χρέω δέ σε πάντα πυθέσθαι,
   ἠμὲν ἀληθείης εὐπειθέος ἀτρεμὲς ἦτορ,
30 ἠδὲ βρότων δόξας τῆς οὐκ ἔνι πίστις ἀληθής.
   ἀλλ' ἔμπης καὶ ταῦτα μαθήσεαι, ὡς τὰ δοκοῦντα
   χρὴ δοκίμως κρῖναι· διὰ παντὸς πάντα περῶντα.

                    τὰ πρὸς ἀλήθειαν.

   εἰ δ' ἄγ', ἐγὼν ἐρέω, κόμισαι δὲ σὺ μῦθον ἀκούσας,
   αἵπερ ὁδοὶ μοῦναι διζήσιός εἰσι νοῆσαι.
35 ἡ μὲν ὅπως ἔστιν τε καὶ ὡς οὐκ ἔστι μὴ εἶναι

33-40. Prokl. Tim. 105 в.   35-40. Simpl. Phys. 25 r 116, 28.   40b.
Plot. Ennead. v. 1, 8, p. 489; Clem. Al. Strom. 749.

    V. 33: MSS. ἄγε τῶν, corr. Karsten. V. 34: MSS. μοῦσαι, corr.
    Brandis.   V. 38: Prokl. δ' ἤτοι: Simpl. παναπευθέα, Stein
    παναπειθῆ, text follows Prokl. V. 39 Prokl. ἐφικτὸν, text follows
    Simpl.   Stein compares Simpl. D 109, 24; 111, 25.

10 to the light, leaving the realms of night, pushing
aside with the hand the veils from their heads.
There is the gate between the ways of day and night ;
lintel above it, and stone threshold beneath, hold it
in place, and high in air it is fitted with great doors ;
retributive Justice holds the keys that open and
15 shut them.[1]   However, the maidens addressed her
with mild words, and found means to persuade her
to thrust back speedily for them the fastened bolt from
the doors ; and the gate swinging free made the
opening wide, turning in their sockets the bronze
20 hinges, well fastened with bolts and nails ; then
through this the maidens kept horses and chariot
straight on the high-road.   The goddess received
me with kindness, and, taking my right hand in
25 hers, she addressed me with these words :—Youth
joined with drivers immortal, who hast come with
the horses that bear thee, to our dwelling, hail !
since no evil fate has bid thee come on this road
(for it lies far outside the beaten track of men),
but right and justice.   'Tis necessary for thee to
30 learn all things, both the abiding essence of persuasive truth, and men's opinions in which rests
no true belief.   But nevertheless these things also
thou shalt learn, since it is necessary to judge
accurately the things that rest on opinion, passing
all things carefully in review.

Concerning Truth.

Come now I will tell thee—and do thou hear my
word and heed it—what are the only ways of
35 enquiry that lead to knowledge.   The one way,

---

[1] *Archiv f. d. Gesch. d. Phil.* iii. p. 173.

πειθοῦς ἐστι κέλευθος, ἀληθείῃ γὰρ ὀπηδεῖ ·

ἡ δ' ὡς οὐκ ἔστιν τε καὶ ὡς χρεών ἐστι μὴ εἶναι

τὴν δή τοι φράζω παναπειθέα ἔμμεν ἀταρπόν ·

οὔτε γὰρ ἂν γνοίης τό γε μὴ ἐόν · οὐ γὰρ ἀνυστόν ·

40　οὔτε φράσαις.　τὸ γὰρ αὐτὸ νοεῖν ἐστίν τε καὶ εἶναι.

ξυνὸν δέ μοί ἐστιν,

ὁππόθεν ἄρξωμαι, τόθι γὰρ πάλιν ἵξομαι αὖθις.

χρὴ τὸ λέγειν τε νοεῖν τ' ἐὸν ἔμμεναι. ἔστι γὰρ
    εἶναι,

μηδὲν δ' οὐκ εἶναι, τά σ' ἐγὼ φράζεθαι ἄνωγα,

45　πρώτης γάρ σ' ἀφ' ὁδοῦ ταύτης διζήσιος < εἴργω >

αὐτὰρ ἔπειτ' ἀπὸ τῆς, ἣν δὴ βροτοὶ εἰδότες οὐδὲν

πλάζονται δίκρανοι · ἀμηχανίη γὰρ ἐν αὐτῶν

στήθεσιν ἰθύνει πλαγκτὸν νόον · οἱ δὲ φορεῦνται

κωφοὶ ὁμῶς τυφλοί τε τεθηπότες ἄκριτα φῦλα,

50　οἷς τὸ πέλειν τε καὶ οὐκ εἶναι τὠυτὸν νενόμισται

κοὐ τὠυτόν, πάντων δὲ παλίντροπός ἐστι κέλευθος.

οὐ γὰρ μή ποτε τοῦτο δαμῇ, φησιν, εἶναι μὴ ἐόντα

ἀλλὰ σὺ τῆσδ' ἀφ' ὁδοῦ διζήσιος εἶργε νόημα ·

41-42. Prokl. *Parm.* ii. 120 ; Vulg. ἄρξωμαι corr. Karst.

43-51. Simpl. *Phys.* 25 r 117, 4. 43-44. *Ibid.* 19 r 86, 27. 45. Cf. *Ibid.*
17 r 78, 6.　50. *Ibid.* 17 r 78, 3.

V. 43: *F* τέον, a*DE* (19 : 86) τὸ ὄν.　V. 44: MSS. (19 : 86) and a
(25 : 117) : *D* μὴ δὲ οἶδ', *F* οἶδ', *E* μὴ δέοι δ' : f εἶναι, *DEF* (25 :
117) ἔστι.　V. 45: Diels supplies εἴργω, Stein concludes the
line like v. 52.　V. 47 *DEF* πλάττονται, text follows a. Vv. 50,
51 : Diels ταὐτόν.

53-58a follow 1-32 in Sext. Emp.　52-53. Plato, *Soph.* 237 A, 258 D ;
Arist. *Met.* xiii. 1089 a ; Simpl. *Phys.* 29 v 135, 21 ; 31 r 143, 31 ; 53 v
244, 1.　53. Simpl. *Phys.* 11 r 78, 6 ; 152 v 650, 13.　54-56. Diog. Laer.
ix. 22.

V. 52 : Plato, τοῦτ' οὐδαμῇ, Arist. τοῦτο δαῇς Simpl. δαμῇ, corr. Stein.
Karsten omits v. 52.　V. 55 : Bergk εὔσκοπον.　V. 56 : *CRV*
κρίνε, *G* κριναν : *L* πολύπειρον.　Vulg. λόγῳ, corr. Burnet. Stein
rejects v. 53, and transfers 54-57a to the prooemium following
32.

assuming that being is and that it is impossible for
it not to be, is the trustworthy path, for truth
attends it.   The other, that not-being is and that
it necessarily is, I call a wholly incredible course,
40 since thou canst not recognise not-being (for this is
impossible), nor couldst thou speak of it, for thought
and being are the same thing.

It makes no difference to me at what point I
begin, for I shall always come back again to this.

It is necessary both to say and to think that being
is ; for it is possible that being is, and it is impos-
45 sible that not-being is ; this is what I bid thee
ponder.   I restrain thee from this first course of
investigation ; and from that course also along
which mortals knowing nothing wander aimlessly,
since helplessness directs the roaming thought in
their bosoms, and they are borne on deaf and like-
50 wise blind, amazed, headstrong races, they who
consider being and not-being as the same and not
the same ; and that all things follow a back-turning
course.[1]

That things which are not are, shall never
prevail, she said, but do thou restrain thy mind
from this course of investigation.

[1] Stein, *Symbol.* p. 782; Bernays, *Rhein. Mus.* vii. 115; Zeller, 738
and n. 1.

μηδέ σ' ἔθος πολύπειρον ὁδὸν κατὰ τήνδε βιάσθω
55 νωμᾶν ἄσκοπον ὄμμα καὶ ἠχήεσσαν ἀκουήν
καὶ γλῶσσαν, κρῖναι δὲ λόγων πολύδηριν ἔλεγχον
ἐξ ἐμέθεν ῥηθέντα. μόνος δ' ἔτι μῦθος ὁδοῖο
λείπεται, ὡς ἔστιν. ταύτῃ δ' ἐπὶ σήματ' ἔασι
πολλὰ μάλ', ὡς ἀγένητον ἐὸν καὶ ἀνώλεθρόν ἐστιν,
60 οὖλον μουνογενές τε καὶ ἀτρεμὲς ἠδ' ἀτέλεστον.
οὐδέ ποτ' ἦν οὐδ' ἔσται ἐπεὶ νῦν ἔστιν ὁμοῦ πᾶν,
ἕν, ξυνεχές· τίνα γὰρ γένναν διζήσεαι αὐτοῦ ;
πῆ πόθεν αὐξηθέν ; οὔτ' ἐκ μὴ ἐόντος ἐάσω
φάσθαι σ' οὐδὲ νοεῖν· οὐ γὰρ φατὸν οὐδὲ νοητὸν
65 ἐστὶν ὅπως οὐκ ἔστι. τί δ' ἄν μιν καὶ χρέος ὦρσεν,
ὕστερον ἢ πρόσθεν τοῦ μηδενὸς ἀρξάμενον φῦν ;
οὕτως ἢ πάμπαν πέλεναι χρεών ἐστιν ἢ οὐχί.
οὐδέ ποτ' ἔκ πη ἐόντος ἐφήσει πίστιος ἰσχύς
γίνεσθαί τι παρ' αὐτό· τοῦ εἵνεκεν οὔτε γενέσθαι
70 οὔτ' ὄλλυσθαι ἀνῆκε Δίκη χαλάσασα πέδησιν
ἀλλ' ἔχει.

[ἡ δὲ κρίσις περὶ τούτων ἐν τῷδ' ἔνεστιν]

---

57 b–112 (except 90–93). Simpl. *Phys.* 31 : 145–146. 57 b–59. *Ibid.* 31 r 142, 34. 57 b–70. *Ibid.* 17 r 78, 12. 59–60. Clem. Al. *Strom.* v. 716 ; Euseb. *Praep.* xiii. 680 c. 59–61. Simpl. *Phys.* 7 r 30, 1.   60. Plut. *adv. Col.* 1114 D ; Euseb. *Praep.* i. 23 ; Theod. *Ther. Ser.* iv. 7 ; Phil. *Phys.* B 5 r : 65 ; Simpl. *de Caelo* 557, 17 ; *Phys.* 26 r 120, 23.   60a. Simpl. *Phys.* 19 r 87, 21 ; Plut. *Strom.* 5 ; *Dox.* 580.   61. Ammon. on Herm. D 7 (= Cramer A. P. 1388) ; Philop. *Phys.* 5 r : 65 ; Prokl. *Parm.* iv. 62. 62–66. Simpl. *Phys.* 34 v 162, 18.   62–65. Simpl. *de Caelo*, 137, 1.

V. 57 : Stein μόνης : V δέ τι, CH δὲ τοι, FG δέ γε.   V. 60 : Plut. *Strom.* 5 reads μοῦνον for οὖλον : a (17 : 78) ἀτέλευτον, MSS. (26 : 120) and *Dox.* 284 and 580 ἀγένητον.   V. 62 : F διζήσεται. V. 66 : D (31 : 145) μηδαμῶς : E (31 : 145) αὐξάμενον : Da (17 : 78) a (31 : 145) φῦναι, E φῦν. Cf. Stein, p. 786.   V. 68 : MSS. ἔκ γε μὴ ὄντος, DE om. γε, Karst. ἐκ τοῦ ἐόντος, Stein ἔκ γε πέλοντος. Corr. Diels, paraphrasing Simpl. 78, 27.   V. 70 : EF' Bergk, Diels πέδησιν.   V. 71b : v. Stein, *Symbol.* 787. V. 73 : aDE ἀνόνητον ; text follows F.   V. 75 : MSS. ἔπειτα πέλοι το, corr. Karsten, Stein ἀπόλοιτο πέλον : MSS. ἄν, corr. Stein.   V. 76 : EF ἐγένετ', D ἔγετ', corr. Bergk.

And let not long-practised habit compel thee
55 along this path, thine eye careless, thine ear and thy
tongue overpowered by noise; but do thou weigh
the much contested refutation of their words, which
I have uttered.

There is left but this single path to tell thee of:
namely, that being is. And on this path there
are many proofs that being is without beginning and
60 indestructible; it is universal, existing alone, immovable and without end; nor ever was it nor will it
be, since it now *is*, all together, one, and continuous.
For what generating of it wilt thou seek out? From
what did it grow, and how? I will not permit
thee to say or to think that it came from not-being;
for it is impossible to think or to say that not-being
65 is. What thing would then have stirred it into
activity that it should arise from not-being later
rather than earlier? So it is necessary that being
either is absolutely or is not. Nor will the force
of the argument permit that anything spring from
70 being except being itself. Therefore justice does
not slacken her fetters to permit generation or destruction, but holds being firm.

(The decision as to these things comes in at
this point.)

ἔστιν ἢ οὐκ ἔστιν. κέκριται δ' οὖν ὥσπερ ἀνάγκη,
τὴν μὲν ἐᾶν ἀνόητον, ἀνώνυμον· οὐ γὰρ ἀληθὴς
ἐστὶν ὁδός· τὴν δ' ὥστε πέλειν καὶ ἐτήτυμον εἶναι.
75 πῶς δ' ἂν ἔπειτ' ἀπόλοιτο ἐόν; πῶς δ' αὖ κε γένοιτο;
εἰ γὰρ ἐγέντ' οὐκ ἔστ' οὐδ' εἴ ποτε μέλλει ἔσεσθαι.
τὼς γένεσις μὲν ἀπέσβεσται καὶ ἄπυστος ὄλεθρος.
οὐδὲ διαίρετόν ἐστιν, ἐπεὶ πᾶν ἐστιν ὁμοῖον·
οὐδέ τι τῇ μᾶλλον, τό κεν εἴργοι μιν συνέχεσθαι,
80 οὐδέ τι χειρότερον, πᾶν δ' ἔμπλεόν ἐστιν ἐόντος.
τῷ ξυνεχὲς πᾶν ἐστιν, ἐὸν γὰρ ἐόντι πελάζει.
αὐτὰρ ἀκίνητον μεγάλων ἐν πείρασι δεσμῶν
ἔστιν, ἄναρχον, ἄπαυστον, ἐπεὶ γένεσις καὶ ὄλεθρος
τῆλε μάλ' ἐπλάγχθησαν, ἀπῶσε δὲ πίστις ἀληθής.
85 τωὐτόν τ' ἐν τωὐτῷ τε μένον καθ' ἑωυτό τε κεῖται,
χοὔτως ἔμπεδον αὖθι μένει· κρατερὴ γὰρ ἀνάγκη
πείρατος ἐν δεσμοῖσιν ἔχει, τό μιν ἀμφὶς ἐέργει.
οὕνεκεν οὐκ ἀτελεύτητον τὸ ἐὸν θέμις εἶναι·
ἐστὶ γὰρ οὐκ ἐπιδευές, ἐὸν δ' ἂν παντὸς ἐδεῖτο.

90 λεῦσσε δ' ὅμως ἀπεόντα νόῳ παρεόντα βεβαίως·
οὐ γὰρ ἀποτμήξεις τῇ ἐὸν τῇ ἐόντος ἔχεσθαι

---

77. De Caelo, 559, 115.   78. Simpl. Phys. 19 r 86, 24, 31 r 143, 3;
81. Simpl. Phys. 86, 22 ; 87, 23.   Plot. Ennead. vi. 4, 4, 648 A ; Prokl.
Parm. ii. 62 and 120 ; Philop. B 5: 65. 82-89 (except 85). Simpl. Phys.
9 r 39, 26.   82-84. Ibid. 17 v 79, 32. 85-89.   Ibid. 7 r 30, 6 ; 9 r 40, 3.
85. Prokl. Parm. iv. 32.   Simpl. Phys. 31 r 143, 15.

V. 78: Ϝδιαιρέτεον.   V. 79: For μᾶλλον Stein reads κεν ἐόν.   V.
80: Ϝ δὲ πλέον.   V. 82: D ἀκινήτων.   V. 84: MSS. τῆδε, corr.
Scal.   DEF ἐπλάχθησαν, corr. a.   V. 85: Diels ταὐτόν,
ταὐτῷ, ἐαυτό. Simpl. 30, 6 omits the last τε.   V. 86: C οὐχ οὕτως,
a οὕτως, text from DF.   V. 88: Stein πέλον.   V. 89: Simpl.
μὴ ἐὸν δὲ ἂν παντὸς.   Karsten reads ἐπιδευές in three syllables
and puts κε for ἂν.   Preller omits μή.   Stein considers these
views untenable, and finds a break, probably longer than one
line, after ἐπιδευές.

90-93. Clem. Al. Strom. v. 2, 653.   90. Theod. Ther. Ser. i. 13.

V. 90: Stein suggests ἀπεόν τε νόῳ παρεόν τε βεβαίῳ.   V. 91:
Stein πέλον: Vulg. ἀποτμήξει, corr. Brandis.   MSS. τὸ ἐὸν τοῦ,
corr. Preller, comparing vv. 105 and 108.

Either being exists or it does not exist. It has been decided in accordance with necessity to leave the unthinkable, unspeakable path, as this is not the true path, but that the other path exists and is true.
75 How then should being suffer destruction? How come into existence? If it came into existence, it is not being, nor will it be if it ever is to come into existence. . . . So its generation is extinguished, and its destruction is proved incredible.

Nor is it subject to division, for it is all alike; nor is anything more in it, so as to prevent its co-hesion, nor anything less, but all is full of being;
80 therefore the all is continuous, for being is con-tiguous to being.

Farther it is unmoved, in the hold of great chains, without beginning or end, since generation and destruction have completely disappeared and
85 true belief has rejected them. It lies the same, abiding in the same state and by itself; accordingly it abides fixed in the same spot. For powerful neces-sity holds it in confining bonds, which restrain it on all sides. Therefore divine right does not permit being to have any end; but it is lacking in nothing, for if it lacked anything it would lack everything.[1]

90   Nevertheless, behold steadfastly all absent things as present to thy mind; for thou canst not separate

[1] Following Karsten and Preller; Stein rejects the interpretation.

οὔτε σκιδνάμενον πάντῃ πάντως κατὰ κόσμον
οὔτε συνιστάμενον.
τωὐτὸν δ' ἐστὶ νοεῖν τε καὶ οὔνεκέν ἐστι νόημα.
95 οὐ γὰρ ἄνευ τοῦ ἐόντος, ἐν ᾧ πεφατισμένον ἐστίν,
εὑρήσεις τὸ νοεῖν. οὐδὲν χρέος ἔστιν ἢ ἔσται
ἄλλο πάρεξ τοῦ ἐόντος, ἐπεὶ τό γε μοῖρ' ἐπέδησεν
οὖλον ἀκίνητόν τ' ἔμεναι. τῷ πάντ' ὄνομ' ἔσται
ὅσσα βροτοὶ κατέθεντο, πεποιθότες εἶναι ἀληθῆ,
100 γίνεσθαί τε καὶ ὄλλυσθαι, εἶναί τε καὶ οὐκί,
καὶ τόπον ἀλλάσσειν διά τε χρόα φανὸν ἀμείβειν.
αὐτὰρ ἐπεὶ πεῖρας πύματον, τετελεσμένον ἐστὶ
πάντοθεν, εὐκύκλου σφαίρης ἐναλίγκιον ὄγκῳ,
μεσσόθεν ἰσοπαλὲς πάντῃ· τὸ γὰρ οὔτε τι μεῖζον
105 οὔτε τι βαιότερον πέλεναι χρεών ἐστι τῇ ἢ τῇ.
οὔτε γὰρ οὐκ ἐόν ἐστι, τό κεν παύοι μιν ἱκνεῖσθαι
εἰς ὁμόν, οὔτ' ἐὸν ἔστιν ὅπως εἴη κεν ἐόντος
τῇ μᾶλλον τῇ δ' ἧσσον, ἐπεὶ πᾶν ἐστιν ἄσυλον.
εἰ γὰρ πάντοθεν ἶσον ὁμῶς ἐν πείρασι κύρει.

τὰ πρὸς δόξαν.

110 ἐν τῷ σοι παύσω πιστὸν λόγον ἠδὲ νόημα
ἀμφὶς ἀληθείης· δόξας δ' ἀπὸ τοῦδε βροτείας

94-112. Simpl. *Phys.* 31 v 146, 7.   94-98. *Ibid.* 19 r 87, 13 and 86, 31.
94-96. *Ibid.* 31 r 143, 22.   98. Plat. *Theaet.* 180 E, and from this Simpl.
Phys. 7 r 29, 18.   103-105. Plat. *Soph.* 244 E ; from Plato, Simpl. *Phys.*
12 r 52, 23 ; 19 v 89, 22 ; Stob. *Ecl.* i. 15, p. 352.   103-104. Arist. *de*
X.Z.G. ch. 2 and 4 ; Prokl. *Tim.* 160 D ; Simpl. *Phys.* 27 r 126,
22 and 127, 31 ; 29 v 137, 16.   104-105. Prokl. *Parm.* iv. p. 62.

V. 95 : *DE* (87, 15) πεφωτισμένον.   V. 96 : (19 : 86, 13) οὐδὲν γάρ
ἐστιν, (31 : 146) οὐδ' εἰ χρόνος ἐστίν, corr. Stein.   V. 98 : Text
from Simpl. 19 : 87.   Simpl. 31 : 146 πάντ' ὠνόμασται.   Plato
οἷον ἀκίνητον †τελέθει τῷ πάντι† ὄνομ' εἶναι.   V. 100 : MSS.
οὐχί, corr. Karst.   V. 105 : *E* and Plato χρεόν.   V. 102 : Karsten αὐτὰρ ἐπί, Stein αὐτὰρ ἐόν.   V. 106 : *DEF* παύοι, text
from a : *F* κινεῖσθαι, Stein ἱκέσθαι.   V. 107 : MSS. οὔτε ὄν,
corr. a.   *DEF* καὶ ἕν, a κενὸν, corr. Karsten.   V. 109 : *DEF* οἱ
γάρ, a ἢ γάο, Diels εἰ γάρ or ᾗ γάρ : MSS. κυρεῖ, corr. Stein.

being in one place from contact with being in another place; it is not scattered here and there
through the universe, nor is it compounded of parts.

Therefore thinking and that by reason of which
95 thought exists are one and the same thing, for thou
wilt not find thinking without the *being* from which
it receives its name.   Nor is there nor will there be
anything apart from being; for fate has linked it
together, so that it is a whole and immovable.
Wherefore all these things will be but a name, all
these things which mortals determined in the belief
that they were true, viz. that things arise and perish,
100 that they are and are not, that they change their
position and vary in colour.

But since there is a final limit, it is perfected on
every side, like the mass of a rounded sphere,
equally distant from the centre at every point.   For
105 it is necessary that it should neither be greater at
all nor less anywhere, since there is no not-being
which can prevent it from arriving at equality, nor
is being such that there may ever be more than
what is in one part and less in another, since the
whole is inviolate.   For if it is equal on all sides,
it abides in equality within its limits.

CONCERNING OPINIONS.

110   At this point I cease trustworthy discourse and
the thought about truth; from here on, learn the
opinions of mortals, hearing of the illusive order of
my verses.

II

μάνθανε, κόσμον ἐμῶν ἐπέων ἀπατηλὸν ἀκούων.
μορφὰς γὰρ κατέθεντο δύο γνώμαις ὀνομάζειν
τῶν μίαν οὐ χρεών ἐστιν, ἐν ᾧ πεπλανημένοι εἰσίν.
115 ἀντία δ' ἐκρίναντο δέμας καὶ σήματ' ἔθεντο
χωρὶς ἀπ' ἀλλήλων, τῇ μὲν φλογὸς αἰθέριον πῦρ
ἤπιον ἔμμεν ἀραιόν, ἑαυτῷ πάντοσε τωὐτόν,
τῷ δ' ἑτέρῳ μὴ τωὐτόν· ἀτὰρ κἀκεῖνο κατ' αὐτοῦ
ἀντία νύκτ' ἀδαῆ, πυκινὸν δέμας ἐμβριθές τε.
120 τῶν σοι ἐγὼ διάκοσμον ἐοικότα πάντα φατίζω,
ὡς οὐ μή ποτέ τίς σε βροτῶν γνώμῃ παρελάσῃ.

αὐτὰρ ἐπειδὴ πάντα φάος καὶ νὺξ ὀνόμασται
καὶ τὰ κατὰ σφετέρας δυνάμεις ἐπὶ τοῖσί τε καὶ τοῖς,
πᾶν πλέον ἐστὶν ὁμοῦ φάεος καὶ νυκτὸς ἀφάντου,
125 ἴσων ἀμφοτέρων, ἐπεὶ οὐδετέρῳ μέτα μηδέν.

αἱ γὰρ στεινότεραι πλῆνται πυρὸς ἀκρήτοιο,
αἱ δ' ἐπὶ ταῖς νυκτός, μετὰ δὲ φλογὸς ἵεται αἶσα,
ἐν δὲ μέσῳ τούτων δαίμων, ἣ πάντα κυβερνᾷ.

110-121. Simpl. *Phys.* 9 r 38, 30. 110-119. *Ibid.* 7 v 30, 4. 113-119.
Ibid. 38 r 180, 1. 110-113. Simpl. *de Coelo* 138, Peyr. 55 sq.

V. 113 : (9 r 38) *DEF* γνώμας. 110-111. *Phys.* 9 r 41, 8 (7 v 30 and
38 r 180 all MSS. give γνώμαις and Stein prefers this, p. 794). V.
117 : (9 r 39) *DE*, (39 r 180) *DEF* ἤπιον ἀραιὸν ἐλαφρόν (ἔστιν a),
7 r 30, and (9 r 39) a*F* ἤπιον ὂν μέγ' ἀραιὸν ἐλαφρόν, RP λεπτὸν
ἀραιὸν ἐλαφρὸν, text follows Stein V. 118 : (9 r 39) a*EF*
(39 r 180) a*F*, (7 v 31) MSS. κατ' αὐτό· (9 r 39) *DE* κατὰ
ταὐτον, text follows Stein, who uses first letter of the next line.
V. 119 : *F* κατ' αὐτό τἀντια, a*DE* τἀναντια, text from Stein by
change of τ to τ. V. 120 : MSS. τὸν, corr. Karsten. V. 121 :
Stein reads γνώμῃ.

122-125. Simpl. *Phys.* 39 r 180, 9.

V. 125 : D ἴσον, Stein suggests ἀμφότερον.

126-128. *Ibid.* 9 r 39, 14. 127-131. *Ibid.* 7 v 31, 13.

V. 126 : E¹D¹ πάηντο, D²E πύηντο, a ποίηντο, corr. Bergk : DE¹
ἀκρήτοις, a ἀκρίτοιο, corr. Stein. V. 127 : E³ οἴεται. V. 129 :
MSS. πάντα, Mullach πάντῃ, Stein πᾶσιν : aF ἀρχῃ, text
follows *DE*. V. 130 : Stein suggests μιγῆν, τό τ'.

Men have determined in their minds to name two principles [*lit.* forms]; but one of these they ought

115 not to name, and in so doing they have erred. They distinguish them as antithetic in character, and give them each character and attributes distinct from those of the other. On the one hand there is the aethereal flame of fire, fine, rarefied, everywhere identical with itself and not identical with its opposite; and on the other hand, opposed to the first, is

120 the second principle, flameless darkness, dense and heavy in character. Of these two principles I declare to thee every arrangement as it appears to men, so that no knowledge among mortals may surpass thine.

But since all things are called light and darkness, and the peculiar properties of these are predicated of one thing and another, everything is at the same time full of light and of obscure darkness, of both

125 equally, since neither has anything in common with the other.

And the smaller circles are filled with unmixed fire, and those next them with darkness into which their portion of light penetrates; in the midst of these is the divinity who directs the course of all.

πάντη γὰρ στυγεροῖο τόκου καὶ μίξιος ἄρχει
130 πέμπουσ᾽ ἄρσενι θῆλυ μιγὲν τό τ᾽ ἐνάντιον αὖθις
ἄρσεν θηλυτέρῳ.

πρώτιστον μὲν Ἔρωτα θεῶν μητίσατο πάντων.

εἴσῃ δ᾽ αἰθερίαν τε φύσιν τά τ᾽ ἐν αἰθέρι πάντα
σήματα καὶ καθαρᾶς εὐαγέος ἠελίοιο
135 λαμπάδος ἔργ᾽ ἀίδηλα καὶ ὁππόθεν ἐξεγένοντο,
ἔργα τε κύκλωπος πεύσῃ περίφοιτα σελήνης
καὶ φύσιν. εἰδήσεις τε καὶ οὐρανὸν ἀμφὶς ἔχοντα,
ἔνθεν ἔφυ τε, καὶ ὥς μιν ἄγουσ᾽ ἐπέδησεν Ἀνάγκη
πείρατ᾽ ἔχειν ἄστρων.

140   πῶς γαῖα καὶ ἥλιος ἠδὲ σελήνη
αἰθήρ τε ξυνὸς γάλα τ᾽ οὐράνιον καὶ Ὄλυμπος
ἔσχατος ἠδ᾽ ἄστρων θερμὸν μένος ὡρμήθησαν
γίνεσθαι.
νυκτιφαὲς περὶ γαῖαν ἀλώμενον ἀλλότριον φῶς

145 αἰεὶ παπταίνουσα πρὸς αὐγὰς ἠελίοιο

ὡς γὰρ ἑκάστοτ᾽ ἔχει κρᾶσις μελέων πολυκάμπτων,
τὼς νόος ἀνθρώποισι παρέστηκεν· τὸ γὰρ αὐτὸ
ἔστιν ὅπερ φρονέει μελέων φύσις ἀνθρώποισιν
καὶ πᾶσιν καὶ παντί· τὸ γὰρ πλέον ἐστὶ νόημα.

150 δεξιτεροῖσιν μὲν κούρους, λαοῖσι δὲ κούρας.

132. Plato, *Symp.* 178 B ; Arist. *Met.* i. 4, 984 b 26 ; Plut. *Amat.* 756 F ;
Sext. Emp. *Math.* ix. 9 ; Stob. *Ecl.* i. 10, p. 274 ; Simpl. *Phys.* 9 r 39, 18.
133-139. Clem. Al. *Strom.* v. 14, 732.   Stein assigns to Empedokles.
140-143. Simpl. *de Coelo* f. 138 ; Peyr. 55 sqq., Brandis 510a.
  V. 140 : Stein introduces λέγειν before πως from what precedes.
144. Plut. *Colot.* p. 1116 A.
145. Plut. *Quaest. Rom.* 282 A ; *de fac. lun.* 929 A.
146-149. Arist. *Met.* iii. 5, 1009 b 17 ; Theophr. *de sens.* 3 ; *Dox.* 499.
  V. 146 : Text follows Arist. SBᵇCᵇ, Theophr. PF ; Vulg. ἑκαστος :
MSS. κρᾶσιν, corr. Stephan.   V. 147 : Arist. παρίσταται ; text
follows Theophr.
150. Galen, Hipp. *Epid.* vi. 48 ; Comm. ii. (ix. p. 430 Char).

For she controls dreaded birth and coition in every
130 part of the universe, sending female to join with
male, and again male to female.

First of all the gods she devised love.

Thou shalt know the nature of the heavens and
135 all signs that are in the sky, the destructive deeds of
the pure bright torch of the sun and whence they
arose, and thou shalt learn the wandering deeds of the
round-eyed moon and its nature. Thou shalt know
also the sky surrounding all, whence it arose, and
how necessity took it and chained it so as to serve as
140 a limit to the courses of the stars.   How earth and
sun and moon and common sky and the milky way
of the heavens and highest Olympos and the burning
(might of the) stars began to be.

It (the moon) wanders about the earth, shining
145 at night with borrowed light.   She is always gazing
earnestly toward the rays of the sun.

For as at any time is the blending of very complex members in a man, so is the mind in men constituted; for that which thinks is the same in all
men and in every man, *viz.* the essence of the
members of the body; and the element that is in
150 excess is thought.

On the right hand boys, on the left hand girls.

So, according to men's opinions, did things
arise, and so they are now, and from this state when
they shall have reached maturity shall they perish.
For each of these men has determined a name as
a distinguishing mark.

K.   When male and female mingle seed of Venus
150 in the form [the body] of one, the excellence from
the two different bloods, if it preserves harmony,
fashions a well-formed body ; but if when the seed is
mingled the excellencies fight against each other

οὕτω τοι κατὰ δόξαν ἔφυν τάδε νῦν τε ἔασι,
καὶ μετέπειτ' ἀπὸ τοῦδε τελευτήσουσι τραφέντα.
τοῖς δ' ὄνομα ἄνθρωποι κατέθεντ' ἐπίσημον ἑκάστῳ.

Kars. (150) Femina virque simul Veneris cum germina
    miscent
  unius in formam diverso ex sanguine virtus
  temperiem servans bene condita corpora fingit.
  at si virtutes permixto semine pugnent
  nec faciant unam permixto in corpore dirae
  nascentem gemino vexabunt semine sexum.

Simpl. *Phys.* 7, v. 31, 4. ἐπὶ τῷδέ ἐστι τὸ ἀραιὸν καὶ
τὸ θερμὸν καὶ τὸ φάος καὶ τὸ μαλθακὸν καὶ τὸ κουφὸν, ἐπὶ
δὲ πυκνῷ ὠνόμασται τὸ ψυχρὸν καὶ ὁ ζόφος καὶ σκληρὸν
καὶ βαρύ· ταῦτα γὰρ ἀπεκρίθη ἑκατέρως ἑκατέρα.

151-153. Simpl. *de Coelo* f. 138; Peyr. 55 sq., Gaisf. *Poet. Min.* 287.
    V. 151: MSS. ἔφυ, corr. Stein. MSS. (καὶ) νῦν ἔασι, Peyr. νῦν τε
    ἔασι, Stein νῦν καὶ ἔασι. V. 153: Text follows Oxford MS.:
    Turin MS. transposes last two words.

150-155. (Karsten) Coelius Aurel. *de Morb. Chron.* iv. 9, p. 545
Wet. RP. 102 c. V. (151) Vulg. *venis informans*, corr. Diels, Dox. 193,
n. 1.

and do not unite into one, they will distress the sex
that is coming into existence, as the twofold seed is
mingled in the body of the unfortunate woman.
    With this there are fineness and heat and light
and softness and brightness; and with the dense
are classed cold and darkness and hardness and
weight, for these are separated the ones on one
side, the others on the other.

b) Passages relating to Parmenides in Plato and Aristotle.

Plato, *Theaet.* 180 D. I almost forgot, Theodoros, that there were others who asserted opinions the very opposite of these : ' the all is alone, unmoved ; to this all names apply,' and the other emphatic statements in opposition to those referred to, which the school of Melissos and Parmenides make, to the effect that all things are one, and that the all stands itself in itself, not having space in which it is moved.

Ibid. 183 E. Feeling ashamed before Melissos and the rest who assert that the all is one being, for fear we should examine the matter somewhat crudely, I am even more ashamed in view of the fact that Parmenides is one of them. Parmenides seems to me, in the words of Homer, a man to be reverenced and at the same time feared. For when I was a mere youth and he a very old man, I conversed with him, and he seemed to me to have an exceedingly wonderful depth of mind. I fear lest we may not understand what he said, and that we may fail still more to understand his thoughts in saying it ; and, what is most important, I fear lest the question before us should fail to receive due consideration. . . . [1]

Soph. 238 c (concluding a discussion of Parmenides). You understand then that it is really impossible to speak of not-being or to say anything about it or to conceive it by itself, but it is inconceivable, not to be spoken of or mentioned, and irrational.

Parm. 150 E. Accordingly the unity itself in relation to itself is as follows : Having in itself neither greatness nor littleness, it could not be exceeded by itself nor could it exceed itself, but being equal it would be equal to itself.

[1] Cf. *Soph.* 217 c.

Ibid. 163 c. This statement : It does not exist, means absolutely that it does not exist anywhere in any way, nor does not-being have any share at all in being. Accordingly not-being could not exist, nor in any other way could it have a share in being.

(*Symp.* 178 B, 195 c : Reference to the stories which Hesiod and Parmenides told about the gods.   Line 132 is quoted.)

Arist. Phys. i. 2 ; 184 b 16. The first principle must be one, unmoved, as Parmenides and Melissos say, . . .

Ibid. i. 3 ; 186 a 4. To those proceeding after this impossible manner things seem to be one, and it is not difficult to refute them from their own statements. For both of them reason in a fallacious manner, both Parmenides and Melissos ; for they make false assumptions, and at the same time their course of reasoning is not logical. . . . And the same sort of arguments are used by Parmenides, although he has some others of his own, and the refutation consists in showing both that he makes mistakes of fact and that he does not draw his conclusions correctly.   He makes a mistake in assuming that being is to be spoken of absolutely, speaking of it thus many times ; and he draws the false conclusion that, in case only whites are considered, white meaning one thing, none the less there are many whites and not one ; since neither in the succession of things nor in the argument will whiteness be one.   For what is predicated of white will not be the same as what is predicated of the object which is white, and nothing except white will be separated from the object ; since there is no other ground of separation except the fact that the white is different from the object in which the white exists.   But Parmenides had not yet arrived at the knowledge of this.

Ibid. i. 5 ; 188 a 20. Parmenides also makes heat

and cold first principles; and he calls them fire and earth.

Ibid. iii. 6; 207 a 15. Wherefore we must regard Parmenides as a more acute thinker than Melissos, for the latter says that the infinite is the all, but the former asserts that the all is limited, equally distant from the centre [on every side].[1]

Gen. Corr. i. 3; 318 b 6. Parmenides says that the two exist, both being and not being—*i.e.* earth and water.

Metaph. i. 3; 984 b 1. None of those who have affirmed that the all is one have, it happens, seen the nature of such a cause clearly, except, perhaps, Parmenides, and he in so far as he sometimes asserts that there is not one cause alone, but two causes.

Metaph. i. 5; 986 b 18. For Parmenides seemed to lay hold of a unity according to reason, and Melissos according to matter; wherefore the former says it is limited, the latter that it is unlimited. Xenophanes first taught the unity of things (Parmenides is said to have been his pupil), but he did not make anything clear, nor did he seem to get at the nature of either finiteness or infinity, but, looking up into the broad heavens, he said, the unity is god. These, as we said, are to be dismissed from the present investigation, two of them entirely as being somewhat more crude, Xenophanes and Melissos; but Parmenides seems to speak in some places with greater care. For believing that not-being does not exist in addition to being, of necessity he thinks that being is one and that there is nothing else, . . . and being compelled to account for phenomena, and assuming that things are one from the standpoint of reason, plural from the standpoint of sense, he again asserts that there are two causes and two first principles, heat and

[1] V. Parmenides, Frag. v. 104.

cold, or, as he calls them, fire and earth ; of these he regards heat as being, its opposite as not-being.

Metaph. ii. 4 ; 1001 a 32. There is nothing different from being, so that it is necessary to agree with the reasoning of Parmenides that all things are one, and that this is being.

(c) Passages relating to Parmenides in the Doxographists.

Theophrastos, Fr. 6 ; Alexander *Metaph.* p. 24, 5 Bon.; *Dox.* 482. And succeeding him Parmenides, son of Pyres, the Eleatic—Theophrastos adds the name of Xenophanes—followed both ways. For in declaring that the all is eternal, and in attempting to explain the genesis of things, he expresses different opinions according to the two standpoints :—from the standpoint of truth he supposes the all to be one and not generated and spheroidal in form, while from the standpoint of popular opinion, in order to explain generation of phenomena, he uses two first principles, fire and earth, the one as matter, the other as cause and agent.

Theophrastos, Fr. 6a ; Laer. Diog. ix. 21, 22 ; *Dox.* 482. Parmenides, son of Pyres, the Eleatic, was a pupil of Xenophanes, yet he did not accept his doctrines. . . . He was the first to declare that the earth is spheroidal and situated in the middle of the universe. He said that there are two elements, fire and earth ; the one has the office of demiurge, the other that of matter. Men first arose from mud ; heat and cold are the elements of which all things are composed. He holds that intelligence and life are the same, as Theophrastos records in his book on physics, where he put down the opinions of almost everybody. He said that philosophy has a two-fold office, to understand both the truth and also what men believe.   Accordingly he says: (Vv. 28–30), ' 'Tis necessary for thee to learn all things, both the abiding essence of persuasive truth, and men's opinions in which rests no true belief.'

Theoph. Fr. 17; Diog. Laer. viii. 48; *Dox.* 492. Theophrastos says that Parmenides was the first to call the heavens a universe and the earth spheroidal.

Theoph. *de Sens.* 3; *Dox.* 499. Parmenides does not make any definite statements as to sensation, except that knowledge is in proportion to the excess of one of the two elements.   Intelligence varies as the heat or the cold is in excess, and it is better and purer by reason of heat; but nevertheless it has need of a certain symmetry. (Vv. 146–149) 'For,' he says, ' as at any time is the blending of very complex members in a man, so is the mind in men constituted; for that which thinks is the same in all men and in every man, viz., the essence of the members of the body; and the element that is in excess is thought.' He says that perceiving and thinking are the same thing, and that remembering and forgetting come from these [1] as the result of mixture, but he does not say definitely whether, if they enter into the mixture in equal quantities, thought will arise or not, nor what the disposition should be.   But it is evident that he believes sensation to take place by the presence of some quality in contrast with its opposite, where he says that a corpse does not perceive light and heat and sound by reason of the absence of fire, but that it perceives cold and silence and the similar contrasted qualities, and in general that being as a whole has a certain knowledge.   So in his statements he seems to do away with what is difficult by leaving it out.

Theophr. Fr. 7; Simpl. *Phys.* 25 r 115; *Dox.* 483. In

---

[1] Karsten understands 'heat and cold,' Diels 'perceiving and thinking.'

the first book of his physics Theophrastos gives as the
opinion of Parmenides : That which is outside of being
is not-being, not-being is nothing, accordingly being is
one.

Hipp. *Phil.* 11 ; *Dox.* 564. Parmenides supposes that
the all is one and eternal, and without beginning and
spheroidal in form ; but even he does not escape the
opinion of the many, for he speaks of fire and earth as
first principles of the all, of earth as matter, and of
fire as agent and cause, and he says that the earth will
come to an end, but in what way he does not say.   He
says that the all is eternal, and not generated, and
spherical, and homogeneous, not having place in itself,
and unmoved, and limited.[1]

Plut. *Strom.* 5 ; *Dox.* 580.   Parmenides the Eleatic,
the companion of Xenophanes, both laid claim to his
opinions, and at the same time took the opposite standpoint.   For he declared the all to be eternal and immovable according to the real state of the case ; for it is
alone, existing alone, immovable and without beginning
(v. 60) ; but there is a generation of the things that
seem to be according to false opinion, and he excepts
sense perceptions from the truth.   He says that if anything exists besides being, this is not-being, but not-
being does not exist at all.   So there is left the being
that has no beginning ; and he says that the earth was
formed by the precipitation of dense air.

Epiph. *adv. Haer.* iii. 10 ; *Dox.* 590.   Parmenides,
the son of Pyres, himself also of the Eleatic school, said
that the first principle of all things is the infinite.

Cic. *de Nat. Deor.* i. 11 ; *Dox.* 534.   For Parmenides
devised a sort of contrivance like a crown (he applied
to it the word στεφάνη), an orb of light with continuous heat, which arched the sky, and this he called

[1] V. Herm. *Irr. Gen. Phil.* 6 ; *Dox.* 652.

god, but in it no one could suspect a divine form or a
divine sentiment, and he made many monstrosities of
this sort; moreover, he raised to the rank of gods War,
Discord, Desire, and many other things which disease or
sleep or forgetfulness or old age destroys; and similarly
with reference to the stars he expresses opinions which
have been criticised elsewhere and are omitted here.

Aet. i. 3; *Dox.* 284. Parmenides, the Eleatic, son of
Pyrrhes, was a companion of Xenophanes, and in his
first book the doctrines agree with those of his master;
for here that verse occurs: (v. 60), Universal, existing
alone, immovable and without beginning. He said that
the cause of all things is not earth alone, as his master
said, but also fire. 7; 303. The world is immovable and
limited, and spheroidal in form. 24; 320. Parmenides
and Melissos did away with generation and destruction,
because they thought that the all is unmoved. 25; 321.
All things are controlled by necessity; this is fated, it is
justice and forethought, and the producer of the world.

Aet. ii. 1; *Dox.* 327. The world is one. 4; 332. It
is without beginning and eternal and indestructible.
7; 335. Parmenides taught that there were crowns
encircling one another in close succession,[1] one of rarefied matter, another of dense, and between these other
mixed crowns of light and darkness; and that which
surrounded all was solid like a wall, and under this was
a crown of fire; and the centre of all the crowns was
solid, and around it was a circle of fire; and of the mixed
crowns the one nearest the centre was the source of
motion and generation for all, and this 'the goddess
who directs the helm and holds the keys,'[2] he calls
'justice and necessity.' The air is that which is
separated from the earth, being evaporated by the

---

[1] Cf. vv. 123-131.
[2] V. Simpl. *Phys.* 8: 34, 14.

forcible pressure of the earth; the sun and the circle of
the milky way are the exhalation of fire, and the moon
is the mixture of both, namely of air and fire. The aether
stands highest of all and surrounding all, and beneath this
is ranged the fiery element which we call the heavens,
and beneath this are the things of earth. 11 ; 339. The
revolving vault highest above the earth is the heavens.
340. The heavens are of a fiery nature. 13 ; 342. The
stars are masses of fire. 15 ; 345. He ranks the
morning star, which he considers the same as the
evening star, first in the aether; and after this the sun,
and beneath this the stars in the fiery vault which he
calls the heavens. 17 ; 346. Stars are fed from the
exhalations of the earth. 20 ; 349. The sun is of a fiery
nature. The sun and the moon are separated from the
milky way, the one from the thinner mixture, which is
hot, the other from the denser, which is cold. 25 ;
356. The moon is of a fiery nature. 26 ; 357. The
moon is of the same size as the sun, and derives its light
from it. 30 ; 361. (The moon appears dark) because
darkness is mingled with its fiery nature, whence he
calls it the star that shines with a false light.

Aet. iii. 1 ; 365. The mixture of dense and thin gives
its milk-like appearance to the milky way. 11 ; 377.
Parmenides first defined the inhabited parts of the earth
by the two tropical zones. 15 ; 380. Because the earth
is equally distant on all sides from other bodies, and so
rests in an equilibrium, not having any reason for sway-
ing one way rather than another; on this account it only
shakes and does not move from its place.

Aet. iv. 3 ; 388. The soul is of a fiery nature.
5 ; 391. The reason is in the whole breast. 392. Life
and intelligence are the same thing, nor could there be
any living being entirely without reason. 9 ; 397. Sensations arise part by part according to the symmetry of

the pores, each particular object of sense being adapted to each sense (organ).   398. Desire is produced by lack of nourishment.

Aet. v. 7; 419. Parmenides holds the opposite opinion; males are produced in the northern part, for this shares the greater density; and females in the southern part by reason of its rarefied state. 420. Some descend from the right side to the right parts of the womb, others from the left to the left parts of the womb; but if they cross in the descent females are born.   11; 422. When the child comes from the right side of the womb, it resembles the father; when it comes from the left side, the mother.   30; 443. Old age attends the failure of heat.

VII.

THE ELEATIC SCHOOL : ZENO.

ZENO of Elea, son of Teleutagoras, was born early in the fifth century B.C.   He was the pupil of Parmenides, and his relations with him were so intimate that Plato calls him Parmenides's son (*Soph.* 241 D).   Strabo (vi. 1, 1) applies to him as well as to his master the name Pythagorean, and gives him the credit of advancing the cause of law and order in Elea.   Several writers say that he taught in Athens for a while.   There are numerous accounts of his capture as party to a conspiracy ; these accounts differ widely from each other, and the only point of agreement between them has reference to his determination in shielding his fellow conspirators.   We find reference to one book which he wrote in prose (Plato, *Parm.* 127 c), each section of which showed the absurdity of some element in the popular belief.

Literature : Lohse,   Halis   1794 ;   Gerling,   *de Zenonis Paralogismis*, Marburg 1825 ; Wellmann, *Zenos Beweise*, G.-Pr. Frkf. a. O. 1870 ; Raab, *d. Zenonische Beweise*, Schweinf. 1880 ; Schneider, *Philol.* xxxv. 1876 ; Tannery, *Rev. Philos.* Oct. 1885 ; Dunan, *Les arguments de Zénon*, Paris 1884 ; Brochard, *Les arguments de Zénon*, Paris 1888 ; Frontera, *Étude sur les arguments de Zénon*, Paris 1891.

(a) FRAGMENTS OF ZENO, FROM SIMPLICIUS ON THE PHYSICS.

1. Simpl. *Phys.* 30 r 139, 11. εἰ γὰρ ἄλλῳ ὄντι προσγένοιτο, οὐδὲν ἂν μεῖζον ποιήσειεν· μεγέθους γὰρ μηδενὸς ὄντος, προσγενομένου δὲ οὐδὲν οἷόν τε εἰς μέγεθος ἐπιδοῦναι. καὶ οὕτως ἂν ἤδη τὸ προσγινόμενον οὐδὲν εἴη. εἰ δὲ ἀπογινομένου τὸ ἕτερον μηδὲν ἔλαττόν ἐστι, μηδὲ αὖ προσγινομένου αὐξήσεται, δῆλον ὅτι τὸ προσγενόμενον οὐδὲν ἦν οὐδὲ τὸ ἀπογενόμενον.

2. Simpl. *Phys.* 30 r 140, 29. εἰ πολλά ἐστιν, ἀνάγκη τοσαῦτα εἶναι ὅσα ἐστὶ καὶ οὔτε πλείονα αὐτῶν οὔτε ἐλάττονα. εἰ δὲ τοσαῦτά ἐστιν ὅσα ἐστί, πεπερασμένα ἂν εἴη. εἰ πολλά ἐστιν, ἄπειρα τὰ ὄντα ἐστίν. ἀεὶ γὰρ ἕτερα μεταξὺ τῶν ὄντων ἐστί, καὶ πάλιν ἐκείνων ἕτερα μεταξύ. καὶ οὕτως ἄπειρα τὰ ὄντα ἐστί.

3. Simpl. *Phys.* 30 v 141, 1. εἰ μὴ ἔχοι μέγεθος τὸ ὂν οὐδ' ἂν εἴη, εἰ δὲ ἔστιν, ἀνάγκη ἕκαστον μέγεθός τι ἔχειν καὶ πάχος καὶ ἀπέχειν αὐτοῦ τὸ ἕτερον ἀπὸ τοῦ ἑτέρου. καὶ περὶ τοῦ προύχοντος ὁ αὐτὸς λόγος. καὶ γὰρ ἐκεῖνο ἕξει μέγεθος καὶ προέξει αὐτοῦ τι. ὅμοιον δὴ τοῦτο ἅπαξ τε εἰπεῖν καὶ ἀεὶ λέγειν· οὐδὲν γὰρ αὐτοῦ τοιοῦτον ἔσχατον ἔσται οὔτε ἕτερον πρὸς ἕτερον οὐκ ἔσται. οὕτως εἰ πολλά ἐστιν, ἀνάγκη αὐτὰ μικρά τε εἶναι καὶ μεγάλα, μικρὰ μὲν ὥστε μὴ ἔχειν μέγεθος, μεγάλα δὲ ὥστε ἄπειρα εἶναι.

4. Simpl. *Phys.* 130 v 562, 4. εἰ ἔστιν ὁ τόπος, ἔν τινι ἔσται· πᾶν γὰρ ὂν ἔν τινι· τὸ δὲ ἔν τινι καὶ ἐν τόπῳ. ἔσται ἄρα καὶ ὁ τόπος ἐν τόπῳ καὶ τοῦτο ἐπ' ἄπειρον· οὐκ ἄρα ἔστιν ὁ τόπος.

Sources and Critical Notes.

Fr. 1. D εἰ γὰρ, EF οὐ γὰρ, a οὐ γὰρ εἰ: E ἄλλων. προσγενομένου δὲ]
Zeller, *Vorsokr. Phil.* 591, n. 2, strikes out δὲ: F οἴονται εἰς: E gives οὐ
διὰ for οὐδὲ: DEF ἀπογινόμενον.

Fr. 2. a adds καὶ πάλιν after ἂν εἴη.

Fr. 3. DF ἔχοι, aE ἔχει.

Fr. 4. E omits καὶ after ἄρα.

30 r 138, 30. For Eudemos says in his Physics,
'Then does not this exist, and is there any *one*?
This was the problem. He reports Zeno as saying that
if any one explains to him the *one*, what it is, he can
tell him what things are. But he is puzzled, it seems,
because each of the senses declares that there are
many things, both absolutely, and as the result of
division, but no one establishes the mathematical point.
He thinks that what is not increased by receiving additions, or decreased as parts are taken away, is not one
of the things that are.' It was natural that Zeno, who,
as if for the sake of exercise, argued both sides of a case
(so that he is called double-tongued), should utter such
statements raising difficulties about the one ; but in his
book which has many arguments in regard to each point,
he shows that a man who affirms multiplicity naturally
falls into contradictions. Among these arguments is one
by which he shows that if there are many things, these
are both small and great—great enough to be infinite in
size, and small enough to be nothing in size. By this
he shows that what has neither greatness nor thickness
nor bulk could not even be.   (Fr. 1) [1] 'For if, he says,
anything were added to another being, it could not
make it any greater ; for since greatness does not exist,
it is impossible to increase the greatness of a thing by
adding to it. So that which is added would be nothing.
If when something is taken away that which is left is no
less, and if it becomes no greater by receiving additions,
evidently that which has been added or taken away is
nothing.' These things Zeno says, not denying the
one, but holding that each thing has the greatness of

---

[1] Cf. Arist. *Metaph.* ii. 4 ; 1001 b 8.

many and infinite things, since there is always something before that which is apprehended, by reason of its
infinite divisibility; and this he proves by first showing
that nothing has any greatness because each thing of
the many is identical with itself and is one.

Ibid. 30 v 140, 27.   And why is it necessary to say
that there is a multiplicity of things when it is set
forth in Zeno's own book?   For again in showing
that, if there is a multiplicity of things, the same things
are both finite and infinite, Zeno writes as follows, to
use his own words: (Fr. 2) 'If there is a multiplicity of
things, it is necessary that these should be just as many
as exist, and not more nor fewer.   If there are just as
many as there are, then the number would be finite.   If
there is a multiplicity at all, the number is infinite, for
there are always others between any two, and yet others
between each pair of these.   So the number of things
is infinite.'   So by the process of division he shows that
their number is infinite.   And as to magnitude, he begins
with this same argument.   For first showing that (Fr.
3) 'if being did not have magnitude, it would not exist
at all,' he goes on, 'if anything exists, it is necessary
that each thing should have some magnitude and thickness, and that one part of it should be separated from
another.   The same argument applies to the thing that
precedes this.   That also will have magnitude and will
have something before it.   The same may be said of each
thing once for all, for there will be no such thing as
last, nor will one thing differ from another.   So if there
is a multiplicity of things, it is necessary that these
should be great and small—small enough not to have
any magnitude, and great enough to be infinite.' [1]

Ibid. 130 v 562, 3.   Zeno's argument seems to deny
that place exists, putting the question as follows: (Fr. 4)

---

[1] Cf. Diels, *Archiv f. d. Gesch. d. Phil.* i. 245; Zeller, i.³ 593 n. 1.

'If there is such a thing as place, it will be in something, for all being is in something, and that which is
in something is in some place. Then this place will be
in a place, and so on indefinitely. Accordingly there is
no such thing as place.'

  Ibid. 131 r 563, 17. Eudemos' account of Zeno's
opinion runs as follows :—' Zeno's problem seems to
come to the same thing. For it is natural that all
being should be somewhere, and if there is a place for
things, where would this place be ? In some other
place, and that in another, and so on indefinitely.'

  Ibid. 236 v. Zeno's argument that when anything
is in a space equal to itself, it is either in motion or at
rest, and that nothing is moved in the present moment,
and that the moving body is always in a space equal to
itself at each present moment, may, I think, be put in
a syllogism as follows : The arrow which is moving
forward is at every present moment in a space equal
to itself, accordingly it is < in a space equal to itself
in all time ; but that which is in a space equal
to itself in the present moment is not in motion.
Accordingly it is in a state of rest, since it is not moved
in the present moment, and that which is not moving is
at rest, since everything is either in motion or at rest.
So the arrow which is moving forward is at rest while
it is moving forward, in every moment of its motion.

  237 r. The Achilles argument is so named because
Achilles is named in it as the example, and the argument shows that if he pursued a tortoise it would be
impossible for him to overtake it.

  255 r. Aristotle accordingly solves the problem of
Zeno the Eleatic, which he propounded to Protagoras
the Sophist.[1] Tell me, Protagoras, said he, does one
grain of millet make a noise when it falls, or does the

---

[1] Arist. *Phys.* vii. 5, 250ᵃ, 20.

ten-thousandth part of a grain ?   On receiving the
answer that it does not, he went on : Does a measure of
millet grains make a noise when it falls, or not ?   He
answered, it does make a noise.   Well, said Zeno, does
not the statement about the measure of millet apply to
the one grain and the ten-thousandth part of a grain ?
He assented, and Zeno continued, Are not the statements as to the noise the same in regard to each ?   For
as are the things that make a noise, so are the noises.
Since this is the case, if the measure of millet makes a
noise, the one grain and the ten-thousandth part of a
grain make a noise.

(b) Zeno's arguments as described by Aristotle.

Phys. iv. 1 ; 209 a 23.   Zeno's problem demands
some consideration ; if all being is in some place, evidently there must be a place of this place, and so on
indefinitely.   3 ; 210 b 22.   It is not difficult to solve
Zeno's problem, that if place is anything, it will be in
some place ; there is no reason why the first place should
not be in something else, not however as in that place,
but just as health exists in warm beings as a state while
warmth exists in matter as a property of it.   So it is not
necessary to assume an indefinite series of places.

vi. 2 ; 233 a 24.   (Time and space are continuous
. . . . the divisions of time and space are the same.)
Accordingly Zeno's argument is erroneous, that it is
not possible to traverse infinite spaces, or to come in
contact with infinite spaces successively in a finite time.
Both space and time can be called infinite in two ways,
either absolutely as a continuous whole, or by division
into the smallest parts.   With infinites in point of quantity, it is not possible for anything to come in contact in
a finite time, but it is possible in the case of the infinites

reached by division, for time itself is infinite from this
standpoint. So the result is that it traverses the infinite
in an infinite, not a finite time, and that infinites, not
finites, come in contact with infinites.

vi. 9 ; 239 b 5. And Zeno's reasoning is fallacious.
For if, he says, everything is at rest [or in motion] when
it is in a space equal to itself, and the moving body is
always in the present moment · in a space equal to
itself, then the moving arrow is still. This is false ;
for time is not composed of present moments that are
indivisible, nor indeed is any other quantity. Zeno pre-
sents four arguments concerning motion which involve
puzzles to be solved, and the first of these shows that
motion does not exist because the moving body must go
half the distance before it goes the whole distance ; of
this we have spoken before (*Phys.* viii. 8 ; 263 a 5). And
the second is called the Achilles argument ; it is this : —
The slow runner will never be overtaken by the swiftest,
for it is necessary that the pursuer should first reach the
point from which the pursued started, so that necessarily the slower is always somewhat in advance. This
argument is the same as the preceding, the only
difference being that the distance is not divided each
time into halves. . . . His opinion is false that the one
in advance is not overtaken ; he is not indeed overtaken
while he is in advance ; but nevertheless he is overtaken,
if you will grant that he passes through the limited
space. These are the first two arguments, and the third
is the one that has been alluded to, that the arrow in
its flight is stationary. This depends on the assumption
that time is composed of present moments ; there will
be no syllogism if this is not granted. And the fourth
argument is with reference to equal bodies moving in
opposite directions past equal bodies in the stadium with
equal speed, some from the end of the stadium, others from

the middle ; in which case he thinks half the time equal to twice the time. The fallacy lies in the fact that while he postulates that bodies of equal size move forward with equal speed for an equal time, he compares the one with something in motion, the other with something at rest.

(c) Passages relating to Zeno in the Doxographists.

Plut. *Strom.* 6 ; *Dox.* 581. Zeno the Eleatic brought out nothing peculiar to himself, but he started farther difficulties about these things.

Epiph. *adv. Haer.* iii. 11; *Dox.* 590. Zeno the Eleatic, a dialectician equal to the other Zeno, says that the earth does not move, and that no space is void of content. He speaks as follows :--That which is moved is moved in the place in which it is, or in the place in which it is not; it is neither moved in the place in which it is, nor in the place in which it is not; accordingly it is not moved at all.

Galen, *Hist. Phil.* 3 ; *Dox.* 601. Zeno the Eleatic is said to have introduced the dialectic philosophy. 7 ; *Dox.* 604. He was a skeptic.

Aet. i. 7 ; *Dox.* 303. Melissos and Zeno say that the one is universal, and that it exists alone, eternal, and unlimited. And this one is necessity [*Heeren inserts here the name* Empedokles], and the material of it is the four elements, and the forms are strife and love. He says that the elements are gods, and the mixture of them is the world. The uniform will be resolved into them ;[1] he thinks that souls are divine, and that pure men who share these things in a pure way are divine. 23 : 320. Zeno et al. denied generation and destruction, because they thought that the all is unmoved.

---

[1] Reading πρὸς ταῦτα λυθήσεται, which, as Mr. G. D. Lord suggests to me, is probably the source of the corruption προσταυλυθήσεται. The Vatican vulgate combines both readings.

VIII.

THE ELEATIC SCHOOL : MELISSOS.

MELISSOS of Samos, son of Ithagenes, was a contemporary of Zeno, though he may have been slightly younger. Parmenides is said to have been his teacher, and it is possible that he may have made the acquaintance of Herakleitos. According to Diogenes, he was a respected statesman, and there seems to be good evidence (Plutarch, *Perikles* 26, after Aristotle) that he commanded the Samian fleet at its victory over the Athenians, 440 B.C. He wrote a book which later writers refer to under various titles.

> Literature : The fragments are treated by Brandis, *Commen. Eleat.* iii. and by Mullach *de Melisso X. G.* p. 80 ; Pabst, *de Meliss. Fragmentis*, Bonn 1889, disputes the authenticity of Fr. 1–5. Spalding, *Vindic. philos. Megar.* Berlin 1793, first showed that the first two chapters of the book called *de Xenophane, Zenone, Gorgia*, refer to Melissos. Cf. also Fr. Kern, *Zur Würdigung des Melissos*, Festschrift d. stettin. Stadtgym. 1880.

Sources and Critical Notes.

Fr. 1–5. The passage giving these fragments, as they have been called, contains little that is not found in the remaining fragments, and in spite of the fact that it is given as a direct quotation, it seems best to regard it as a condensed statement of the opinions of Melissos. V. Zeller, *Vorsokr. Phil.* 607, n. 1, and Pabst, *de Meliss. Fragmentis*, Bonn 1889.

(a) Fragments of Melissos mainly from Simplicius on the Physics.

Simpl. *Phys.* 23 v 109, 20 (Fr. 7). ὅτε τοίνυν οὐκ ἐγένετο, ἔστι δέ, ἀεὶ ἦν καὶ ἀεὶ ἔσται καὶ ἀρχὴν οὐκ ἔχει οὐδὲ τελευτήν, ἀλλ' ἄπειρόν ἐστιν. εἰ μὲν γὰρ ἐγένετο, ἀρχὴν ἂν εἶχεν· ἤρξατο γὰρ ἄν ποτε γινόμενον· καὶ τελευτήν· ἐτελεύτησε γὰρ ἄν ποτε γινόμενον· εἰ δὲ μήτε ἤρξατο μήτε ἐτελεύτησεν ἀεί τε ἦν καὶ ἀεὶ ἔσται, οὐκ ἔχει ἀρχὴν οὐδὲ τελευτήν· οὐ γὰρ ἀεὶ εἶναι ἀνυστὸν ὅ τι μὴ πᾶν ἐστι. l. 31. (Fr. 8.) ἀλλ' ὥσπερ ἔστιν ἀεί, οὕτω καὶ τὸ μέγεθος ἄπειρον ἀεὶ χρὴ εἶναι. l. 33. (Fr. 15.) εἰ γὰρ διῄρηται τὸ ἐόν, κινεῖται. κινούμενον δὲ οὐκ ἂν εἴη ἅμα.

Phys. 24 r 110, 1. (Fr. 16.) εἰ μὲν ὂν εἴη, δεῖ αὐτὸ ἓν εἶναι· ἓν δὲ ὂν δεῖ αὐτὸ σῶμα μὴ ἔχειν. (19 r 87, 6) εἰ δὲ ἔχοι πάθος, ἔχοι ἂν μόρια καὶ οὐκέτι ἓν εἴη. l. 3. (Fr. 9.) ἀρχήν τε καὶ τέλος ἔχον οὐδὲν οὔτε ἀίδιον οὔτε ἄπειρόν ἐστιν. l. 5. (Fr. 10.) εἰ μὴ ἓν εἴη, περανεῖ πρὸς ἄλλο.

Phys. 24 r 111, 19. (Fr. 11.) οὕτως οὖν ἀίδιόν ἐστι καὶ ἄπειρον· καὶ ἓν καὶ ὅμοιον πᾶν. καὶ οὔτ' ἂν ἀπόλοιτο οὔτε μεῖζον γίνοιτο οὔτε μετακοσμέοιτο οὔτε ἀλγεῖ οὔτε ἀνιᾶται. εἰ γάρ τι τούτων πάσχοι, οὐκ ἂν ἔτι ἓν εἴη. εἰ γὰρ ἑτεροιοῦται, ἀνάγκη τὸ ἐὸν μὴ ὅμοιον εἶναι, ἀλλὰ ἀπόλλυσθαι τὸ πρόσθεν ἐόν, τὸ δὲ οὐκ ἐὸν γίνεσθαι. εἰ τοίνυν τριχὶ μιῇ μυρίοις ἔτεσιν ἑτεροῖον γίνοιτο τὸ πᾶν,

---

Fr. 7. *D* omits καὶ . . . γινόμενον. Simplicius writes γινόμενον, Diels would restore γενόμενον regularly, and compares Spengel ad Eudem. fr. p. 18, 18. *DE* ἔχει, a*F* ἔχον.

Fr. 15. a*F* ἅμα, *E* ἀλλά.

Fr. 16. a*D* ὂν εἴη, *EF* οὖν εἴη, Brandis suggests ὂν ἐστι. *F* δὲ μὴ ὄν. Cf. 19 r 87, 6.

Fr. 11. a*F* γίγνοιτο. *E* οὐκέτι, omits ἄν. *F* omits δὲ after τὸ. a*D* (*F*) τριχὶ μιῇ, *E* τρὶ μὴ ἤ. Vulg. from Brandis εἰ τοίνυν τρισμυρίοισι ἔτεσι. *F* παρόντι for παντί.

ὀλεῖται ἂν ἐν τῷ παντὶ χρόνῳ. 1. 24. (Fr. 12.) ἀλλ' οὐδὲ
μετακοσμηθῆναι ἀνυστόν· ὁ γὰρ κόσμος ὁ πρόσθεν ἐὼν
οὐκ ἀπόλλυται οὔτε ὁ μὴ ἐὼν γίνεται.   ὅτε δὲ μήτε
προσγίνεται μηδὲν μήτε ἀπόλλυται μήτε ἑτεροιοῦται,
πῶς ἂν μετακοσμηθὲν τῶν ἐόντων τι ᾖ; εἰ μὲν γάρ τι
ἐγίνετο ἑτεροῖον, ἤδη ἂν καὶ μετακοσμηθείη· οὐδὲ ἀλγεῖ
οὐ γὰρ ἂν πᾶν εἴη ἀλγέον· οὐ γὰρ ἂν δύναιτο ἀεὶ εἶναι
χρῆμα ἀλγέον οὐδὲ ἔχει ἴσην δύναμιν τῷ ὑγιεῖ· οὔτ' ἂν
ὅμοιον εἴη, εἰ ἀλγέοι· ἀπογινομένου γάρ τευ ἂν ἀλγέοι ἢ
προσγινομένου, κοὐκ ἂν ἔτι ὅμοιον εἴη.   οὐδ' ἂν τὸ ὑγιὲς
ἀλγῆσαι δύναιτο· ἀπὸ γὰρ ἂν ὄλοιτο τὸ ὑγιὲς καὶ τὸ ἐόν,
τὸ δὲ οὐκ ἐὸν γένοιτο. καὶ περὶ τοῦ ἀνιᾶσθαι ὡὐτὸς
λόγος τῷ ἀλγέοντι. 1. 6. (Fr. 14.) οὐδὲ κενεόν ἐστιν οὐδέν·
τὸ γὰρ κενεὸν οὐδέν ἐστιν· οὐκ ἂν οὖν εἴη τό γε μηδέν.
οὐδὲ κινεῖται· ὑποχωρῆσαι γὰρ οὐκ ἔχει οὐδαμῇ, ἀλλὰ
πλέων ἐστίν. εἰ μὲν γὰρ κενεὸν ἦν, ὑπεχωρεῖ ἂν εἰς τὸ
κενόν· κενοῦ δὲ μὴ ἐόντος οὐκ ἔχει ὅκῃ ὑποχωρήσει.
πυκνὸν δὲ καὶ ἀραιὸν οὐκ ἂν εἴη· τὸ γὰρ ἀραιὸν οὐκ
ἀνυστὸν πλέων εἶναι ὁμοίως τῷ πυκνῷ, ἀλλ' ἤδη τὸ
ἀραιόν γε κενεώτερον γίνεται τοῦ πυκνοῦ. κρίσιν δὲ
ταύτην χρὴ ποιήσασθαι τοῦ πλέω καὶ τοῦ μὴ πλέω· εἰ
μὲν οὖν χωρεῖ τι ἢ εἰσδέχεται, οὐ πλέων· εἰ δὲ μήτε
χωρεῖ μήτε εἰσδέχεται, πλέων. ἀνάγκη τοίνυν πλέων
εἶναι, εἰ κενὸν μὴ ἔστιν. εἰ τοίνυν πλέων ἐστίν, οὐ
κινεῖται.

Phys. 34 v 162, 24. (Fr. 6.) ἀεὶ ἦν ὅ τι ἦν καὶ ἀεὶ
ἔσται. εἰ γὰρ ἐγένετο, ἀναγκαῖόν ἐστι πρὶν γενέσθαι
εἶναι μηδέν. †εἰ τύχοι νῦν μηδὲν ἦν, οὐδαμὰ ἂν γένοιτο
οὐδὲν ἐκ μηδενός.

Fr. 12. D μετὰ τὸ κοσμηθῆναι: a ἀπολεῖται: DF μετακοσμηθέντων
ἐόντων: a γάρ, DFE γε: a ἀλγεινόν (twice): D οὐκ for κοὐκ: DF ὡὐτὸς,
aE ὁ αὐτός.

Fr. 14. Cf. Simpl. 40, 12.   E πλέον et passim, Text follows aD:
DF κενώτερον, E κοινότερον: a omits οὖν.

Fr. 6. E εἰ τύχοι νῦν, D εἰ τύχῃ, aF εἰ τοίνυν. Diels suggests ὅτε
τοίνυν; cf. 109, 20.   DE οὐδὲν, aF μηδέν.

Simpl. *de Coelo*, 137 r ; Schol. Aristot. 509 b 18 ; cf.
Aristokl. Euseb. *Pr. Ev.* xiv. 17.   (Fr. 17.) μέγιστον μὲν
οὖν σημεῖον οὗτος ὁ λόγος ὅτι ἓν μόνον ἐστίν. ἀτὰρ καὶ
τάδε σημεῖα· εἰ γὰρ ἦν πολλά, τοιαῦτα χρῆν αὐτὰ εἶναι,
οἷόν περ ἐγώ φημι τὸ ἓν εἶναι. εἰ γὰρ ἔστι γῆ καὶ ὕδωρ καὶ
ἀὴρ καὶ σίδηρος καὶ χρυσὸς καὶ πῦρ καὶ τὸ μὲν ζῶον τὸ δὲ
τεθνηκὸς καὶ μέλαν καὶ λευκὸν καὶ τὰ ὅσα φασὶν οἱ
ἄνθρωποι εἶναι ἀληθῆ,—εἰ δὴ ταῦτα ἔστι καὶ ἡμεῖς ὀρθῶς
ὁρῶμεν καὶ ἀκούομεν, εἶναι χρὴ ἕκαστον τοιοῦτον οἷόν
περ τὸ πρῶτον ἔδοξεν ἡμῖν, καὶ μὴ μεταπίπτειν μηδὲ
γίνεσθαι ἑτεροῖον, ἀλλ' αἰεὶ εἶναι ἕκαστον οἷόν περ ἔστιν·
νῦν δέ φαμεν ὀρθῶς ὁρᾶν καὶ ἀκούειν καὶ συνιέναι, δοκεῖ
δὲ ἡμῖν τό τε θερμὸν ψυχρὸν γίνεσθαι καὶ τὸ ψυχρὸν
θερμὸν καὶ τὸ σκληρὸν μαλθακὸν καὶ τὸ μαλθακὸν
σκληρόν, καὶ τὸ ζῶον ἀποθνήσκειν καὶ ἐκ μὴ ζῶντος
γίνεσθαι, καὶ ταῦτα πάντα ἑτεροιοῦσθαι, καὶ ὅ τι ἦν τε
καὶ ὃ νῦν οὐδὲν ὅμοιον εἶναι, ἀλλ' ὅ τε σίδηρος σκληρὸς
ἐὼν τῷ δακτύλῳ κατατρίβεσθαι † ὁμοῦ ῥέων καὶ χρυσὸς
καὶ λίθος καὶ ἄλλο ὅ τι ἰσχυρὸν δοκεῖ εἶναι πᾶν, ὥστε
συμβαίνει μήτε ὁρᾶν μήτε τὰ ὄντα γινώσκειν· ἐξ ὕδατός
τε γῆ καὶ λίθος γίνεσθαι. οὐ τοίνυν ταῦτα ἀλλήλοις
ὁμολογεῖ· φαμένοις γὰρ εἶναι πολλὰ καὶ ἀίδια καὶ εἴδη
τε καὶ ἴσχυν ἔχοντα, πάντα ἑτεροιοῦσθαι ἡμῖν δοκεῖ καὶ
μεταπίπτειν ἐκ τοῦ ἑκάστοτε ὁρωμένου. δῆλον τοίνυν
ὅτι οὐκ ὀρθῶς ἑωρῶμεν οὐδὲ ἐκεῖνα πολλὰ ὀρθῶς δοκεῖ
εἶναι. οὐ γὰρ ἂν μετέπιπτεν εἰ ἀληθῆ ἦν, ἀλλ' ἦν οἷόν
περ ἐδόκει ἕκαστον τοιοῦτον· τοῦ γὰρ ἐόντος ἀληθινοῦ
κρεῖσσον οὐδέν. ἢν δὲ μεταπέσῃ, τὸ μὲν ἐὸν ἀπώλετο,
τὸ δὲ οὐκ ἐὸν γέγονεν. οὕτως οὖν εἰ πολλὰ εἴη, τοιαῦτα
χρὴ εἶναι οἷόν περ τὸ ἕν.

Fr. 17. Vulg. χρή: Simpl. ζῶον, Aristokl. ζῶν (twice): Aristokl. εἶναι
ἐγρῆν, καὶ τὸ ἐὸν τοιοῦτον, οἷον πρῶτον ἔδοξεν ἡμῖν εἶναι, Simpl. omits
πάντα and ἀληθῆ: Aristokl. ἕτερον, ἀλλ' εἶναι ὅμοιον, οἷόν περ ἐστὶ ἕκαστον,
Simpl. omits ἔστιν: Bergk ὁμουρέων, digito conterminus, aptatus,
MSS. τὸ μέσον, corr. Brandis, *Gesch. d. Phil.* i. 403 : Vulg. εἴη.

SIMPLICIUS'S ACCOUNT OF MELISSOS, INCLUDING THE
TRANSLATION OF THE FRAGMENTS.

22; 103, 13. Now let us glance at Melissos' argument, which we ran across a few lines back. Melissos,
making use of the axioms of the physicists, in regard to
generation and destruction, begins his book as follows :
(Fr. 1) If nothing is, how could this be spoken of
as though something is ? And if anything is, either
it has come into being, or else it always has been. If
it came into being, it sprung either from being or from
not-being; but it is impossible that any such thing
should have sprung from not-being (for nothing else
that is could have sprung from it, much less pure
being) ; nor could it have sprung from being, for in that
case it < would simply be, and would not have come
into existence. So then being is not generated ; being
always is, nor will it be destroyed. For being could
not be changed into not-being (this also is conceded by
the physicists), nor into being ; for then it would abide
as it is, and would not be destroyed. Accordingly being
was not generated, nor will it be destroyed ; so it always
was and always will be.   (Fr. 2) But while that which
comes into existence has a beginning, that which does
not come into existence does not have a beginning,
and being which did not come into existence would not
have a beginning. Farther, that which is destroyed has
an end ; but if anything is not subject to destruction, it
does not have an end ; and that which has neither beginning nor end is of course infinite ; so being is infinite.
(Fr. 3) And if it is infinite, it is one ; for if being were
two, both parts could not be infinite, but each would
be limited by the other. But being is infinite ; there
could not be several beings ; accordingly being is one.
(Fr. 4) Farther, if being is one it does not move ; for the

one is always homogeneous [*lit.* like itself]; and that which is homogeneous could not perish or become greater or change its arrangement or suffer pain or annoyance. If it experienced any of these things it would not be one; for that which is moved with any sort of motion changes something from one thing into something different; but there is nothing else except being, so this will not be moved.   (Fr. 5) To follow another line of argument : there is no place void of being, for the void is nothing; but that which is nothing could not exist; so then being is not moved: it is impossible for it to go anywhere, if there is no void. Nor is it possible for it to contract into itself, for in that case different degrees of density would arise, and this is impossible; for it is impossible that the rare should be as full as the dense ; but the rare is more empty than the dense, and there is no such thing as emptiness.   It is necessary to judge whether being is full or not by its capacity to receive something else : if it will not receive anything it is full; if it will receive something it is not full.   Now if the void does not exist, it must of necessity be full ; and if this is the case it does not move, not because it is impossible for it to move through space already filled, as we say of bodies, but because all being cannot be moved into being (for there is nothing besides itself), nor can being be moved into not-being, for not-being does not exist.

23 ; 109, 7. Melissos also is blamed because in his frequent references to the beginning he does not use the word to mean a beginning in time which applies to that which comes into existence, but rather to mean a logical beginning which does not apply to the things that are changing collectively.   He seems to have seen clearly before Aristotle that all matter, even that which is eternal, being limited has a limited capacity,

and in itself is always at the end of time, and because
of the ever-moving beginning of that which passes,
it is always at the beginning, and remains eternal,
so that that which has beginning and end in quantity
has also beginning and end in time, and the reverse ;
for that which has beginning and end in time is not
everything simultaneously.   So he bases his proof on
beginning and end in time.   Accordingly he says
that that which is not everything—*i.e.* which is not
the whole simultaneously—is not without beginning or
end ; what applies to things that are indivisible and
infinite in their being, applies so much the more to pure
being ; and that all applies to being.   Melissos puts it
as follows : (Fr. 7) Since then it did not come into being
but *is*, it always was and always will be, and has
neither beginning nor end, but is infinite.   For if it had
come into existence it would have had a beginning (for
that which once came into existence would have a beginning) and an end (for that which once came into existence would come to an end) ; if it neither had a beginning
nor came to an end, it always was and always will be ;
it has not beginning or end ; but it is impossible
that anything which is not the whole should always
exist. . . . . l. 31. (Fr. 8) But as it always exists, so
it is necessary also that it be always infinite in magnitude.
l. 33. (Fr. 15) If being is separated it moves ; and
that which moves could not exist simultaneously.

24 ; 110, 1 (Fr. 16) If being exists it must be one,
and being one it is necessary that it should not itself
have body ; (19 ; 87, 6) and if it should have thickness,
it would have parts and would no longer be a unity.
l. 3 (Fr. 9) Nothing which has beginning and end is
either eternal or infinite. l. 5 (Fr. 10) If it were not
one, it would be bounded by something else.[1]

---

[1] The paraphrase above (Fr. 3) gives the argument in fuller form.

24 ; 111, 18. Melissos bringing his previous topic to a conclusion goes on to consider motion. (Fr. 11) So then the all is eternal and infinite and homogeneous ; and it could neither perish nor become greater nor change its arrangement nor suffer pain or distress. If it experienced any of these things it would no longer be one ; for if it becomes different, it is necessary that being should not be homogeneous, but that which was before must perish, and that which was not must come into existence.   If then the all should become different by a single hair in ten thousand years, it would perish in the whole of time.   (Fr. 12) And it is impossible for its order to change, for the order existing before does not perish, nor does another which did not exist come into being ; and since nothing is added to it or subtracted from it or made different, how could any of the things that are change their order ?   But if anything became different, its order would already have been changed. (Fr. 13) Nor does it suffer pain, for the all could not be pained ; it would be impossible for anything suffering pain always to be ; nor does it have power equal to the power of what is healthy.   It would not be homogeneous if it suffered pain ; it would suffer pain whenever anything was added or taken away, and it would no longer be homogeneous. Nor could what is healthy suffer a pang of pain, for both the healthy and *being* would perish, and not-being would come into existence.   The same reasoning that applies to pain applies also to distress.   (Fr. 14) Nor is there any void, for the void is nothing, and that which is nothing could not be.   Nor does it move, for it has nowhere to go to, since it is full ; for if there were a void it could go into the void, but since there is no void it has nowhere to go to.   It could not be rare and dense, for it is not possible for the rare to be as full as the dense, but the rare is already more empty than the dense.

This is the test of what is full and what is not full: if it
has room for anything, or admits anything into it, it is
not full; if it does not have room for anything, or admit
anything into it, it is full. If no void exists it must be
full; if then it is full it does not move. These are the
doctrines of Melissos.

34; 162, 24. (Fr. 6) What was, always was and
always will be; for if it had come into existence, it
necessarily would have been nothing before it came into
existence. If now there were nothing existing, nothing
would ever have come into existence from nothing.

Simpl. *de Coelo* 137 r; Schol. Aristot. 509 b; cf.
Aristokl. Euseb. *Pr. Er.* xiv. 17. (Fr. 17) This argument
is the strongest proof that being is one only. And the
proofs are as follows: For if a multiplicity of things
existed it would be necessary that these things should be
just such as I say the one is. For if earth exists, and
water and air and iron and gold and fire and the living
and the dead and black and white, and everything else
which men say is real,—if these things exist and we see
and hear them correctly, it is necessary that each thing
should be such as we first determined, namely, it should
not change its character or become different, but should
always be each thing what it is. Now we say that we see
and hear and understand correctly; but it seems to us
that hot becomes cold and cold hot, that hard becomes
soft and soft hard, that the living being dies and life
comes from what is not living; and that all these things
become different, and what they are is not like what
they were. It seems to us that iron, being hard to the
touch, wastes away †becoming liquefied,†[1] and so does
gold, and rock, and whatever else seems to be strong,
so that we conclude that we do not see or know things

[1] Zeller i.⁵ 613 n. 1 suggests ὑπ' ἰοῦ ῥέων, 'passing away because of
rust.'

that are. And earth and rock arise from water. These
things then do not harmonise with each other. Though
we said that many things are eternal, and have forms
and strength, it seems that they all become different and
change their character each time they are seen. Evidently we do not see correctly, nor is the appearance of
multiplicity correct; for they would not change their
character if they were real, but would remain each thing
as it seemed, for nothing is nobler than that which is
real. But if they change their character, being perishes
and not-being comes into existence. So then if a multiplicity of things exist, it is necessary that they should be
such as the one is.

(*b*) ARISTOTLE'S ACCOUNT OF MELISSOS.

Phys. i. 3 ; 186 a 6.   Both Melissos and Parmenides
argue fallaciously, and they make false assumptions and
their reasonings are not logical ; but the argument of
Melissos is the more wearisome, for it sets no problem,
but granted one strange thing, others follow ; and there
is no difficulty in this.   The error in the reasoning of
Melissos is plain, for he thinks that if everything which
has come into being has a beginning, he can assume
that that which has not come into being does not have
a beginning.   This, then, is strange, that he should
think that everything has a beginning except time, and
this does not, and that simple generation has no beginning but change alone begins, as though change as a
whole did not come into being.   Even if the all is
a unity, why then should it not move ? Why should
not the whole be moved even as a part of it which is a
unity, namely water, is moved in itself ?   Then why
should there not be change ? It is not possible that
being should be one in form, but only in its source.

K

Soph. Elen. 5; 163 b 13. The same is true of syllogisms, as for instance in the case of Melissos' argument that the all is infinite; in this he assumes that the all is not generated (for nothing is generated from not-being), and that that which is generated, is generated from a beginning. If then the all was not generated, it does not have a beginning, so it is infinite. It is not necessary to assent to this, for even if everything which is generated has a beginning, it does not follow that if anything has a beginning it was generated, as a man with a fever is warm, but one who is warm may not have a fever.

Soph. Elen. 6; 164 b 35. Or again, as Melissos assumes in his argument that generation and having a beginning are the same thing, or that that which is generated from equals has the same size. The two statements, that what is generated has a beginning, and that what has a beginning is generated, he deems equivalent, so that the generated and the limited are both the same in that they each have a beginning. Because what is generated has a beginning, he postulates that what has a beginning is generated, as though both that which is generated and that which is finite were the same in having a beginning.

(*c*) Passages relating to Melissos in the Doxographists.

Epiph. *adv. Haer.* iii. 12; *Dox.* 590. Melissos of Samos, son of Ithagenes, said that the all is one in kind, but that nothing is fixed in its nature, for all things are potentially destructible.

Aet. *Plac.* i. 3; *Dox.* 285. Melissos of Miletos, son of Ithagenes, became his companion, but he did not preserve in its purity the doctrine that was transmitted to

him. For he said in regard to the infinite that the
world of those things that appear is limited. i. 7 ; 303.
Melissos and Zeno say that the one is universal, **and
that it exists** alone, eternal, and unlimited. And
this unity is necessity [*Heeren inserts here the name*
Empedokles], and the material of which it consists
is the four elements, and the forms are love and strife.
He calls the elements gods, and the mixture of them the
world. And the uniform will be resolved. He thinks
that souls are divine, and that pure men who share
these things in a pure way are divine. i. 24 ; 320.
Melissos (et al.) deny generation and destruction, because
they think that the all is unmoved.

Aet. ii. 1 ; 327. Melissos (et al.): The universe is one.
328. The all is infinite, but the world is limited. 4 ; 332.
Melissos (et al.) : The world is not generated, not to be
destroyed, eternal.

Aet. iv. 9 ; 396. Melissos (et al.) : Sensations are
deceptive.

IX.

PYTHAGORAS AND THE PYTHAGOREANS.

PYTHAGORAS, son of Mnesarchos, a native of Samos, left his fatherland to escape the tyranny of Polykrates (533/2 or 529/8 B.C.). He made his home for many years in Kroton in southern Italy, where his political views gained control in the city. At length he and his followers were banished by an opposing party, and he died at Metapontum. Many stories are told of his travels into Egypt and more widely, but there is no evidence on which the stories can be accepted. He was a mystic thinker and religious reformer quite as much as a philosopher, but there is no reason for denying that the doctrines of the school originated with him. Of his disciples, Archytas, in southern Italy, and Philolaos and Lysis, at Thebes, are the best known. It is the doctrine of the school, not the teaching of Pythagoras himself, which is known to us through the writings of Aristotle.

Literature :—On Pythagoras: Krische, *De societatis a Pythagora conditae scopo politico*, 1830 ; E. Rohde, *Rhein. Mus.* xxvi. 565 sqq. ; xxvii. 23 sqq.; Diels, *Rhein. Mus.* xxxi. 25 sq. ; Zeller, *Sitz. d. kgl. preus. Akad.* 1889, 45, p. 985 sqq.; Chaignet, *Pythagore*, 1873, and the excellent account in Burnett.
Philolaos : Boeckh, *Philolaos Lehren, nebst den Bruchstücken seines Werkes,* 1819 ; V. Rose, *Comment. de Arist. libr. ord. et auct.* Berlin 1854 ; Schaarschmidt, *Die angebliche Schriftstellerei des Phil.* Bonn 1864 ; Zeller, *Gesch. d. griech. Phil.* 4 Auf. 261, 341, 886 ; *Hermes* x. 178 ; Bywater, *Journal of Philol.* i. 21 sqq.

Archytas : Hartenstein, *de Archyt. Tar. fragm.* Lips.
1833 ; Gruppe, *Die Fragm. d. Archyt.* Berlin 1840 ;
Petersen, *Zeitschr. f. Altertumsk.* 1836 ; Chaignet,
Pythagore, 1873, pp. 191, 255.

Passages in Plato referring to the Pythagoreans.

Phaedo 62 B. The saying that is uttered in secret
rites, to the effect that we men are in a sort of prison,
and that one ought not to loose himself from it nor yet
to run away, seems to me something great and not easy
to see through ; but this at least I think is well said, that
it is the gods who care for us, and we men are one of the
possessions of the gods.

Kratyl. 400 B. For some say that it (the body) is
the tomb of the soul—I think it was the followers of
Orpheus in particular who introduced this word—which
has this enclosure like a prison in order that it may be
kept safe.

Gorg. 493 A. I once heard one of the wise men say
that now we are dead and the body is our tomb, and that
that part of the soul where desires are, it so happens,
is open to persuasion, and moves upward or downward.
And, indeed, a clever man—perhaps some inhabitant
of Sicily or Italy—speaking allegorically, and taking
the word from credible' ($\pi i\theta a\nu os$) and 'persuadable'
($\pi\iota\sigma\tau\iota\kappa\acute{o}s$), called this a jar ($\pi i\theta os$) ; and he called those
without intelligence uninitiated, and that part of the
soul of uninitiated persons where the desires are, he
called its intemperateness, and said it was not watertight, as a jar might be pierced with holes—using the
simile because of its insatiate desires.

Gorg. 507 E. And the wise men say that one com-
munity embraces heaven and earth and gods and men
and friendship and order and temperance and righteous-
ness, and for that reason they call this whole a universe,

my friend, for it is not without order nor yet is there excess. It seems to me that you do not pay attention to these things, though you are wise in regard to them. But it has escaped your notice that geometrical equality prevails widely among both gods and men.

PASSAGES IN ARISTOTLE REFERRING TO THE PYTHAGOREANS.

Phys. iii. 4 ; 203 a 1. For all who think they have worthily applied themselves to such philosophy, have discoursed concerning the infinite, and they all have asserted some first principle of things—some, like the Pythagoreans and Plato, a first principle existing by itself, not connected with anything else, but being itself the infinite in its essence. Only the Pythagoreans found it among things perceived by sense (for they say that number is not an abstraction), and they held that it was the infinite outside the heavens.

iii. 4 ; 204 a 33. (The Pythagoreans) both hold that the infinite is being, and divide it.

iv. 6 ; 213 b 22. And the Pythagoreans say that there is a void, and that it enters into the heaven itself from the infinite air, as though it (the heaven) were breathing ; and this void defines the natures of things, inasmuch as it is a certain separation and definition of things that lie together ; and this is true first in the case of numbers, for the void defines the nature of these.

De coel. i. 1 ; 268 a 10. For as the Pythagoreans say, the all and all things are defined by threes ; for end and middle and beginning constitute the number of the all, and also the number of the triad.

ii. 2 ; 284 b 6. And since there are some who say that there is a right and left of the heavens, as, for instance, those that are called Pythagoreans (for such is their doctrine), we must investigate whether it is as they say.

ii. 2 ; 285 a 10.   Wherefore one of the Pythagoreans might be surprised in that they say that there are only these two first principles, the right and the left, and they pass over four of them as not having the least validity ; for there is no less difference up and down, and front and back than there is right and left in all creatures.

ii. 2 ; 285 b 23.   And some are dwelling in the upper hemisphere and to the right, while we dwell below and to the left, which is the opposite to what the Pytha-goreans say ; for they put us above and to the right, while the others are below and at the left.

ii. 9 ; 290 b 15.   Some think it necessary that noise should arise when so great bodies are in motion, since sound does arise from bodies among us which are not so large and do not move so swiftly ; and from the sun and moon and from the stars in so great number, and of so great size, moving so swiftly, there must necessarily arise a sound inconceivably great.   Assuming these things and that the swiftness has the principle of harmony by reason of the intervals, they say that the sound of the stars moving on in a circle becomes musical. And since it seems unreasonable that we also do not hear this sound, they say that the reason for this is that the noise exists in the very nature of things, so as not to be distinguishable from the opposite silence; for the dis-tinction of sound and silence lies in their contrast with each other, so that as blacksmiths think there is no difference between them because they are accustomed to the sound, so the same thing happens to men.

ii. 9 ; 291 a 7.   What occasions the difficulty and makes the Pythagoreans say that there is a harmony of the bodies as they move, is a proof.   For whatever things move themselves make a sound and noise; but whatever things are fastened in what moves or exist in it as the parts in a ship, cannot make a noise, nor yet does the ship if it moves in a river.

ii. 13 ; 293 a 19.   They say that the whole heaven is limited, the opposite to what those of Italy, called the Pythagoreans, say; for these say that fire is at the centre and that the earth is one of the stars, and that moving in a circle about the centre it produces night and day. And they assume yet another earth opposite this which they call the counter-earth [ἀντίχθων], not seeking reasons and causes for phenomena, but stretching phenomena to meet certain assumptions and opinions of theirs and attempting to arrange them in a system. . . . And farther the Pythagoreans say that the most authoritative part of the All stands guard, because it is specially fitting that it should, and this part is the centre; and this place that the fire occupies, they call the guard of Zeus, as it is called simply the centre, that is, the centre of space and the centre of matter and of nature.

iii. 1 ; 300 a 15.   The same holds true for those who construct the heaven out of numbers; for some construct nature out of numbers, as do certain of the Pythagoreans.

Metaphys. i. 5 ; 985 b 23–986 b 8.   With these and before them (Anaxagoras, Empedokles, Atomists) those called Pythagoreans applying themselves to the sciences, first developed them ; and being brought up in them they thought that the first principles of these (*i.e.* numbers) were the first principles of all things.   And since of these (sciences) numbers are by nature the first, in numbers rather than in fire and earth and water they thought they saw many likenesses to things that are and that are coming to be, as, for instance, justice is such a property of numbers, and soul and mind are such a property, and another is opportunity, and of other things one may say the same of each one.

†And further, discerning in numbers the conditions and reasons of harmonies also†; since, moreover, other things seemed to be like numbers in their entire nature, and numbers were the first of every nature, they assumed that the elements of numbers were the elements of all things, and that the whole heavens were harmony and number. And whatever characteristics in numbers and harmonies they could show were in agreement with the properties of the heavens and its parts and with its whole arrangement, these they collected and adapted; and if there chanced to be any gap anywhere, they eagerly sought that the whole system might be connected with these (stray phenomena). To give an example of my meaning : inasmuch as ten seemed to be the perfect number and to embrace the whole nature of numbers, they asserted that the number of bodies moving through the heavens were ten, and when only nine were visible, for the reason just stated they postulated the counter-earth as the tenth. We have given a more definite account of these thinkers in other parts of our writings. But we have referred to them here with this purpose in view, that we might ascertain from them what they asserted as the first principles and in what manner they came upon the causes that have been enumerated. They certainly seem to consider number as the first principle and as it were the matter in things and in their conditions and states ; and the odd and the even are elements of number, and of these the one is infinite and the other finite, and unity is the product of both of them, for it is both odd and even, and number arises from unity, and the whole heaven, as has been said, is numbers.

A different party in this same school say that the

first principles are ten, named according to the following table :—finite and infinite, even and odd, one and many, right and left, male and female, rest and motion, straight and crooked, light and darkness, good and bad, square and oblong.   After this manner Alkmaeon of Kroton seems to have conceived them, and either he received this doctrine from them or they from him ; for Alkmaeon arrived at maturity when Pythagoras was an old man, and his teachings resembled theirs.   For he says that most human affairs are twofold, not meaning opposites reached by definition, as did the former party, but opposites by chance — as, for example, white-black, sweet-bitter, good-bad, small-great.   This philosopher let fall his opinions indefinitely about the rest, but the Pythagoreans declared the number of the opposites and what they were.   From both one may learn this much, that opposites are the first principles of things ; but from the latter he may learn the number of these, and what they are.   But how it is possible to bring them into relation with the causes of which we have spoken if they have not clearly worked out ; but they seem to range their elements under the category of matter, for they say that being is compounded and formed from them, and that they inhere in it.

987 a 9–27.   Down to the Italian philosophers and with the exception of them the rest have spoken more reasonably about these principles, except that, as we said, they do indeed use two principles, and the one of these, whence is motion, some regard as one and others as twofold.   The Pythagoreans, however, while they in similar manner assume two first principles, add this which is peculiar to themselves : that they do not think that the finite and the infinite and the one are certain other things by nature, such as fire or earth or any other such thing, but the infinite itself and unity itself are

the essence of the things of which they are predicated,
and so they make number the essence of all things.   So
they taught after this manner about them, and began
to discourse and to define what being is, but they made
it altogether too simple a matter.   For they made their
definitions superficially, and to whatever first the definition might apply, this they thought to be the essence of
the matter ; as if one should say that twofold and two
were the same, because the twofold subsists in the two.
But undoubtedly the two and the twofold are not the
same ; otherwise the one will be many—a consequence
which even they would not draw.   So much then may
be learned from the earlier philosophers and from their
successors.

i. 6 ; 987 b 10.   And Plato only changed the name,
for the Pythagoreans say that things exist by imitation
of numbers, but Plato, by sharing the nature of numbers.

i. 6 ; 987 b 22.   But that the one is the real essence of
things, and not something else with unity as an attribute,
he affirms, agreeing with the Pythagoreans ; and in
harmony with them he affirms that numbers are the
principles of being for other things.   But it is peculiar
to him that instead of a single infinite he posits a double
infinite, an infinite of greatness and of littleness ; and it
is also peculiar to him that he separates numbers from
things that are seen, while they say that numbers
are the things themselves, and do not interpose mathematical objects between them.   This separation of the one
and numbers from things, in contrast with the position
of the Pythagoreans, and the introduction of ideas, are
the consequence of his investigation by concepts.

i. 8 ; 989 b 32–990 a 32.   Those, however, who carry
on their investigation with reference to all things, and
divide things into what are perceived and what are not
perceived by sense, evidently examine both classes, so

one must delay a little longer over what they say. They
speak correctly and incorrectly in reference to the questions now before us. Now those who are called Pythagoreans use principles and elements yet stranger than
those of the physicists, in that they do not take them
from the sphere of sense, for mathematical objects are
without motion, except in the case of astronomy.˙ Still,
they discourse about everything in nature and study it ;
they construct the heaven, they observe what happens in
its parts †and their states and motions† ; they apply to
these their first principles and causes, as though they
agreed entirely with˙the other physicists that being is only
what is perceptible and what that which is called heaven
includes. But their causes and first principles, they say,
are such as to lead up to the higher parts of reality, and
are in harmony with this rather than with the doctrines
of nature. In what manner motion will take place when
finite and infinite, odd and even, are the only underlying
realities, they do not say ; nor how it is possible for
genesis and destruction to take place without motion and
change, or for the heavenly bodies to revolve. Farther,
if one grant to them that greatness arises from these
principles, or if this could be proved, nevertheless, how
will it be that some bodies are light and some heavy ?
For their postulates and statements apply no more to
mathematical objects than to things of sense ; accordingly they have said nothing at all about fire or earth
or any such objects, because I think they have no distinctive doctrine about things of sense. Farther, how
is it necessary to assume that number and states of
number are the causes of what is in the heavens and
what is taking place there from the beginning and now,
and that there is no other number than that out of
which the world is composed ? For when opinion and
opportune time are at a certain point in the heavens,

and a little farther up or down are injustice and judgment or a mixture of them, and they bring forward as proof that each one of these is number, and the result then is that at this place there is already a multitude of compounded quantities because those states of number have each their place—is this number in heaven the same which it is necessary to assume that each of these things is, or is it something different ? Plato says it is different ; still, he thinks that both these things and the causes of them are numbers ; but the one class are ideal causes, and the others are sense causes.

ii. 1 ; 996 a 4. And the most difficult and perplexing question of all is whether unity and being are not, as Plato and the Pythagoreans say, something different from things but their very essence, or whether the underlying substance is something different, friendship, as Empedokles says, or as another says, fire, or water, or air.

ii. 4 ; 1001 a 9. Plato and the Pythagoreans assert that neither being nor yet unity is something different from things, but that it is the very nature of them, as though essence itself consisted in unity and existence.

1036 b 17. So it turns out that many things of which the forms appear different have one form, as the Pythagoreans discovered ; and one can say that there is one form for everything, and the others are not forms ; and thus all things will be one.

ix. 2 ; 1053 b 11. Whether the one itself is a sort of essence, as first the Pythagoreans and later Plato affirmed. . .

xi. 7 ; 1072 b 31. And they are wrong who assume, as do the Pythagoreans and Speusippos, that the most beautiful and the best is not in the first principle, because the first principles of plants and animals are indeed causes ; for that which is beautiful and perfect is in what comes from these first principles.

xii. 4 ; 1078 b 21. The Pythagoreans (before Demokritos) only defined a few things, the concepts of which
they reduced to numbers, as for instance opportunity or
justice or marriage. . .

xii. 6 ; 1080 b 16. The Pythagoreans say that there
is but one number, the mathematical, but things of
sense are not separated from this, for they are composed of it ; indeed, they construct the whole heaven
out of numbers, but not out of unit numbers, for they
assume that the unities have quantity ; but how the
first unity was so constituted as to have quantity, they
seem at a loss to say. b 31. All, as many as regard
the one as the element and first principle of things, except
the Pythagoreans, assert that numbers are based on
the unit ; but the Pythagoreans assert, as has been
remarked, that numbers have quantity.

xii. 8 ; 1083 b 9. The Pythagorean standpoint has on
the one hand fewer difficulties than those that have
been discussed, but it has new difficulties of its own.
The fact that they do not regard number as separate,
removes many of the contradictions ; but it is impossible
that bodies should consist of numbers, and that this
number should be mathematical. Nor is it true that
indivisible elements have quantity ; but, granted that
they have this quality of indivisibility, the units have no
quantity ; for how can quantity be composed of indivisible
elements ? but arithmetical number consists of units.
But these say that things are number ; at least, they
adapt their speculations to such bodies as consist of
elements which are numbers.

xiii. 3 ; 1090 a 20. On the other hand the Pythagoreans, because they see many qualities of numbers in
bodies perceived by sense, regard objects as numbers,
not as separate numbers, but as derived from numbers.
And why ? Because the qualities of numbers exist in

harmony both in the heaven and in many other things. But for those who hold that number is mathematical only, it is impossible on the basis of their hypothesis to say any such thing; and it has already been remarked that there can be no science of these numbers. But we say, as above, that there is a science of numbers. Evidently the mathematical does not exist apart by itself, for in that case its qualities could not exist in bodies. In such a matter the Pythagoreans are restrained by nothing ; when, however, they construct out of numbers physical bodies—out of numbers that have neither weight nor lightness, bodies that have weight and lightness—they seem to be speaking about another heaven and other bodies than those perceived by sense.

Eth. i. 4 ; 1096 b 5. And the Pythagoreans seem to speak more persuasively about it, putting the unity in the co-ordination of good things.

ii. 5 ; 1106 b 29. The evil partakes of the nature of the infinite, the good of the finite, as the Pythagoreans conjectured.

v. 8 ; 1132 b 21. Reciprocity seems to some to be absolutely just, as the Pythagoreans say; for these defined the just as that which is reciprocal to another.

Mor. i. 1 ; 1182 a 11. First Pythagoras attempted to speak concerning virtue, but he did not speak correctly ; for bringing virtues into correspondence with numbers, he did not make any distinct.

PYTHAGORAS AND THE PYTHAGOREANS : PASSAGES IN
THE DOXOGRAPHISTS.

Aet. *Plac.* i. 3 ; *Dox.* 280. And again from another starting-point, Pythagoras, son of Mnesarchos, a Samian, who was the first to call this matter by the name of philosophy, assumed as first principles the numbers and

the symmetries existing in them, which he calls harmonies, and the elements compounded of both, that are
called geometrical. And again he includes the monad
and the undefined dyad among the first principles; and
for him one of the first principles tends toward the
creative and form-giving cause, which is intelligence,
that is god, and the other tends toward the passive and
material cause, which is the visible universe. And he
says that the starting-point of number is the decad; for
all Greeks and all barbarians count as far as ten, and
when they get as far as this they return to the monad.
And again, he says, the power of the ten is in the four
and the tetrad. And the reason is this: if any one
†returning† from the monad adds the numbers in a
series as far as the four, he will fill out the number
ten (i.e. $1+2+3+4=10$); but if he goes beyond the
number of the tetrad, he will exceed the ten. Just
as if one should add one and two and should add to
these three and four, he will fill out the number ten; so
that according to the monad number is in the ten, but
potentially in the four. Wherefore the Pythagoreans
were wont to speak as though the greatest oath were
the tetrad: ‘By him that transmitted to our soul the
tetraktys, which has the spring and root of ever-flowing
nature.’ And our soul, he says, is composed of the
tetrad; for it is intelligence, understanding, opinion,
sense, from which things come every art and science,
and we ourselves become reasoning beings. The monad,
however, is intelligence, for intelligence sees according
to the monad. As for example, men are made up of
many parts, and part by part they are devoid of sense
and comprehension and experience, yet we perceive
that man as one alone, whom no being resembles,
possesses these qualities; and we perceive that a horse
is one, but part by part it is without experience.

For these are all forms and classes according to monads.
Wherefore, assigning this limit with reference to each
one of these, they speak of a reasoning being and a
neighing being.   On this account then the monad is
intelligence by which we perceive these things.   And
the undefined dyad is science; fittingly, for all proof and
all persuasion is part of science, and farther every
syllogism brings together what is questioned out of some
things that are agreed upon, and easily proves something
else; and science is the comprehension of these things,
wherefore it would be the dyad.   And opinion as the
result of comprehending them is the triad; fittingly,
for opinion has to do with many things; and the triad
is quantity, as 'The thrice-blessed Danaoi.'   On this
account then he includes the triad. . . .   And their
sect is called Italic because Pythagoras taught in Italy,
for he removed from Samos, his fatherland, because of
dissatisfaction with the tyranny of Polykrates.

Aet. i. 7; *Dox.* 302. Pythagoras held that one of the
first principles, the monad, is god and the good, which
is the origin of the One, and is itself intelligence; but
the undefined dyad is a divinity and the bad, surrounding
which is the mass of matter.   i. 8; 307. Divine spirits
[δαίμονες] are psychical beings; and heroes are souls
separated from bodies, good heroes are good souls, bad
heroes are bad souls.   i. 9; 307. The followers of
Thales and Pythagoras and the Stoics held that matter
is variable and changeable and transformable and in a
state of flux, the whole through the whole.   i. 10; 309.
Pythagoras asserted that the so-called forms and ideas
exist in numbers and their harmonies, and in what are
called geometrical objects, apart from bodies.   i. 11; 310.
Pythagoras and Aristotle asserted that the first causes
are immaterial, but that other causes involve a union
or contact with material substance [so that the world is

material]. i. 14 ; 312. The followers of Pythagoras held
that the universe is a sphere according to the form of
the four elements ; but the highest fire alone is conical.
i. 15 ; 314. The Pythagoreans call colour the manifesta-
tion of matter. i. 16 ; 314. Bodies are subject to change
of condition, and are divisible to infinity. i. 18 ; 316.
(After quotation from Arist. *Phys.* iv. 4 ; 212 a 20)
And in his first book on the philosophy of Pythagoras
he writes that the heaven is one, and that time and
wind and the void which always defines the places of
each thing, are introduced from the infinite.   And
among other things he says that place is the immovable
limit of what surrounds the world, or that in which
bodies abide and are moved ; and that it is full when it
surrounds body on every side, and empty when it has
absolutely nothing in itself.   Accordingly it is necessary
for place to exist, and body ; and it is never empty except
only from the standpoint of thought, for the nature of it
in perpetuity is destructive of the interrelation of things
and of the combination of bodies ; and motions arise
according to place of bodies that surround and oppose
each other ; and no infiniteness is lacking, either of
quantity or of extent.   i. 20; 318. Pythagoras said
that time is the sphere of what surrounds the world.
i. 21; 318.   Pythagoras, Plato : Motion is a certain
otherness or difference in matter.   [This is the common
limit of all motion.]   i. 24 ; 320. Pythagoras and all
that assume that matter is subject to change assert that
genesis and destruction in an absolute sense take place ;
for from change of the elements and modification and
separation of them there take place juxtaposition and
mixture, and intermingling and melting together.

Aet. *Plac.* ii. 1 ; 327. Pythagoras first named the
circumference of all things the universe by reason of the
order in it. ii. 4 ; 330. Pythagoras, Plato, and the Stoics

held that the universe is brought into being by god. And it is perishable so far as its nature is concerned, for it is perceived by sense, and therefore material; it will not however be destroyed in accordance with the foreknowledge and plan of god. ii. 6; 334. Pythagoras: The universe is made from five solid figures, which are called also mathematical; of these he says that earth has arisen from the cube, fire from the pyramid, air from the octahedron, and water from the icosahedron, and the sphere of the all from the dodecahedron. ii. 9; 338. The followers of Pythagoras hold that there is a void outside the universe into which the universe breathes forth, and from which it breathes in. ii. 10; 339. Pythagoras, Plato, Aristotle: The right hand side of the universe is the eastern part from which comes the beginning of motion, and the left hand side is the west. They say the universe has neither height nor depth, in which statement height means distance from below upwards, and depth from above downwards. For none of the distances thus described exist for the universe, inasmuch as it is disposed around the middle of itself, from which it extends toward the all, and with reference to which it is the same on every side. ii. 12; 340. Thales, Pythagoras, and their followers: The sphere of the whole heaven is divided into five circles, which they call zones; the first of these is called the arctic zone and is ever visible ; the second the summer solstice, the third the equinoctial, the fourth the winter solstice, and fifth the antarctic zone, which is invisible. And the ecliptic called the zodiac in the three middle ones is projected to touch the three middle ones. And the meridian crosses all these from the north to the opposite quarter at right angles. It is said that Pythagoras was the first to recognise the slant of the zodiacal circle which Oenopides of Chios appropriated as his own discovery. ii. 13 ; 343. Herakleides and the Pythagoreans asserted that each world [κόσμος] of the stars is air and aether surrounding earth in the infinite aether. And these doctrines are brought out in the Orphic writings, for they construct each world of the stars. ii. 22 ; 352. The Pythagoreans : The sun is spherical. ii. 23 ; 353. Plato, Pythagoras, Aristotle : The solstices lie along the slant of the zodiacal circle, through which the sun goes along the zodiac, and with the accompaniment of the tropic circles ; and all these things also the globe shows. ii. 24 ; 354. An eclipse takes place when the moon comes past. ii. 25 ; 357. Pythagoras : The moon is a mirror-like body. ii. 29 ; 360. Some of the Pythagoreans (according to the Aristotelian account and the statement of Philip the Opuntian) said that an eclipse of the moon takes place, sometimes by the interposition of the earth, sometimes by the interposition of the counter-earth [ἀντίχθων]. But it seems to some more recent thinkers that it takes place by a spreading of the flame little by little as it is gradually kindled, until it gives the complete full moon, and again, in like manner, it grows less until the conjunction, when it is completely extinguished. ii. 30 ; 361. Some of the Pythagoreans, among them Philolaos, said that the earthy appearance of the moon is due to its being inhabited by animals and by plants, like those on our earth, only greater and more beautiful ; for the animals on it are fifteen times as powerful, not having any sort of excrement, and their day is fifteen times as long as ours. But others said that the outward appearance in the moon is a reflection on the other side of the inflamed circle of the sea that is on our earth. ii. 32 ; 364. Some regard the greater year . . . . as the sixty year period, among whom are Oenopides and Pythagoras.

Aet. *Plac.* iii. 1 ; *Dox.* 364. Some of the Pythagoreans

said that the milky way is the burning of a star that fell
from its own foundation, setting on fire the region
through which it passed in a circle, as Phaethon was
burned.   And others say that the course of the sun
arose in this manner at the first.   And certain ones say
that the appearance of the sun is like a mirror reflecting
its rays toward the heaven, and therefore it happens at
times to reflect its rays on the rainbow in the clouds.

Aet. iii. 2 ; 366. Some of the followers of Pythagoras
say that the comet is one of the stars that are not
always shining, but emit their light periodically through
a certain definite time; but others say that it is the
reflection of our vision into the sun, like reflected
images.   iii. 14; 378. Pythagoras: The earth, after the
analogy of the sphere of the all, is divided into five
zones, arctic, antarctic, summer, winter, and equinoctial ;
of these the middle one he defines to be the middle of the
earth, called for this very reason the torrid zone ; but
the inhabited one [the one between the arctic and the
torrid zones] being well-tempered. . . .

Aet. iv. 2 ; *Dox.* 386. Pythagoras holds that number
moves itself, and he takes number as an equivalent for
intelligence.   iv. 4; 389. Pythagoras, Plato: According
to a superficial account the soul is of two parts, the one
possessing, the other lacking, reason ; but according to
close and exact examination, of three parts; for the
unreasoning part they divide into the emotions and the
desires.   (Theodor. v. 20); *Dox.* 390. The successors of
Pythagoras saying that body is a mixture of five elements
(for they ranked the aether as a· fifth along with the
four) held that the powers of the soul are of the same
number as these.   And these they name intelligence
and wisdom and understanding and opinion and sense-
perception.   iv. 5; 391. Pythagoras: The principle of
life is about the heart, but the principle of reason and

intelligence is about the head. iv. 5; 392. Pythagoras et
al. : The intelligence enters from without. iv. 7; 392.
Pythagoras, Plato : The soul is imperishable. iv. 9;
396.   Pythagoras et al. : The sense-perceptions are
deceptive. iv. 9; 397. Pythagoras, Plato : Each of the
sensations is pure, proceeding from each single element.
With reference to vision, it was of the nature of aether ;
hearing, of the nature of wind; smell, of the nature
of fire ; taste, of the nature of moisture ; touch, of the
nature of earth. iv. 14; 405. The followers of Pythagoras and of the mathematicians on reflections of vision :
For vision moves directly as it were against the bronze
[of a mirror], and meeting with a firm smooth surface
it is turned and bent back on itself, meeting some such
experience as when the arm is extended and then bent
back to the shoulder. iv. 20; 409. Pythagoras, Plato,
Aristotle : Sound is immaterial. For it is not air, but
it is the form about the air and the appearance
[ἐπιφανεία] after some sort of percussion which becomes
sound ; and every appearance is immaterial ; for it moves
with bodies, but is itself absolutely immaterial ; [1] as in
the case of a bent rod the surface-appearance suffers
no change, but the matter is what is bent.

Aet. *Plac.* v. 1 ; 415.   Pythagoras did not admit the
sacrificial part alone (of augury). v. 3 ; 417. Pythagoras : The seed is foam of the best part of the blood,
a secretion from the nourishment, like blood and marrow.
v. 4 ; 417. Pythagoras, Plato, Aristotle : The power of
seed is immaterial, like intelligence, the moving power ;
but the matter that is poured forth is material. v. 20 ;
432. Pythagoras, Plato : The souls of animals called
unreasoning are reasonable, not however with active
reasoning powers, because of an imperfect mixture of
the bodies and because they do not have the power of

---

[1] Cf. Galen, 27 ; *Dox.* 615 sq.

speech, as in the case of apes and dogs; for these have intelligence but not the power of speech.

Ar. Did. *Ep.* Fr. 32; *Dox.* 467. Apollodoros in the second book *Concerning the gods*: It is the Pythagorean opinion that the morning and the evening star are the same.

Theophr. *Phys. Op.* Fr. 17; *Dox.* 492. Favorinus says that he (Pythagoras) was the first to call the heavens a universe and the earth round [στρογγύλην].

Cic. *de Deor. Nat.* i. 11; Philod. *piet.* Fr. c 4 b; *Dox.* 533. For Pythagoras, who held that soul is extended through all the nature of things and mingled with them, and that from this our souls are taken, did not see that god would be separated and torn apart by the separation of human souls; and when souls are wretched, as might happen to many, then part of god would be wretched; a thing which could not happen.

Hippol. *Phil.* 2; *Dox.* 555. There is a second philosophy not far distant from the same time, of which Pythagoras, whom some call a Samian, was the first representative. And this they call the Italian philosophy because Pythagoras fled the rule of Polykrates over the Samians and settled in a city of Italy where he spent his life. The successive leaders of this sect shared the same spirit. And he in his studies of nature mingled astronomy and geometry and music <and arithmetic>. And thus he asserted that god is a monad, and examining the nature of number with especial care, he said that the universe produces melody and is put together with harmony, and he first proved the motion of the seven stars to be rhythm and melody. And in wonder at the structure of the universe, he decreed that at first his disciples should be silent, as it were mystae who were coming into the order of the all; then when he thought they had sufficient education

in the principles of truth, and had sought wisdom
sufficiently in regard to stars and in regard to nature,
he pronounced them pure and then bade them speak.
He separated his disciples into two groups, and called
one esoteric, and the other exoteric.   To the former
he entrusted the more perfect sciences, to the latter
the more moderate.   And he dealt with magic, as they
say, and himself discovered the art of physiognomy.
Postulating both numbers and measures he was wont
to say that the first principle of arithmetic em-
braced philosophy by combination, after the following
manner :

Number is the first principle, a thing which is undefined, incomprehensible, having in itself all numbers
which could reach infinity in amount.   And the first
principle of numbers is in substance the first monad,
which is a male monad, begetting as a father all other
numbers.   Secondly the dyad is female number, and
the same is called by the arithmeticians even.   Thirdly
the triad is male number ; this the arithmeticians have
been wont to call odd.   Finally the tetrad is a female
number, and the same is called even because it is
female.

All numbers, then, taken by classes are fours (for
number is undefined in reference to class), of which is
composed the perfect number, the decad.   For the
series, one two three and four, becomes ten, if its own
name is kept in its essence by each of the numbers.
Pythagoras said that this sacred tetraktys is 'the spring
having the roots of ever-flowing nature' in itself, and
from this numbers have their first principle.   For the
eleven and the twelve and the rest derive from the
ten the first principle of their being.   The four parts of
the decad, this perfect number, are called number,
monad, power, and cube.   And the interweavings and

minglings of these in the origin of growth are what
naturally completes nascent number ; for when a power
is multiplied upon itself, it is the power of a power ;
and when a power is multiplied on a cube, it is the
power of a cube ; and when a cube is multiplied on a
cube, the cube of a cube ; thus all numbers, from which
arises the genesis of what arises, are seven :—number,
monad, power, cube, power of a power, power of a cube,
cube of a cube.

He said that the soul is immortal, and that it changes
from one body to another ;[1] so he was wont to say that
he himself had been born before the Trojan war as
Aethalides, and at the time of the Trojan war as
Euphorbos, and after that as Hermotimos of Samos,
then as Pyrrhos of Delos, fifth as Pythagoras. And
Diodoros of Eretria and Aristoxenos the musician say
that Pythagoras had come into Zaratas of Chaldaea ;
and he set forth that in his view there were from the
beginning two causes of things, father and mother ;
and the father is light and the mother darkness ; and
the parts of light are warm, dry, light, swift ; and of
darkness are cold, moist, heavy, slow ; and of these all
the universe is composed, of male and female. And he
says that the universe exists in accordance with musical
harmony, so the sun also makes an harmonious period.
And concerning the things that arise from the earth
and the universe they say that Zaratas spoke as follows :
There are two divinities, one of the heavens and the
other of the earth ; the one of the earth produces
things from the earth, and it is water ; and the divinity
of the heavens is fire with a portion of air, warm, and
cold ; wherefore he says that none of these things will
destroy or even pollute the soul, for these are the essence
of all things. And it is said that Zaratas forbade men

[1] Cf. Epiph. *Haer.* i. 7; *Dox.* 589.

to eat beans because he said that at the beginning and composition of all things when the earth was still a whole, the bean arose. And he says that the proof of this is that if one chews a bean to a pulp and exposes it to the sun for a certain time (for the sun will affect it quickly), it gives out the odour of human seed. And he says that there is another and clearer proof: if when a bean is in flower we were to take the bean and its flower, and putting it into a pitcher moisten it and then bury it in the earth, and after a few days dig it up again, we should see in the first place that it had the form of a womb, and examining it closely we should find the head of a child growing with it.

He perished in a conflagration with his disciples in Kroton in Italy. And it was the custom when one became a disciple for him to burn his property and to leave his money under a seal with Pythagoras, and he remained in silence sometimes three years, sometimes five years, and studied. And immediately on being released from this he mingled with the others and continued a disciple and made his home with them; otherwise he took his money and was sent off. The esoteric class were called Pythagoreans, and the others Pythagoristae. And those of the disciples who escaped the conflagration were Lysis and Archippos and Zalmoxis the slave of Pythagoras, who is said to have taught the Pythagorean philosophy to the Druids among the Celts.[1] It is said that Pythagoras learned numbers and measures from the Egyptians; astonished at the wisdom of the priests, which was deserving of belief and full of fancies and difficult to buy, he imitated it and himself also taught his disciples to be silent, and obliged the student to remain quietly in rooms underneath the earth.

Epiph. *Pro.* i.; *Dox.* 587.   Pythagoras laid down

[1] Cf. 25; *Dox.* 574.

the doctrine of the monad and of foreknowledge and the interdict on sacrificing to the gods then believed on, and he bade men not to partake of beings that had life, and to refrain from wine. And he drew a line between the things from the moon upwards, calling these immortal, and those below, which he called mortal; and he taught the transmigration of souls from bodies into bodies even as far as animals and beasts. And he used to teach his followers to observe silence for a period of five years. Finally he named himself a god.

Epiph. *Haer.* iii. 8; *Dox.* 390.   Pythagoras the Samian, son of Mnesarchos, said that the monad is god, and that nothing has been brought into being apart from this. He was wont to say that wise men ought not to sacrifice animals to the gods, nor yet to eat what had life, or beans, nor to drink wine. And he was wont to say that all things from the moon downward were subject to change, while from the moon upward they were not. And he said that the soul goes at death into other animals. And he bade his disciples to keep silence for a period of five years, and finally he named himself a god.

Herm. *I.G.P.* 16; *Dox.* 655.   Others then from the ancient tribe, Pythagoras and his fellow-tribesmen, revered and taciturn, transmitted other dogmas to me as mysteries, and this is the great and unspeakable *ipse-dixit*: the monad is the first principle of all things. From its forms and from numbers the elements arose. And he declared that the number and form and measure of each of these is somehow as follows:—Fire is composed of twenty-four right-angled triangles, surrounded by four equilaterals. And each equilateral consists of six right-angled triangles, whence they compare it to the pyramid. Air is composed of forty-eight triangles, surrounded by eight equilaterals. And it is compared to the octahedron, which is surrounded by eight equilateral triangles, each of which is separated into six right-angled triangles so as to become forty-eight in all. And water is composed of one hundred and twenty triangles, surrounded by twenty equilaterals, and it is compared to the icosahedron, which is composed of one hundred and twenty equilateral triangles. And aether is composed of twelve equilateral pentagons, and is like a dodecahedron. And earth is composed of forty-eight triangles, and is surrounded by six equilateral pentagons, and it is like a cube. For the cube is surrounded by six tetragons, each of which is separated into eight triangles, so that they become in all forty-eight.

X.

EMPEDOKLES.

EMPEDOKLES, son of Meton, grandson of an Empedokles who was a victor at Olympia, made his home at Akragas in Sicily. He was born about 494 B.C., and lived to the age of sixty. The only sure date in his life is his visit to Thourioi soon after its foundation (444). Various stories are told of his political activity, which may be genuine traditions; these illustrate a democratic tendency. At the same time he claimed almost the homage due to a god, and many miracles are attributed to him. His writings in some parts are said to imitate Orphic verses, and apparently his religious activity was in line with this sect. His death occurred away from Sicily—probably in the Peloponnesos.

Literature:—Sturz, *Emped. vita et phil. carm. rell.* Lips. 1805; Karsten, *Emped. carm. rell.* Amst. 1838; Bergk, *Kleine Schriften*, Berl. 1839; Panzerbieter, *Beitr. z. Kritik u. Erkl. d. Emped.* Meining. 1844; Stein, *Emped. Frag.* Bonn 1852; Schneidewin, *Philol.* xv.; H. Diels; *Hermes* xv. pp. 161–179; *Gorgias und Empedocles*, Acad. Berol. 1884; Unger, *Philol. Suppl.* 1883, pp. 511–550; O. Kern, *Archiv f. d. Gesch. d. Philos.* i. 498 ff.; Knatz, 'Empedoclea' in *Schedae Phil. H. Usener oblatae*, Bonn 1891; A. Platt, *Journal of Philology*, xxiv. p. 246; Bidez, *Archiv*, ix. 190; Gomperz, *Hermes*, xxxi. p. 469.

NOTE.—I print Stein's numbers at the left of the Greek text, Karsten's numbers at the right.

FRAGMENTS OF EMPEDOKLES.

ΠΕΡΙ ΦΥΣΕΩΣ ΠΡΩΤΟΣ.

Παυσανία, σὺ δὲ κλῦθι, δαΐφρονος Ἀγχίτου υἱέ.　54

στεινωποὶ μὲν γὰρ παλάμαι κατὰ γυῖα κέχυνται·　32
πολλὰ δὲ δειλ' ἔμπαια, τά τ' ἀμβλύνουσι
　μερίμνας.
παῦρον δὲ ζωῆς ἀβίου μέρος ἀθρήσαντες
5 ὠκύμοροι καπνοῖο δίκην ἀρθέντες ἀπέπταν,　35
αὐτὸ μόνον πεισθέντες, ὅτῳ προσέκυρσεν ἕκαστος
πάντοσ' ἐλαυνόμενος, τὸ δ' ὅλον μὰψ εὔχεται
　εὑρεῖν·
οὕτως οὔτ' ἐπιδερκτὰ τάδ' ἀνδράσιν οὐδ' ἐπα-
　κουστὰ
οὔτε νόῳ περιληπτά.　σὺ δ' οὖν, ἐπεὶ ὧδ' ἐλιά-
　σθης,
10 πεύσεαι οὐ πλέον ἠὲ βροτείη μῆτις ὄπωπεν.　40

ἀλλά, θεοί, τῶν μὲν μανίην ἀποτρέψατε γλώσ-
　σης,
ἐκ δ' ὁσίων στομάτων καθαρὴν ὀχετεύσατε
　πηγήν.
καὶ σέ, πολυμνήστη λευκώλενε παρθένε Μοῦσα,
ἄντομαι, ὧν θέμις ἐστὶν ἐφημερίοισιν ἀκούειν,
15 πέμπε παρ' εὐσεβίης, ἐλάουσ' εὐήνιον ἅρμα·　45

Sources and Critical Notes.

1. Diog. Laer. viii. 60.　2-10. Sext. Emp. *Math.* vii. 123-124.
3. Prokl. on *Tim.* p. 175.　5. Plut. *Mor.* 360 c.　6. Diog. Laer. ix. 73 ;
8-9a. Plut. *Mor.* 17 ᴇ.

　　3. MSS. δειλεμπέα, corr. Emperius. Prokl. δειν' ἔπεα.　4. MSS. ζωῆσι
βίου, corr. Scaliger.　*CFR* ἀθροίσαντος.　7. MSS. ἐλαυνόμενοι,
τὸ δ' ὅλον εὔχεται, corr. Stein.　9. Bergk adds δ' after σὺ.
10.　MSS. πλεῖόν γε, Karsten πλέον' ἠὲ, Stein πλέον : MSS.
ὄρωρεν, corr. Panzerbieter.

　11-23. Sext. Emp. *Math.* vii. 125.　16-17. Clem. Al. *Strom.* p. 682.
18. Prokl. *Tim.* 106 ; Plut. *Mor.* 93 ᴅ.

　　12. MSS. ὀχεύσατε, corr. Steph.　16. MSS. σέ, Stein μέ.　17. Sext.

Book I.

1. And do thou hear me, Pausanias, son of wise Anchites.

2. For scant means of acquiring knowledge are scattered among the members of the body; and many are the evils that break in to blunt the edge of studious thought. And gazing on a little portion of life that is not life, swift to meet their fate, they rise and are borne away like smoke, persuaded only of that on which each one chances as he is driven this way and that, but the whole he vainly boasts he has found. Thus these things are neither seen nor heard distinctly by men, nor comprehended by the mind. And thou, now that thou hast withdrawn hither, shalt learn no more than what mortal mind has seen.

11. But, ye gods, avert the madness of those men from my tongue, and from lips that are holy cause a pure stream to flow. And thee I pray, much-wooed white-armed maiden Muse, in what things it is right for beings of a day to hear, do thou, and Piety, driving obedient car, conduct me on. Nor yet shall the flowers of honour

μηδὲ μέ γ' εὐδόξοιο βιήσεται ἄνθεα τιμῆς
πρὸς θνητῶν ἀνελέσθαι, ἐφ' ᾧ θ' ὁσίης πλέον
εἰπεῖν
θάρσει καὶ τότε δὴ σοφίης ἐπ' ἄκροισι θοάζειν.
ἀλλ' ἄγ' ἄθρει πάσῃ παλάμῃ πῇ δῆλον ἕκαστον,
20 μήτε τιν' ὄψιν ἔχων πίστει πλέον ἢ κατ' ἀκουὴν   50
μήτ' ἀκοὴν ἐρίδουπον ὑπὲρ τρανώματα γλώσσης,
μήτε τι τῶν ἄλλων, ὁπόσων πόρος ἐστὶ νοῆσαι,
γυίων πίστιν ἔρυκε, νόει δ' ᾗ δῆλον ἕκαστον.

φάρμακα δ' ὅσσα γεγᾶσι κακῶν καὶ γήραος ἄλκαρ
25 πεύσῃ, ἐπεὶ μούνῳ σοὶ ἐγὼ κρανέω τάδε πάντα.   425
παύσεις δ' ἀκαμάτων ἀνέμων μένος οἵ τ' ἐπὶ
γαῖαν
ὀρνύμενοι πνοιαῖσι καταφθινύθουσιν ἀρούρας·
καὶ πάλιν, εὖτ' ἐθέλῃσθα, παλίσσυτα πνεύματ'
ἐπάξεις·
θήσεις δ' ἐξ ὄμβροιο κελαινοῦ καίριον αὐχμὸν
30 ἀνθρώποις, θήσεις δὲ καὶ ἐξ αὐχμοῖο θερείου   430
ῥεύματα δενδρεόθρεπτα κατ' αἰθέρος ἀΐσσοντα·
ἄξεις δ' ἐξ Ἀΐδαο καταφθιμένου μένος ἀνδρός.

τέσσαρα τῶν πάντων ῥιζώματα πρῶτον ἄκουε·   55
Ζεὺς ἀργὴς Ἥρη τε φερέσβιος ἠδ' Ἀϊδωνεὺς

MSS. ἐφωθοείης, corr. Steph. Clem. confirms correction. 18. MSS.
θοάζει, Plut. θαμίζειν, corr. Hermann.   19. MSS. ἀλλὰ γὰρ ἄθρει
πᾶς, corr. Bergk.   20. Bergk τι . . . πιστίν, Gomperz, ὄψει
ἔχων πίστιν πλέον'.   22. MSS. ὀπόσῃ, corr. Stein.   23. MSS. ᾗ',
Karsten δ'.

24-32. Diog. Laer. viii. 59 from Satyros; Suidas under ἔκνους;
Eudocia, p. 170; Tzetzes, Chil. ii. 906 f.; Iriarte, Catal. Matrit. p.
450.   26-28. Clem. Al. Strom. p. 754.

27. Clem. θνητοῖσι; Clem., Diog. Laer. Vin. MS., Tzt. ἀρούρας. Elsewhere ἄρουραν.   28. Clem. εὖτ', others ἤν κ'.   Diog., Clem.
παλίντιτα, corr. Stein.   29. Tzt. στήσεις, Suidas στήσει.
30. Tzt. στήσεις.   31. Diog. τὰ δ' ἐν θέρει ἀΐσαντα, Hermann
τά τ' αἰθέρι αἰθύσσονται, corr. Stein.

33-35. Sext. Emp. Math. ix. 362, and x. 315; Plut. Mor. 878 A
(Eus. Pr. Evang. xiv. p. 749); Probus on Verg. Ecl. vi. 31; Hipp. Ref.

well esteemed compel me to pluck them from mortal hands, on condition that I speak boldly more than is holy and only then sit on the heights of wisdom.

19. But come, examine by every means each thing how it is clear, neither putting greater faith in anything seen than in what is heard, nor in a thundering sound more than in the clear assertions of the tongue, nor keep from trusting any of the other members in which there lies means of knowledge, but know each thing in the way in which it is clear.

24. Cures for evils whatever there are, and protection against old age shalt thou learn, since for thee alone will I accomplish all these things. Thou shalt break the power of untiring gales which rising against the earth blow down the crops and destroy them; and, again, whenever thou wilt, thou shalt bring their blasts back; and thou shalt bring seasonable drought out of dark storm for men, and out of summer drought thou shalt bring streams pouring down from heaven to nurture the trees; and thou shalt lead out of Hades the spirit of a man that is dead.

33. Hear first the four roots of all things: bright Zeus, life-giving Hera (air), and Aidoneus (earth), and Nestis who moistens the springs of men with her tears.[1]

[1] Cf. *Dox.* p. 90, n. 3.

35 Νῆστίς θ' ἢ δακρύοις τέγγει κρούνωμα βρότειον.

ἄλλο δέ τοι ἐρέω· φύσις οὐδενός ἐστιν ἁπάντων
θνητῶν, οὐδέ τις οὐλομένου θανάτοιο τελευτή,
ἀλλὰ μόνον μεῖξίς τε διάλλαξίς τε μιγέντων
ἐστὶ, φύσις δ' ἐπὶ τοῖς ὀνομάζεται ἀνθρώποισιν.   80

40 οἱ δ' ὅτε κεν κατὰ φῶτα μιγὲν φῶς αἰθέρι <ἵκη>
ἢ κατὰ θηρῶν ἀγροτέρων γένος ἢ κατὰ θάμνων
ἠὲ κατ' οἰωνῶν, τότε μὲν τὰ λέγουσι γενέσθαι·
εὖτε δ' ἀποκριθέωσι, τὰ δ' αὖ δυσδαίμονα πότμον,   345
ἢ θέμις ἐστί, καλοῦσι, νόμῳ δ' ἐπίφημι καὶ αὐτός.

45 νήπιοι· οὐ γάρ σφιν δολιχόφρονές εἰσι μέριμναι,
οἳ δὴ γίγνεσθαι πάρος οὐκ ἐὸν ἐλπίζουσιν
ἤ τι καταθνήσκειν τε καὶ ἐξόλλυσθαι ἁπάντη.
ἔκ τε γὰρ οὐδάμ' ἐόντος ἀμήχανόν ἐστι γενέσθαι,   81

---

haer. 246; Stob. *Ecl.* i. 10, p. 287.   34-35. Athenag. *Legatio*, p. 22;
Diog. Laer. viii. 76; Herakl. *Alleg. Hom.* 443 σ.   Clem. Al. *Strom.*
p. 746 joins 33, 78, and 104.

33. τῶν, Sext. γάρ, Prob. δή.   Last word Prob. ἐῶσιν.   34. Plut.
Ζεὺς αἰθήρ.   35. Diog. Laer. ἐπιπικροῖ ὕμμα βρότειον, Prob. γε
πικροῖς νωμα (νωμᾷ?) βρότειον γένος.

36-39. Plut. *Mor.* 1111 ϝ, 885 D.   36 b, 38. Arist. *Gen. Corr.* I. 1;
314 b 7; *Meta.* iv. 4; 1015 a 1.   38, 39. Arist. *de X.Z.G.* c. 2 975 b 7.

36. Plut. *de placit.* οὐδὲν, adv. Colot. ἑκάστου.   Ar. *Meta.* ἐόντων.
37. Plut. *adv. Col.* οὐλομένη θ. γενέθλη.   39. Plut. *de placit.*
φύσις δὲ βροτοῖς.

40-44. Plut. *Colot.* 1113 c.   44. Plut. *Mor.* 820 ϝ.

40. MSS. ὅτε μὲν . . . φῶς αἰθέρι, Mul. δ τι κεν, Panz. αἰθέρος κη.
42. MSS. τὸν γενέσθαι, Reiske τὸ λέγουσι γεν., Karst. δοκέουσι
γεν. 43. MSS. ἀποκριθῶσι, corr. Ritschl.   44. MSS. εἶναι καλέουσι·
ὅμως.   Plut. *Mor.* 820 ϝ gives the line as in the text.   Duebner
suggests εἰκαίως for εἶναι here.

45-47. Plut. *Colot.* 1113 c.

47. MS. ἤτοι, corr. Reiske.   MS. πάντη, corr. Steph.

48-50. Arist. *de X.Z.G.* 2; 975 a 36.   48-49. Philo, *de incorr. mundi*
p. 488.

48. Vulg. ἔκ τε μή, Cd. Lps. Syl. ἐκ τοῦ μή, Philo ἐκ τοῦ γὰρ
οὐδαμῆ.   49. MS. τό τε ὄν, Stein καί τ' ἐὸν.   Arist. ἄπρηκτον,
Philo ἄπαυστον.   Text from Diels, *Hermes* xv. p. 161.   50. MS.
θήσεσθαι, corr. Karst.

36. And a second thing I will tell thee: There is no origination of anything that is mortal, nor yet any end in baneful death; but only mixture and separation of what is mixed, but men call this 'origination.'

40. But when light is mingled with air in human form, or in form like the race of wild beasts or of plants or of birds, then men say that these things have come into being; and when they are separated, they call them evil fate; this is the established practice, and I myself also call it so in accordance with the custom.

45. Fools! for they have no far-reaching studious thoughts who think that what was not before comes into being or that anything dies and perishes utterly.

48. For from what does not exist at all it is impossible that anything come into being, and it is neither possible nor perceivable that being should perish completely; for things will always stand wherever one in each case shall put them.

καί τ᾽ ἐὸν ἐξαπολέσθαι ἀνήνυστον καὶ ἄπυστον·
50 αἰεὶ γὰρ στήσονται ὅπη κέ τις αἰὲν ἐρείδῃ.

οὐκ ἂν ἀνὴρ τοιαῦτα σοφὸς φρεσὶ μαντεύσαιτο,   350
ὡς ὄφρα μέν τε βιοῦσι, τὸ δὴ βίοτον καλέουσι,
τόφρα μὲν οὖν εἰσὶν καί σφιν πάρα δειλὰ καὶ
  ἐσθλά,
πρὶν δὲ πάγεν τε βροτοὶ καὶ ἐπεὶ λύθεν, οὐδὲν
  ἄρ᾽ εἰσίν.

55 ἀλλὰ κακοῖς μὲν κάρτα πέλει κρατέουσιν
  ἀπιστεῖν.   81
ὡς δὲ παρ᾽ ἡμετέρης κέλεται πιστώματα Μούσης,
γνῶθι, διατμηθέντος ἐνὶ σπλάγχνοισι λόγοιο.

  κορυφὰς ἑτέρας ἑτέρῃσι προσάπτων   447
μύθων, μήτε τελεῖν ἀτραπὸν μίαν·
60 δὶς γὰρ καὶ τρὶς δεῖ ὅ τι δὴ καλόν ἐστιν ἐνίσπειν.   446
    [πείρατα μύθων]   87
δίπλ᾽ ἐρέω· τοτὲ μὲν γὰρ ἓν ηὐξήθη μόνον εἶναι

51–54. Plut. *Colot.* 1113 D.

53. MSS. εἰσὶ καί σφι, corr. Karst.   MSS. δεινα, corr. Bergk.

55–57. Clem. Al. *Strom.* 656.   56–57. Theod. *Serm.* 476 Sch.

56. Theod. ὧδε γὰρ.

58–59. Plut. *de orac. def.* 418 c.   Arranged in verse by Xylander.
MSS. μήτε λέγειν corr. Knatz, *Empedoclea*, p. 7.

60. Plut. *non pos. suav. viv.* 1103 y δὶς γὰρ ὃ δεῖ καλόν ἐστιν ἀκοῦσαι,
Schol. Plat. *Gorg.* 124 Ruhnk. δὶς καὶ τρὶς τὸ καλόν. . . 'Εμπεδ. τὸ ἔπος
" καὶ δὶς γὰρ ὃ δεῖ καλόν ἐστιν ἐνίσπειν."   Text from Sturz.

61–73. Simpl. in Arist. *Phys.* 34 r 158, 1 sq.   66–68. Tzetzes, *Hom.*
58 Sch.   67–73. Simpl. *de caelo* Peyr. p. 47 sq.   67–68. Simpl. *Phys.*
6 v 25, 29, and 310 r. Diog. Laer. viii. 76; Stob. *Ecl.* i. 11, p.290;
vit. Hom. p. 327 Gal.   69–73. Arist. *Phys* viii. 1; 250 b 30.

61. Karst. supplies πείρατα μύθων from v. 75.   62. Cf. 104.   65. *E*
δρυφθεῖσα, MS. δρεπτή.   66–67. Cf. 116–117.   68. Simpl. 158,
8 δίχα πάντα.   Elsewhere as in text.   69. Om. Simpl. 158 b
1.   73. MSS. ἀκίνητοι corr. Bergk.

51. A man of wise mind could not divine such things as these, that so long as men live what indeed they call life, so long they exist and share what is evil and what is excellent, but before they are formed and after they are dissolved, they are really nothing at all.

55. But for base men it is indeed possible to withhold belief from strong proofs; but do thou learn as the pledges of our Muse bid thee, and lay open her word to the very core.

58. Joining one heading to another in discussion, not completing one path (of discourse) . . . for it is right to say what is excellent twice and even thrice.

60. Twofold is the truth I shall speak; for at one time there grew to be one alone out of many, and at another time, however, it separated so that there were many out of the one. Twofold is the coming into being, twofold the passing away, of perishable things; for the latter (*i.e.* passing away) the combining of

ἐκ πλεόνων, τοτὲ δ' αὖ διέφυ πλέον' ἐξ ἑνὸς
εἶναι.

δοιὴ δὲ θνητῶν γένεσις, δοιὴ δ' ἀπόλειψις.　　　　90
τὴν μὲν γὰρ πάντων σύνοδος τίκτει τ' ὀλέκει τε,
65 ἡ δὲ πάλιν διαφυομένων θρεφθεῖσα διέπτη.
καὶ ταῦτ' ἀλλάσσοντα διαμπερὲς οὐδαμὰ λήγει,
ἄλλοτε μὲν Φιλότητι συνερχόμεν' εἰς ἓν ἅπαντα,
ἄλλοτε δ' αὖ δίχ' ἕκαστα φορεύμενα Νείκεος
ἔχθει,　　　　　　　　　　　　　　　　　95
118 εἰς ὅ κεν ἓν συμφύντα τὸ πᾶν ὑπένερθε γένηται.　144
οὕτως ᾗ μὲν ἓν ἐκ πλεόνων μεμάθηκε φύεσθαι
70 ἠδὲ πάλιν διαφύντος ἑνὸς πλέον' ἐκτελέθουσι,
τῇ μὲν γίγνονταί τε καὶ οὔ σφισιν ἔμπεδος αἰών·
ᾗ δὲ τάδ' ἀλλάσσοντα διαμπερὲς οὐδαμὰ λήγει,
ταύτῃ αἰὲν ἔασιν ἀκινητὸν κατὰ κύκλον.　　　100
ἀλλ' ἄγε, μύθων κλῦθι, μάθη γάρ τοι φρένας
αὔξει.
75 ὡς γὰρ καὶ πρὶν ἔειπα πιφαύσκων πείρατα
μύθων,
δίπλ' ἐρέω· τοτὲ μὲν γὰρ ἓν ηὐξήθη μόνον εἶναι

74-95. Simpl. *Phys.* 34 r 158, 13 sq. following the preceding without break.　74. Stob. *Ecl.* App. 34 Gais.; cf. Clem. Al. *Strom.* 697.
77-80. Simpl. *Phys.* 6 v 26, 1; Sext. Emp. *Math.* ix. 10.　78. Plut.
de adult. p. 63 D; Clem. Al. *Strom.* 746 (with v. 33).　79-80. Sext.
Emp. *Math.* x. 317.　79. Plut. *Mor.* 952 D.　80-81. Plut. *Amat.* 756 D.
81. Clem. Al. *Strom.* 653; Simpl. *Phys.* 41 r 188, 26.　91. Cf. Stob. *Ecl.*
i. 18; *Placit.* i. 18 and Theod. iv. 529 c (*Dox.* 316); Galen, *Hist. phil.*
0.　92. Arist. *X.Z.G.* 975 b 10.　Simpl. omits 91.

74. Simpl. μέθη, corr. Bergk from Stob. and Clem.　78. Sext.
ἥπιον, Clem. αἰθέρος, Plut. αἰθέρος ἥπιον.　79. Simpl. ἕκαστον,
Sext. ἀπάντῃ, corr. Panz.　80. Plut. ἐν τοῖς, Sext. φιλίη . . .
ἴσον.　81. Simpl. aF σὺν νῷ; cf. Plut.　82. Simpl. F φυτοῖσιν:
Bergk, Karst. ἐνίζεται.　83. Simpl. DE καὶ ἄρθμια, F καὶ ἄρ'
ὅμοια.　85. Simpl. μετ' ὅσσοισιν, Panz. μεθ' ὅλοισιν, Prel. γ'
ὅσσοισιν. I have suggested μετὰ τοῖσιν.　89. Simpl. καὶ πρὸς τοῖς
οὔτ' ἄρτι. Cf. 159, 8 μηδὲν ἐπιγίνεσθαι μηδ' ἀπολήγειν, corr. Stein.
93. Simpl. DEa κε καὶ κῆρυξ, F omits κε, corr. Stein (notes).
95. D γίνονται. MS. ἄλλοτε, corr. Stein.　DE καὶ ἠνεκὲς (cf.
Hesych.), aF διηνεκὲς.

all things both begets and destroys, and the former (*i.e.* coming into being), which was nurtured again out of parts that were being separated, is itself scattered. 66. And these (elements) never cease changing place continually, now being all united by Love into one, now each borne apart by the hatred engendered of Strife, until they are brought together in the unity of the all, and become subject to it. Thus inasmuch as one has been wont to arise out of many and again with the separation of the one the many arise, so things are continually coming into being and there is no fixed age for them; and farther inasmuch as they [the elements] never cease changing place continually, so they always exist within an immovable circle.

74. But come, hear my words, for truly learning causes the mind to grow. For as I said before in declaring the ends of my words: Twofold is the truth I shall speak; for at one time there grew to be the one

ἐκ πλεόνων, τοτὲ δ' αὖ διέφυ πλέον' ἐξ ἑνὸς εἶναι,
πῦρ καὶ ὕδωρ καὶ γαῖα καὶ αἰθέρος ἄπλετον
    ὕψος ·   105
Νεῖκός τ' οὐλόμενον δίχα τῶν, ἀτάλαντον ἑκάστῳ,
80 καὶ Φιλότης ἐν τοῖσιν ἴση μῆκός τε πλάτος τε.
τὴν σὺ νόῳ δέρκευ μηδ' ὄμμασιν ἧσο τεθηπώς,
ἥτις καὶ θνητοῖσι νομίζεται ἔμφυτος ἄρθροις,
τῇ τε φίλα φρονέουσι καὶ ἄρθμια ἔργα τελεῦσι, 110
γηθοσύνην καλέοντες ἐπώνυμον ἠδ' Ἀφροδίτην·
85 τὴν οὔτις †μετ' ὅσοισιν ἐλισσομένην δεδάηκε
θνητὸς ἀνήρ. σὺ δ' ἄκουε λόγου στόλον οὐκ
    ἀπατηλόν.
ταῦτα γὰρ ἰσά τε πάντα καὶ ἡλίκα γένναν ἔασι,
τιμῆς δ' ἄλλης ἄλλο μέδει, πάρα δ' ἦθος ἑκάστῳ. 115
οὐδὲν γὰρ πρὸς τοῖς ἐπιγίγνεται οὐδ' ἀπολήγει.
90 εἴτε γὰρ ἐφθείροντο διαμπερές, οὐκέτ' ἂν ἦσαν.
οὐδέ τι τοῦ παντὸς κενεὸν πέλει οὐδὲ περισσόν.
τοῦτο δ' ἐπαυξήσειε τὸ πᾶν τί κε καὶ πόθεν
    ἐλθόν;   120
πῆ δέ κε καὶ ἀπολοίατ' ἐπεὶ τῶνδ' οὐδὲν
    ἔρημον ;
112 ἐν δὲ μέρει κρατέουσι περιπλομένοιο κύκλοιο

96-109. Simpl. *Phys.* 34 r 159, 13.   98-107. Simpl. *Phys.* 7 v 33, 8,
98 and 100. Arist. *Gen. Corr.* i. 1, 314 b 19; Philopon. Comment. on this
passage ; Plut. *de prim. frig.* 249 ғ; Galen, vol. xiii. p. 31 Chart.
104-107ᵃ. Arist. *Meta.* ii. 4 ; 1000 a 29.

      98. Arist. Philopon. λευκὸν . . . θερμὸν, Simpl. Galen θερμὸν . . .
λαμπρὸν: Simpl. Arist. δρᾶν, Plut. Aristot. δρα, Simpl. *F* δρᾷ.
99. Simpl. ἔδεται or ἐδεῖτο: Stein ὅσσα πέλει, Diels ὅσσα θέει
τε.   100. Some MSS. Arist. and Plut. ζοφόεντα.   101. Simpl.
θέλημα, a θελίμνα, corr. Sturz: Simpl. 33, 11 στερέωμα.   102.
Simpl. 159, 19 πέλοντα.   104. Simpl. 159, 21 *D* παντὸς ἄτην,
a *F* πάντ' ἦν : Arist. *Met.* ἐξ ὧν πάνθ' ὅσα τ' ἦν ὅσα τ' ἐσθ'
ὅσα τ' ἔσται ὀπίσσω.   105. Simpl. 133, 15 δένδρα τε βεβλάστηκε.
108. *ED* τογον, Diels τό γ' ὄν?   *Hermes* xv. 163 τόσον:
E διάκρασις, *D* διάκρισις. Sturz. διάπτυξις from Simpl. 34 v.
161, 20.   Platt διὰ Κύπρις ἀμείβει *Journ. Philol.* 48, p. 246.
I bracket 108-109 as another form of 94-95.

alone out of many, and at another time it separated so
that there were many out of the one; fire and water
and earth and boundless height of air, and baneful
Strife apart from these, balancing each of them, and
Love among them, their equal in length and breadth.
81. Upon her do thou gaze with thy mind, nor yet sit
dazed in thine eyes; for she is wont to be implanted in
men's members, and through her they have thoughts of
love and accomplish deeds of union, and call her by the
names of Delight, and Aphrodite; no mortal man has
discerned her with them (the elements) as she moves on
her way. But do thou listen to the undeceiving course
of my words.[1] . . .

87. For these (elements) are equal, all of them, and
of like ancient race; and one holds one office, another
another, and each has his own nature. . . . For nothing
is added to them, nor yet does anything pass away from
them; for if they were continually perishing they would
no longer exist. . . . Neither is any part of this all
empty, nor over full. For how should anything cause
this all to increase, and whence should it come? And
whither should they (the elements) perish, since no place
is empty of them? And in their turn they prevail as
the cycle comes round, and they disappear before

[αὐτὰ γάρ ἐστι ταῦτα, δι' ἀλλήλων δὲ θέοντα
109 γίνεται ἀλλοιωπά. †τογον διὰ κρᾶσις ἀμείβει.] 137

[1] Cf. Parmenides v. 112.

113 καὶ φθίνει εἰς ἄλληλα καὶ αὔξεται ἐν μέρει   138
αἴσης.

94 ἀλλ' αὔτ' ἔστιν ταῦτα· δι' ἀλλήλων δὲ θέοντα   122

95 γίνεται ἄλλοθεν ἄλλα καὶ ἠνεκὲς αἰὲν ὁμοῖα.

110 καὶ γὰρ καὶ πάρος ἦν τε καὶ ἔσσεται, οὐδέ ποτ',
οἴω,

111 τούτων ἀμφοτέρων κεινώσεται ἄσπετος αἰών.

96 ἀλλ' ἄγε τῶνδ' ὀάρων προτέρων ἐπιμάρτυρα
δέρκευ,
εἴ τι καὶ ἐν προτέροισι λιπόξυλον ἔπλετο μορφῇ.   125
ἠέλιον μὲν θερμὸν ὁρᾶν καὶ λαμπρὸν ἀπάντη,
ἄμβροτα δ' ὅσσα πέλει τε καὶ ἀργέτι δεύεται
αὐγῇ,

100 ὄμβρον δ' ἐν πᾶσι δνοφόεντά τε ῥιγαλέον τε,
ἐκ δ' αἴης προρέουσι θέλυμνά τε καὶ στερεωπά.
— ἐν δὲ Κότῳ διάμορφα καὶ ἄνδιχα πάντα πέλονται,   130
σὺν δ' ἔβη ἐν Φιλότητι καὶ ἀλλήλοισι ποθεῖται.
ἐκ τούτων γὰρ πάνθ' ὅσα τ' ἦν ὅσα τ' ἔστι καὶ
ἔσται,

105 δένδρεά τ' ἐβλάστησε καὶ ἀνέρες ἠδὲ γυναῖκες
θῆρές τ' οἰωνοί τε καὶ ὑδατοθρέμμονες ἰχθῦς
καί τε θεοὶ δολιχαίωνες τιμῇσι φέριστοι.   135
ὡς δ' ὁπόταν γραφέες ἀναθήματα ποικίλλωσιν

120 ἀνέρες ἀμφὶ τέχνης ὑπὸ μήτιος εὖ δεδαῶτε   155

110-111. Hippol. *Ref. haer.* 247 Mill.

110. MS. εἰ γὰρ . . . ἔσται οὐδέπω τοίω, corr. Schneid. *Phil.* vi. 160.   111. MS. κενώσεται ἄσβεστος, corr. Mill.

112-118. Simpl. *Phys.* 8 r 33, 19.

114. MS. ἰστι, corr. Panz.   115. MS. κηρῶν, Stz. θηρῶν, Bergk θνητῶν.   118. E ἰν, D ὀν, F ὀν, A ἀν, Text *Hermes* xv. 163.

Lines 114-115 are bracketed as a duplication of 94-95, and accordingly 112-113 are inserted before 94-95, where 113 corresponds excellently with 93 ; 116-117 are bracketed as another form of 67-68 (cf. 248), and accordingly 118 finds its proper place after 68.   Cf. "Repetitions in Empedokles," *Classical Review*, Jan. 1898.

each other, and they increase each in its allotted turn.
But these (elements) are the same; and penetrating
through each other they become one thing in one place
and another in another, while ever they remain alike
(*i.e.* the same).

110. For they two (Love and Strife) were before and
shall be, nor yet, I think, will there ever be an unutterably
long time without them both.

96. But come, gaze on the things that bear farther
witness to my former words, if in what was said before
there be anything defective in form. Behold the sun,
warm and bright on all sides, and whatever is immortal
and is bathed in its bright ray, and behold the rain-
cloud, dark and cold on all sides; from the earth there
proceed the foundations of things and solid bodies. In
Strife all things are, endued with form and separate)
from each other, but they come together in Love and
are desired by each other. 104. For from these (elements) come all things that are or have been or shall be;
from these there grew up trees and men and women,
wild beasts and birds and water-nourished fishes, and
the very gods, long-lived, highest in honour.

121. And as when painters are preparing elaborate
votive offerings—men well taught by wisdom in their

---

114 [αὐτὰ γὰρ ἔστιν ταῦτα, δι' ἀλλήλων δὲ θέοντα 140
115 γίνοντ' ἄνθρωποί τε καὶ ἄλλων ἔθνεα κηρῶν,
ἄλλοτε μὲν Φιλότητι συνερχόμεν' εἰς ἕνα κόσμον,
ἄλλοτε δ' αὖ δίχ' ἕκαστα φορεύμενα Νείκεος
ἔχθει,
εἰς ὅ κεν ἐν συμφύντα τὸ πᾶν ὑπένερθε γένηται.]

οἵ τ' ἐπεὶ οὖν μάρψωσι πολύχροα φάρμακα
   χερσίν,
ἁρμονίῃ μίξαντε τὰ μὲν πλέω, ἄλλα δ' ἐλάσσω,
123 ἐκ τῶν εἴδεα πᾶσιν ἀλίγκια πορσύνουσι·

127 οὕτω μή σ' ἀπάτη φρένα καινύτω ἄλλοθεν εἶναι 162
θνητῶν, ὅσσα γε δῆλα γεγᾶσιν ἀάσπετα, πηγήν.
ἀλλὰ τορῶς ταῦτ' ἴσθι θεοῦ πάρα μῦθον
   ἀκούσας. . . .

130 εἰ δ' ἄγε, νῦν τοι ἐγὼ λέξω πρῶθ' ἡλίου ἀρχήν,
ἐξ ὧν δὴ ἐγένοντο τὰ νῦν ἐσορώμενα πάντα,
γαῖά τε καὶ πόντος πολυκύμων ἠδ' ὑγρὸς ἀὴρ
Τιτὰν ἠδ' αἰθὴρ σφίγγων περὶ κύκλον ἅπαντα.   185

[σφαῖρον ἔην.]   64

135 ἔνθ' οὔτ' ἠελίοιο δεδίσκεται ἀγλαὸν εἶδος   72
οὐδὲ μὲν οὐδ' αἴης λάσιον μένος οὐδὲ θάλασσα·
οὕτως ἁρμονίης πυκινῷ κύτει ἐστήρικται   59
σφαῖρος κυκλοτερὴς μονίῃ περιηγέι γαίων.

119-129. Simpl. *Phys.* 34 r 160, 1.

   120. *DEF* ἄμφω: F δεδαωτες.   122. MSS. ἁρμονίη: D μίξαντες, a μόξαν τε.   123. a F πασ' ἐναλίγκια.   124. D κτίζοντες ... ἀνέρες.
   127. F οὕτω μὴν ἀπάτη; a ὡς νύ κεν: Bergk φρένας: καινύτω (Hesych. νικάτω) corr. Blass for MSS. καί νύ τῳ.   128. MSS. γεγάασιν ἄσπετα, corr. Bergk.

130-133. Clem. Al. *Strom.* 674.

   130. εἰ δ' ἄγε τοι λέξω, Pott. εἰ δ' ἄγε τοι μὲν ἐγώ.   131. Gomperz, *Hermes* xxxi, 469 ἐσορῶμεν ἄπαντα.

134. Simpl. *Phys.* 258 r καὶ θεὸν ἐπονομάζει καὶ οὐδετέρως ποτὲ καλεῖ σφαῖρον ἔην. Cf. v. 138.

135-138. Simpl. *Phys.* 272 v.   135-136. Plut. *de fac. in lun.* 926 ε.
138. Simpl. *de caelo*, Peyr. 47 ; M. Antonin. xii. 3 ; Stob. *Ecl. Phys.* i. 15, 354 ; Achilles (Tatius) IN ARAT. 77 Pet. and frag. Schol. p. 96 ; Prokl. in *Tim.* 160.

   135. Simpl. διείδεται ὠκέα γυῖα, Plut. δεδίττεται, corr. Karst.
   136. Plut. MS. γένος, Bergk μένος   137. MS. κρυφῷ or κρύφα, Karst. κρύφῳ, Stein κύτει.   138. Simpl. *Phys.* μονίη περιγηθεὶ αἰών, Text from Simpl. *de caelo*. Stob. Tatius χαίρων. Schol. in Arat. κυκλοτερεῖ μανίᾳ.

art—they take many-coloured pigments to work with, and blend together harmoniously more of one and less of another till they produce likenesses of all things; so let not error overcome thy mind to make thee think there is any other source of mortal things that have likewise come into distinct existence in unspeakable numbers; but know these (elements), for thou didst hear from a god the account of them.

130. But come, I will tell thee now the first principle of the sun, even the sources of all things now visible, earth and billowy sea and damp mist and Titan aether (*i.e.* air) binding all things in its embrace.

135. Then neither is the bright orb of the sun greeted, nor yet either the shaggy might of earth or sea; thus, then, in the firm vessel of harmony is fixed God, a sphere, round, rejoicing in complete solitude.

[δένδρεά τε κτίζοντε καὶ ἀνέρας ἠδὲ γυναῖκας
125 θῆράς τ' οἰωνούς τε καὶ ὑδατοθρέμμονας ἰχθῦς   160
καί τε θεοὺς δολιχαίωνας τιμῇσι φερίστους.]

αὐτὰρ ἐπεὶ μέγα Νεῖκος ἐνὶ μελέεσσιν ἐθρέφθη   66
140 ἐς τιμάς τ' ἀνόρουσε τελειομένοιο χρόνοιο,
    ὅς σφιν ἀμοιβαῖος πλατέος παρελήλαται ὅρκου.

πάντα γὰρ ἐξείης πελεμίζετο γυῖα θεοῖο.   70

χωρὶς γὰρ βαρὺ πᾶν, χωρὶς κοῦφον.   71

        ἄστοργοι καὶ ἄκρητοι.

145   σωρευόμενον μέγεθος.

εἴπερ ἀπείρονα γῆς τε βάθη καὶ δαψιλὸς αἰθήρ, 199
ὡς διὰ πολλῶν δὴ βροτέων ῥηθέντα ματαίως
ἐκκέχυται στομάτων, ὀλίγον τοῦ παντὸς ἰδόν-
των. . . .

ἥλιος ὀξυβελὴς ἠδ' αὖ ἱλάειρα σελήνη. . .   168

150 ἀλλ' ὁ μὲν ἁλισθεὶς μέγαν οὐρανὸν ἀμφιπολεύει. 187
    ἀνταυγεῖν πρὸς Ὄλυμπον ἀταρβήτοισι προσ-
    ώποις.   188

139-141. Arist. *Meta.* ii. 4 ; 1000 b 13 ; Simpl. *Phys.* 272 b.
  139. Arist. ἀλλ' ὅτε δὴ, Simpl. αὐτὰρ ἐπεί.   141. Simpl. ὃ : Arist.
  Ε παρελήλατο.

142. Simpl. *Phys.* 272 v. associated with v. 135.
143-144. Plut. *de fac. lun.* 926 F.
  143. Sturz ends the line ἔθηκεν with object Νεῖκος.   144. MSS.
  ἄκρατοι καὶ ἄστοργοι, corr. Stein.

145. Arist. *Gen. et Corr.* i. 8 ; 325 b 22.
146-148. Arist. *de X.Z.G.* 2 ; 976 a 35 ; *de coelo* ii. 113 ; 294 a 25 ; and
Simpl. on this passage.   147-148. Clem. Al. *Strom.* 817.
  147. Arist. *X.Z.G.* βροτέων, *de coelo* Clem. γλώσσης : Clem.
  ἐλθόντα.   148. Clem. εἰδότων.

149. Plut. *de fac. lun.* 920 c.
  MS. ὀξυμελὴς, Xylander ὀξυβελὴς : MS. ἠδὲ λάινα, corr. G. Dindorf.
    Cf. Hesych. ἱλάειρα ; Preller λάιν' ἠδὲ.

150. Macrob. *Saturn.* i. 17 ; *Etym. Mag.*, Orion *Etym.*, Suidas, under
ἥλιος ; Cramer, *Anec.* ii. 444.
  Macrob. οὕνεκ' ἀναλισθείς, Suid. Cram. ἀλεῖσθαι ; *Et. M. μέσον.*

151. Plut. *Pyth. or.* 400 B ; Galen, *de us. part.* iii. 3.
  Plut. ἀνταυγεῖν, Galen ἀνταυγέω.

139. But when mighty Strife was nurtured in its members and leaped up to honour at the completion of the time, which has been driven on by them both in turn under a mighty oath. . . . .

142. For the limbs of the god were made to tremble, all of them in turn.

143. For all the heavy (he put) by itself, the light by itself.

144. Without affection and not mixed together.

145. Heaped together in greatness.

146. If there were no limit to the depths of the earth and the abundant air, as is poured out in foolish words from the mouths of many mortals who see but little of the all.

149. Swift-darting sun and kindly moon.

150. But gathered together it advances around the great heavens.

151. It shines back to Olympos with untroubled face.

ἡ δὲ φλὸξ ἱλάειρα μινυθαδίης τύχεν αὐγῆς.   193

ὡς αὐγὴ τύψασα σεληναίης κύκλον εὐρύν. .   192

κυκλοτερὲς περὶ γαῖαν ἑλίσσεται ἀλλότριον φῶς 190
155 ἅρματος ὥσπερ ἀν᾽ ἴχνος   189

ἀθρεῖ μὲν γὰρ ἄνακτος ἐναντίον ἀγέα κύκλον.   191

            ἐπεσκέδασεν δέ οἱ αὐγὰς
εἰς αἴθρην καθύπερθεν, ἐπεσκνίφωσε δὲ γαίης   195
τόσσον ὅσον τ᾽ εὖρος γλαυκώπιδος ἔπλετο μήνης.

160 νύκτα δὲ γαῖα τίθησιν ὑφισταμένη φαέεσσιν.   197

νυκτὸς ἐρημαίης ἀλαώπιδος.   198

πολλὰ δ᾽ ἔνερθ᾽ ἔδεος πυρὰ καίεται.   207

---

152. Simpl. *Phys.* 74 v ; 331, 7.

a *DF* ψύχε, *E* τύχε : MSS. γαίης, Stein αὐγῆς.

153. Plut. *de fac. lun.* 929 E.

153a. Diels, *Hermes* xv. 175, constructs the following line from
Philo ed. Aucher, p. 92 :

και μέγαν, αὐτίκ᾽ ἀνῆλθε, θέουσ᾽ ὡς οὐρανὸν ἵκοι.

154. Achill. Tat. *Introd. in Arat.* c. 16 p. 77 Pet.   155. Plut. *de fac.
orb. lun.* 925.

155. Plut. (σελήνη) περιφερομένη πλήσιον, ἅρματος ὥσπερ ἴχνος
ἀνελίσσεται ἧτε περὶ ἄκραν.

156. Bekk. *Anecd.* i. 337.

157-159. Plut. *de fac. lun.* 929 c.

157. MS. ἀπεσκεύασε, Xyl. ἀπεσκέδασεν, Bergk ἀπεσκίασεν.
158. MS. ἔστε γαία, Xyl. ἐς γαῖαν : Stein ἱσταμένη or εἰς αἴθρην :
MS. ἀπεσκνίφωσε, corr. Karst. 159. γλαυκώπιδος, cf. Plut. de
fac. lun. 934 D (Diels, *Hermes* xv. 176).

160. Plut. *Quaest. Plat.* 1006 F.

161. Plut. *Quaest. conv.* 720 E.

MS. ἀγλαώπιδος, corr. Xyl. Cf. Hesych. ἀλαῶπιν · . . . οὐ βλέ-
πουσαν.

162. Prokl. on *Tim.* iii. 141.

MS. οὔδεος, Sturz writes ὔδεος from following. Diels finds connection only with preceding and writes ἔδεος. Cf. Hesych.
ἔδος · . . . γή.

152. The kindly light has a brief period of shining.

153. **As sunlight** striking **the broad circle of the** moon.

154. A borrowed light, circular in form, it revolves about the earth, as if following the track of a chariot.

156. For she beholds opposite to her the sacred circle of her lord.

157. And she scatters his rays into the sky above, and spreads darkness over as much of the earth as the breadth of the gleaming-eyed moon.

160. And night the earth makes by coming in front of the lights.

161. Of night, solitary, blind-eyed.

162. And many fires burn beneath the earth.

φῦλον ἄμουσον ἄγουσα πολυσπερέων καμασή- 205
νων.

ἅλς ἐπάγη ῥιπῇσιν ἐωσμένος ἠελίοιο 206

165   γῆς ἱδρῶτα θάλασσαν.

<ἀλλ'> αἰθὴρ μακρῇσι κατὰ χθόνα δύετο ῥίζαις. 203
οὕτω γὰρ συνέκυρσε θέων τότε, πολλάκι δ'
ἄλλως.

    καρπαλίμως ἀνόπαιον.   202

αὐτὰρ ἐγὼ παλίνορσος ἐλεύσομαι ἐς πόρον ὕμνων, 165
170 τὸν πρότερον κατέλεξα, λόγου λόγον ἐξοχετεύων
κείνου· ἐπεὶ Νεῖκος μὲν ἐνέρτατον ἵκετο βένθος
δίνης, ἐν δὲ μέσῃ Φιλότης στροφάλιγγι γένηται,
ἐν τῇ δὴ τάδε πάντα συνέρχεται ἓν μόνον εἶναι,
οὐκ ἄφαρ, ἀλλὰ θελημὰ συνιστάμεν' ἄλλοθεν
ἄλλα.   170
175 τῶν δὲ συνερχομένων ἐπ' ἔσχατον ἵστατο Νεῖκος.

---

163. Plut. *Quaes. conv.* 685 ᴦ.
 Karst. πολυσπορέων. Cf. 214.

164. Hephaest. *Enchir.* c. 1 p. 4 Gais.

165. Arist. *Meteor.* ii. 3 ; 357 a 26 ; Plut. *Placit. phil.* iii. 13, and *de Is.* 365 ᴅ. Clem. Al. *Strom.* 676. Porphyr. *Vit. Pyth.* c. 41.

166-167. Arist. *de Gen. et Corr.* ii. 6 ; 334 a 3. 167. *Phys.* ii. 4 ; 196 a 22.

166. Diels suggests ῥιπαῖς. Cf. v. 164.

168. Eustath. on *Od.* a 320, p. 1 (from Herodian, περὶ σχημ. Ὁμηρ.). Cf. Arist. *de gen. et corr.* ii. 6 ; 334 a 1.

169-185. Simpl. *de caelo*, Peyron p. 27 ; Gais. *Poet. Min. Gr.* ii. p. xlii ; Schol. Aristot. Brand. p. 507 a. 171-185. Simpl. *Phys.* 7 v 32, 11. 175. Stob. *Ecl.* i. 286. Cf. Arist. *Met.* ii. 4 ; 1000 b 2. 178-181. Simpl. *de caelo*, Peyr. p. 37. 182-183. Theophr. Athen. x. 423 ; Arist. *Poet.* c. 25 ; 1461 a 24. Eust. ad *Iliad.* i. p. 746, 57.

170. MS. λόγῳ, corr. Bergk. Peyr. ὑποχετεύων, Brand. ἐποχ., corr. Bergk. 173. Simpl. *Phys.* ἐν τῇ δὴ, *de caelo* Cd. Taur. Peyr. ἐν τῇ ἠδέ, corr. Bergk. 174. *Phys.* DE θελημὰ, F θέλημα, *de caelo* JP Cd. Taur. ἀλλ' ἐθέλημα. 175. Simpl. repeats 184 instead of 175,

163. (The sea) with its stupid race of fertile fishes.

164. Salt is made solid when struck by the rays of the sun.

165. The sea is the sweat of the earth.

166. But air [1] sinks down beneath the earth with its long roots . . . . For thus it happened to be running at that time, but oftentimes otherwise.

168. (Fire darting) swiftly upwards.

169. But now I shall go back over the course of my verses, which I set out in order before, drawing my present discourse from that discourse. When Strife reached the lowest depth of the eddy and Love comes to be in the midst of the whirl, then all these things come together at this point so as to be one alone, yet not immediately, but joining together at their pleasure, one from one place, another from another. And as they were joining together Strife departed to the utmost boundary. But many things remained unmixed, alter-

---

[1] In Empedokles' verses, αἰθήρ regularly means *air*.

πολλὰ δ' ἄμιχθ' ἔστηκε κεραιομένοισιν ἐναλλάξ,
ὅσσ' ἔτι Νεῖκος ἔρυκε μετάρσιον· οὐ γὰρ ἀμέμφεως
πὼ πᾶν ἐξέστηκεν ἐπ' ἔσχατα τέρματα κύκλου.
ἀλλὰ τὰ μὲν τ' ἐνέμιμνε μελέων, τὰ δέ τ' ἐξεβε-
βήκει.   175

180 ὅσσον δ' αἰὲν ὑπεκπροθέοι, τόσον αἰὲν ἐπῄει
ἠπιόφρων Φιλότητος ἀμεμφέος ἄμβροτος ὁρμή·
αἶψα δὲ θνήτ' ἐφύοντο τὰ πρὶν μάθον ἀθάνατ'
εἶναι,
ζωρά τε τὰ πρὶν ἄκρητα, διαλλάξαντα κελεύθους.
τῶν δέ τε μισγομένων χεῖτ' ἔθνεα μυρία θνητῶν, 180

185 παντοίῃς ἰδέῃσιν ἀρηρότα, θαῦμα ἰδέσθαι.
ἄρθμια μὲν γὰρ ἑαυτὰ ἑαυτῶν πάντα μέρεσσιν   326
ἠλέκτωρ τε χθὼν τι καὶ οὐρανὸς ἠδὲ θάλασσα,
ὅσσα φίλ' ἐν θνητοῖσιν ἀποπλαγχθέντα πέφυκεν.
ὡς δ' αὔτως ὅσα κρᾶσιν ἐπάρτεα μᾶλλον εἶναι,

190 ἀλλήλοις ἐστέρκται ὁμοιωθέντ' Ἀφροδίτῃ.   330
ἐχθρὰ δὲ πλεῖστον ἀπ' ἀλλήλων διέχουσι μάλιστα
γέννᾳ τε κρήσει τε καὶ εἴδεσιν ἐκμακτοῖσιν,
πάντῃ συγγίγνεσθαι ἀήθεα καὶ μάλα λυγρά

---

which is inserted from Stob. by Schneid. 176. *Phys. Ε ἐστι:*
DEF κεκερασμένοισιν, Taur. κεραιζομένοισιν, text from *de caelo.*
177. *de caelo* ἀμφαφέως. 178. *Phys.* aF' πω πᾶν, *DE* οὔπω πᾶν,
de caelo τὸ πᾶν. 180. aF' ὑπεκπρυθέει. 181. *Phys. DE* πίφρων,
F' ἡ περίφρων, *DEF* (*de caelo* P) φιλότητος, *Phys.* ἀμεμφέος, *de
caelo* ἀμφέσσον, Stein φιλότης τε καὶ ἔμπεσεν. 182. Arist. omits
εἶναι. 183. *Phys.* ἄκριτα, Theophr. ἄκρητα: Arist. ζῶα τε πρὶν
κέκριτο Athen. διαλλάττοντα, *Phys.* διαλλάξαντα.

186-194. Simpl. *Phys.* 34 r 160, 28. 191-192. Theophr. *de sens.* § 16.
186. *DE* ἄρθμια, aF ἄρτια: *DE* ἑαυτὰ ἑαυτῶν, aF' αὐτὰ ἑαυτῶν,
Stein suggests πάνθ' αὐτῶν ἐγένοντο, Diels ἔασιν ἑαυτῶν.
188. MS. ὅσσα φιν, Diels ὅσσα φίλ', Hermann ὁσσάκις.
189. MSS. ἐπάρκεα, Karst. ἐπάρτεα. aF ἔχθρα, ED ἔργα:
MS. μάλιστα, Karst. ἄμικτα. 192. *DEF* κρίσει, a κράσει.
193. *DE* δ' ὑγρὰ, a λυγρὰ. 194. MSS. and Simpl. 161, 12
νεικεογεννέστησιν, Panz. νείκεος ἐννεσίῃσι, MS. σφίσι γένναι
ὀργᾷ (a γένναις). Panz. σφίσι γένν' ἄστεργος, Diels ἔοργεν.

nating with those that were mixed, even as many as
Strife, remaining aloft, still retained; for not yet
had it entirely departed to the utmost boundaries of
the circle, but some of its members were remaining
within, and others had gone outside. 180. But, just as
far as it is constantly rushing forth, just so far
there ever kept coming in a gentle immortal stream
of perfect Love; and all at once what before I learned
were immortal were coming into being as mortal things,[1]
what before were unmixed as mixed, changing their
courses. And as they (the elements) were mingled together there flowed forth the myriad species of mortal
things, patterned in every sort of form, a wonder to
behold.

186. For all things are united, themselves with parts
of themselves—the beaming sun and earth and sky and
sea—whatever things are friendly but have separated in
mortal things. And so, in the same way, whatever
things are the more adapted for mixing, these are loved
by each other and made alike by Aphrodite. But whatever things are hostile are separated as far as possible
from each other, both in their origin and in their mixing
and in the forms impressed on them, absolutely unwonted
to unite and very baneful, at the suggestion of Strife,
since it has wrought their birth.

---

[1] θνητά, 'perishable things' in contrast with the elements, might
almost be rendered 'things on the earth.'

Νείκεος ἐννεσίῃσι, ὅτι σφίσι γένναν ἔοργεν.

195 τῇδε μὲν οὖν ἰότητι τύχης πεφρόνηκεν ἅπαντα... 312
καὶ καθ᾽ ὅσον μὲν ἀραιότατα ξυνέκυρσε πεσόντα.

[ὕδατι μὲν γὰρ ὕδωρ,] πυρὶ δ᾽ αὔξεται [ὠγύγιον]
πῦρ   270
αὔξει δὲ χθὼν μὲν σφέτερον δέμας, αἰθέρα
δ᾽ αἰθήρ.

ἡ δὲ χθὼν ἐπίηρος ἐν εὐστέρνοις χοάνοισι   211
200 τὼ δύο τῶν ὀκτὼ μερέων λάχε Νήστιδος αἴγλης.
τέσσαρα δ᾽ Ἡφαίστοιο· τὰ δ᾽ ὀστέα λεύκ᾽
ἐγένοντο
Ἁρμονίης κόλλησιν ἀρηρότα θεσπεσίηθεν.

ἡ δὲ χθὼν τούτοισιν ἴση συνέκυρσε μάλιστα   215
Ἡφαίστῳ τ᾽ Ὄμβρῳ τε καὶ Αἰθέρι παμ-
φανόωντι,
203 Κύπριδος ὁρμισθεῖσα τελείοις ἐν λιμένεσσιν,
εἴτ᾽ ὀλίγον μείζων εἴτε πλεόνεσσιν ἐλάσσων.
ἐκ τῶν αἷμά τε γέντο καὶ ἄλλης εἴδεα σαρκός.

ἄλφιτον ὕδατι κολλήσας. . .   208

σχεδύνην Φιλότητα.

195-196. Simpl. *Phys.* 74 v 331, 12.

195. aF omit οὖν.

197-198. Arist. *de gen. et corr.* ii. 6 ; 333 b 1.

197. Arist. πυρὶ γὰρ αὔξει τὸ πῦρ, corr. Karst.   198. γένος H, δέμας.

199-202. Simpl. *Phys.* 66 v 300, 21.   199-201. Arist. *de anima* i. 5 ;
410 a 4 ; and commentators on this passage.

199. Simpl. aEF εὐτύκτοις, D and Arist. εὐστέρνοις.   200. aF τὰ,
DE τὰς, Diels τὼ: aF μερέων, DE μοιράων.

203-207. Simpl. *Phys.* 7 v 32, 6.   203. 74 v, 331, 5.

205. aDE ὁρμισθεῖσα, F ὁρμισθεῖσα.   206. MS. πλέον ἐστίν, corr.
Panz.   207. aF αἷματ᾽ ἐγένοντο, D αἷμα τέγεντο, E αἷματ᾽
ἔγεντο.

208. Arist. *Meteor.* iv. 4 ; 382 a 1 ; *Probl.* 21, 22 ; 929 b 16 ; cf. Plut.
de prim. frig. 952 B.

209. Plut. *de prim. frig.* 952 B.

195. In this way, by the good favour of Tyche, all things have power of thought.

196. And in so far as what was least dense came together as they fell.

197. For water is increased by water, primeval fire by fire, and earth causes its own substance to increase, and air, air.

199. And the kindly earth in its broad hollows received two out of the eight parts of bright Nestis, and four of Hephaistos, and they became white bones, fitted together marvellously by the glues of Harmony.

203. And the earth met with these in almost equal amounts, with Hephaistos and Ombros and bright-shining Aether (*i.e.* air), being anchored in the perfect harbours of Kypris; either a little more earth, or a little less with more of the others. From these arose blood and various kinds of flesh.

208. . . . glueing barley-meal together with water.

209. (Water) tenacious Love.

ΠΕΡΙ ΦΥΣΕΩΣ ΔΕΥΤΕΡΟΣ

210 Εἰ δέ τί σοι περὶ τῶνδε λιπόξυλος ἔπλετο πίστις, 136
    πῶς ὕδατος γαίης τε καὶ αἰθέρος ἠελίου τε
    κιρναμένων χροιαί τ᾽ εἴδη τε γενοίατο θνητῶν
    τοῖ᾽, ὅσα νῦν γεγάασι συναρμοσθέντ᾽ Ἀφροδίτῃ. .

    πῶς καὶ δένδρεα μακρὰ καὶ εἰνάλιοι καμασῆνες. . 243

215 ὡς δὲ τότε χθόνα Κύπρις, ἐπεί τ᾽ ἐδίηνεν ἐν
        ὄμβρῳ   207
    αἰθέρ᾽ ἐπιπνείουσα θοῷ πυρὶ δῶκε κρατῦναι.

    τῶν δ᾽ ὅσ᾽ ἔσω μὲν πυκνά, τὰ δ᾽ ἔκτοθι μανὰ
        πέπηγε,   230
    Κύπριδος ἐν παλάμῃς πλάδης τοιῆσδε τυχόντα.

    οὕτω δ᾽ ᾠοτοκεῖ μακρὰ δένδρεα πρῶτον ἐλαίας. 245

220 οὕνεκεν ὀψίγονοί τε σίδαι καὶ ὑπέρφλοα μῆλα   246

    οἶνος ὑπὸ φλοιῷ πέλεται σαπὲν ἐν ξύλῳ ὕδωρ.   247

210-213. Simpl. de caelo, Peyr. p. 28 ; Gaisf. Poet. Min. Gr. II. xliii.
Brand. Schol. Arist. 507 a.

210. A εἰ δ᾽ ἔτι σοι, B εἰδέτι σοι, Taur. εἰ δέ τισι.   212. MS. εἴδη
τε γενοίατο χροιάστε, corr. Ritschl.

214. Athen. viii. 334 B.

215-218. Simpl. de caelo a little after 213.   218. Simpl. Phys. 74 v
331, 9.

215. MS. ὡς δὲ . . . ἔπειτ᾽, corr. Karst.: A ἐδίηνεν ἐν, B ἐδείκνυεν
ἐν, Taur. ἐδείκνυεν.   216. A ἡ δέ ἀποπνέουσα, B εἰ δὲ ἀποπνοίουσα,
Taur. ἡ δὲ ἀποπνείουσα, Panz. ἠδὺ δ᾽ ἐπιπνείουσα, corr.
Stein.   217. Phys. E πλάσης, a πλάσιος, text from de caelo.

219. Arist. de gen. anim. i. 23 ; 731 a 5 ; cf. Philop. on this passage
and Theophr. de caus. plant. i. 7, 1.

Philop. and Arist. . . . μικρὰ . . . ἐλα᾽ας.

220. Plut. Quaest. conv. 683 D.

221. Plut. Quaest. nat. 912 c, 919 D ; cf. Arist. Top. iv. 5 ; 127 a 18.
MS. ἀπὸ φλοιοῦ, corr. Meziriacus.

Book II.

210. And if your faith be at all lacking in regard to these (elements), how from water and earth and air and sun (fire) when they are mixed, arose such colours and forms of mortal things, as many as now have arisen under the uniting power of Aphrodite. . . .

214. How both tall trees and fishes of the sea (arose).

215. And thus then Kypris, when she had moistened the earth with water, breathed air on it and gave it to swift fire to be hardened.

217. And all these things which were within were made dense, while those without were made rare, meeting with such moisture in the hands of Kypris.

219. And thus tall trees bear fruit (*lit.* eggs), first of all olives.

220. Wherefore late-born pomegranates and luxuriant apples . . .

221. Wine is water that has fermented in the wood beneath the bark.

εἰ γάρ κέν σφ' ἀδινῇσιν ὑπὸ πραπίδεσσιν ἐρείσας
εὐμενέως καθαρῇσιν ἐποπτεύσῃς μελέτῃσιν,
ταῦτά τέ σοι μάλα πάντα δι' αἰῶνος παρέσονται,
225 ἄλλα τε πόλλ' ἀπὸ τῶνδε κεκτήσεαι· αὐτὰ γὰρ
αὔξει
ταῦτ' εἰς ἦθος ἕκαστον, ὅπῃ φύσις ἐστὶν ἑκάστῳ.
εἰ δέ σύ γ' ἀλλοίων ἐπορέξεαι οἷα κατ' ἄνδρας
μυρία δειλὰ πέλονται, τά τ' ἀμβλύνουσι μερίμνας,
†ζῆν ἄφαρ ἐκλείψουσι περιπλομένοιο χρόνοιο
230 σφῶν αὐτῶν ποθέοντα φίλην ἐπὶ γένναν ἵκεσθαι· †
πάντα γὰρ ἴσθι φρόνησιν ἔχειν καὶ νώματος
αἶσαν.

(χάρις) στυγέει δύστλητον Ἀνάγκην.   69

τοῦτο μὲν ἐν κόγχαισι θαλασσονόμοις βαρυνώ-
τοις   220
καλχῶν κηρύκων τε λιθορρίνων χελύων τε. .

235 ἔνθ' ὄψῃ χθόνα χρωτὸς ὑπέρτατα ναιετάουσαν.

222-231. Hippolyt. *Ref. haer.* 251 Mill; Schneidewin, *Philol.* vi. p. 165.

    222. MS. καὶ ἐν, corr. Mill. MS. σφαδίνησιν . . . corr. Schneid.
223. MS. ἐποπτεύεις, corr. Schneid. 224. MS. ταῦτα δὲ, corr. Schneid. 225. MS. κτ. . . Schneid. κατερχόμεν', corr. Stein.
227. MS. τἄλλ' οἰῶν ἐπιρέξεις, corr. Schneid. 228. MS. δῆλα πέλονται . . . μέριμναι, Schneid. δείλ' ἀπάλαμνα . . . μερίμνας.
229. MS. σῆς, Schneid. ἴσ'. 231. Cf. Sext. E. *Math.* viii. 286. MS. of Hippol. καὶ γνωματοσισον.

232. Plut. *Quaest. conv.* 745 D.
233-235. Plut. *Quaest. conv.* 618 B. 234-235. *de fac. lun.* 927 F.
    234. *Quaest. conv.* καὶ μὴν, *de fac. lun.* καὶ τὴν, Stein μαινῶν, Diels καλχῶν, comparing Nicander, *Alexipharm.* 393 and Schol. Schneid. p. 98 for the interpretation of a fish furnishing a dye. Also Arist. *Hist. anim.* viii. 13; 599 a 10 πορφύραι καὶ κήρυκες.

222. For if thou shalt fix them in all thy close-knit mind and watch over them graciously with pure attention, all these things shall surely be thine for ever, and many others shalt thou possess from them. For these themselves shall cause each to grow into its own character, whatever is the nature[1] of each. But if thou shalt reach out for things of another sort, as is the manner of men, there exist countless evils to blunt your studious thoughts; †soon these latter shall cease to live as time goes on, desiring as they do to arrive at the longed-for generation of themselves.† For know that all things have understanding and their share of intelligence.

232. Favor hates Necessity, hard to endure.

233. This is in the heavy-backed shells found in the sea, of limpets and purple-fish and stone-covered tortoises . . . . there shalt thou see. earth lying uppermost on the surface.

---

[1] φύσις here seems to mean 'nature,' and not 'origin.'

ταὐτὰ τρίχες καὶ φύλλα καὶ οἰωνῶν πτερὰ πυκνὰ 223
καὶ φλονίδες γίγνονται ἐπὶ στιβαροῖσι μέλεσσιν.

αὐτὰρ ἐχίνοις   225
ὀξυβελεῖς χαῖται νώτοις ἐπιπεφρίκασιν.

240 ἐξ ὧν ὄμματ' ἔπηξεν ἀτειρέα δῖ' Ἀφροδίτη.

γόμφοις ἀσκήσασα καταστόργοις Ἀφροδίτη.   228

Κύπριδος ἐν παλάμῃσιν ὅτε ξὺμ πρῶτ' ἐφύοντο. 229

πολυαίματον ἧπαρ.

ᾗ πολλαὶ μὲν κόρσαι ἀναύχενες ἐβλάστησαν,   232
245 γυμνοὶ δ' ἐπλάζοντο βραχίονες εὔνιδες ὤμων,
ὄμματα δ' οἶ' ἐπλανᾶτο πενητεύοντα μετώπων.

τοῦτο μὲν ἐν βροτέων μελέων ἀριδείκετον ὄγκῳ.   335
ἄλλοτε μὲν Φιλότητι συνερχόμεν' εἰς ἓν ἅπαντα
γυῖα τὰ σῶμα λέλογχε βίου θαλέθουσιν ἐν ἀκμῇ·
250 ἄλλοτε δ' αὖτε κακῇσι διατμηθέντ' ἐρίδεσσι
πλάζεται ἄνδιχ' ἕκαστα παρὰ ῥηγμῖνι βίοιο.

236-237. Arist. *Meteor.* iv. 9 387 b 4.

237. MS. λεπίδες, corr. Karst. from a gloss of Hesych.

238-239. Plut. *de fort.* 98 D.

238. MS. ἐχῖνος, corr. Steph.   239. MS. ὀξυβελὴς δέ τε, text follows Cd. Vulc.

240-242. Simpl. *de caelo*, Peyr. 28; Gaisford xliii. Brand. Schol. 512 a. The three lines are cited separately.

242. A ξυμπρώτ', B ξυμπρώταις, corr. Karst.

243. Plut. *Quaest. conv.* 683 E.

244-246. Simpl. *de caelo*, Peyr. 46; Gaisf. xliv. Schol. Brand. 512 a. 244. Ar. *de anim.* iii. 6; 430 a 29; *de gen. an.* i. 18; 722 b 20, and commentators.

244. MS. ᾗ, ἥ, ὡς. 245. πολλαί, πολλῶν ἐμπλάζοντο.

247-253. Simpl. *Phys.* 258 r.

247. MS. τοῦτον μὲν ἂν ... ὄγκον, Vulg. omits ἂν, text from Diels. 249. MS. θαλέθοντος, corr. Karst. 253. Ald. ὀρειμελέεσσιν, corr. Schneider (cf. 438).

236. Hair and leaves and thick feathers of birds are the same thing in origin, and reptiles' scales, too, on strong limbs.

238. But on hedgehogs, sharp-pointed hair bristles on their backs.

240. Out of which divine Aphrodite wrought eyes untiring.

241. Aphrodite fashioning them curiously with bonds of love.

242. When they first grew together in the hands of Aphrodite.

243. The liver well supplied with blood.

244. Where many heads grew up without necks, and arms were wandering about naked, bereft of shoulders, and eyes roamed about alone with no foreheads.

247. This is indeed remarkable in the mass of human members; at one time all the limbs which form the body, united into one by Love, grow vigorously in the prime of life; but yet at another time, separated by evil Strife, they wander each in different directions along the breakers of the sea of life. Just so it is with

ὡς δ' αὔτως θάμνοισι καὶ ἰχθύσιν ὑδρομελάθροις 340
θηρσί τ' ὀρειλεχέεσσιν ἰδὲ πτεροβάμοισι κύμ-
βαις.

αὐτὰρ ἐπεὶ κατὰ μεῖζον ἐμίσγετο δαίμονι δαίμων, 235
255 ταῦτά τε συμπίπτεσκον ὅπη συνέκυρσεν ἕκαστα,
ἄλλα τε πρὸς τοῖς πολλὰ διηνεκῆ ἐξεγένοντο.

πολλὰ μὲν ἀμφιπρόσωπα καὶ ἀμφίστερν' ἐφύοντο,
βουγενῆ ἀνδρόπρωρα, τὰ δ' ἔμπαλιν ἐξανέτελλον 239
ἀνδροφυῆ βούκρανα, μεμιγμένα τῇ μὲν ἀπ' ἀνδρῶν,
260 τῇ δὲ γυναικοφυῆ, στείροις ἠσκημένα γυίοις.

εἰλίποδ' ἀκριτόχειρα.   242
νῦν δ' ἄγ', ὅπως ἀνδρῶν τε πολυκλαύτων τε
γυναικῶν   248
ἐμμυχίους ὄρπηκας ἀνήγαγε κρινόμενον πῦρ,
τῶνδε κλύ'· οὐ γὰρ μῦθος ἀπόσκοπος οὐδ' ἀδαή-
μων.
265 οὐλοφυεῖς μὲν πρῶτα τύποι χθονὸς ἐξανέτελλον,
ἀμφοτέρων ὕδατός τε καὶ εἴδεος αἶσαν ἔχοντες,
τοὺς μὲν πῦρ ἀνέπεμπε θέλον πρὸς ὁμοῖον ἵκε-
σθαι,

254-256. Simpl. de caelo following 246 after a break.

   254. B Taur. omit δαίμονι. 256. B Taur. ἐξεγένετο.

257-260. Aelian, hist. anim. xvi. 29. Cf. Plut. Colot. 1123 D.

   257. MS. φύεσθαι, Karst. ἐφύοντο. 258. MS. ἀνδρόπρωνα . . .
ἐξανατείνειν, corr. Gronovius. 259. MS. ὑπ', corr. Jacobs.
260. MS. σκιεροῖς, corr. Diels.

261. Plut. Colot. 1123 D.

MS. εἰλίποδα κριτόχειρα, corr. Karst. and Duebner.

262-269. Simpl. Phys. 86 v 381, 31.

   263. MS. ἐννυχίους, corr. Panz. cf. Odyssey λ 344 ἀπὸ σκοποῦ,
which perhaps should be restored here. 266. MS. εἴδεος, Stz.
οὔδεος, but cf. Simpl. 382, 7. 269. E οἶά τ', F οὔτ', a οὔτ' αὖ,
Diels οἷόν τ': EF γύων, a γῆρυν, corr. Stein.

plants [1] and with fishes dwelling in watery halls, and beasts whose lair is in the mountains, and birds borne on wings.

254. But as divinity was mingled yet more with divinity, these things kept coming together in whatever way each might chance, and many others also in addition to these continually came into being.

257. Many creatures arose with double faces and double breasts, offspring of oxen with human faces, and again there sprang up children of men with oxen's heads; creatures, too, in which were mixed some parts from men and some of the nature of women, furnished with sterile members.

261. Cattle of trailing gait, with undivided hoofs.

262 But come now, hear of these things; how fire separating caused the hidden offspring of men and weeping women to arise, for it is no tale apart from our subject, or witless. In the first place there sprang up out of the earth forms grown into one whole,[2] having a share of both, of water and of fire. These in truth fire caused to grow up, desiring to reach its like; but they

---

[1] θάμνος, 'bush,' I have rendered regularly 'plant.'
[2] Cf. Aet. v. 19; *Dox.* 430.

οὔτε τί πω μελέων ἐρατὸν δέμας ἐμφαίνοντας,
οὔτ' ἐνοπὴν οἷόν τ' ἐπιχώριον ἀνδράσι γυῖον.　255

270 ἀλλὰ διέσπασται μελέων φύσις· ἡ μὲν ἐν ἀνδρὸς 257
ἡ δὲ γυναικὸς ἐν. . .

τῷ δ' ἐπὶ καὶ πόθος ἦλθε δι' ὄψιος ἀμμιχθέντι.　256

ἐν δ' ἐχύθη καθαροῖσι· τὰ μὲν τελέθουσι γυναῖκες 259
ψύχεος ἀντιάσαντα.

275 λιμένας σχιστοὺς Ἀφροδίτης.　261

ἐν γὰρ θερμοτέρῳ τοκὰς ἄρρενος ἔπλετο γαστήρ, 262
καὶ μέλανες διὰ τοῦτο καὶ ἰνωδέστεροι ἄνδρες
καὶ λαχνήεντες μᾶλλον.

ὡς δ' ὅτ' ὀπὸς γάλα λευκὸν ἐγόμφωσεν καὶ ἔδησε. 265

280 μηνὸς ἐν ὀγδοάτου δεκάτῃ πύον ἔπλετο λευκόν.　266

γνοὺς ὅτι πάντων εἰσίν ἀπορροαὶ ὅσσ' ἐγένοντο.　267

ὣς γλυκὺ μὲν γλυκὺ μάρπτε, πικρὸν δ' ἐπὶ
　πικρὸν ὄρουσεν,　268
ὀξὺ δ' ἐπ' ὀξὺ ἔβη, δαλερὸν δαλερῷ ἐπόχευεν.

---

270. Arist. *de gen. anim.* i. 18 ; 722 b 12 ; *ibid.* i. 1 ; 764 b 17 ; and 270-271 in Philop. on this passage.

270. *Z* omits ἐν.　271. Stein transposes last two words.

272. Plut. *Quaest. nat.* 917 c.

　MS. τῷ δέ τι . . . εἴτε διὰ πέψεως ἀμμίσγων.　Karst, τῷ δ' ἐπὶ . . . δι' ὄψεος ἀντ' ἀίσσων, Stein ἀμμιχθέντι.

273-274. Arist. *de gen. anim.* iv. 1 ; 723 a 24 after 271.
　S ἐλύθη.

275. Schol. Eur. *Phoen.* p. 600 Valck.　Stein transposes first two words.

276-278. Galen in Hippokr. *Epidem.* iv. 2.

　276. MS. τὸ κατ' ἄρρενα ἔπλετο γαίης.　Text from Diels.

279. Plut. *de amic. mult.* 95 λ ; cf. Arist. *de gen. anim.* iv. 4 ; 771 b 23.

280. Arist. *de gen. anim.* iv. 8 ; 777 a 10 ; and Philop. on this passage.

281. Plut. *Quaest. Nat.* 916 D.

282-283. Plut. *Quaest. Conv.* 663 λ.

　282. MS. μὲν ἐπὶ γλυκὺ, corr. Macrob.　283. MS. omits ἔβη and ends δαλεροῦ λαβέτω, corr. Karst.

showed as yet no lovely body formed out of the members, nor voice nor limb such as is natural to men.

270. But the nature of the members (of the child ?) is divided, part in the man's, part in the woman's (body).

271. But desire also came upon him, having been united with . . . by sight.

273. It was poured out in the pure parts, and some meeting with cold became females.

275. The separated harbours of Aphrodite.

276. In its warmer parts the womb is productive of the male, and on this account men are dark and more muscular and more hairy.

279. As when fig-juice curdles and binds white milk.

280. On the tenth day of the eighth month came the white discharge.

281. Knowing that there are exhalations from all things which came into existence.

281. Thus sweet was snatching sweet, and bitter darted to bitter, and sharp went to sharp, and hot coupled with hot.

οἴνῳ ὕδωρ μᾶλλον μὲν ἐνάρθμιον, αὐτὰρ ἐλαίῳ   272
285 οὐκ ἐθέλει.

βύσσῳ δὲ γλαυκῇ κόκκου καταμίσγεται (ἄνθος) 274

ὧδε δ' ἀναπνεῖ πάντα καὶ ἐκπνεῖ· πᾶσι λίφαιμοι 275
σαρκῶν σύρριγγες πύματον κατὰ σῶμα τέτανται,
καί σφιν ἐπὶ στομίοις πύκναις τέτρηνται ἄλοξιν
290 ῥινῶν ἔσχατα τέρθρα διαμπερές, ὥστε φόνον μὲν
κεύθειν, αἰθέρι δ' εὐπορίην διόδοισι τετμῆσθαι.
ἔνθεν ἔπειθ' ὁπόταν μὲν ἀπαΐξῃ τέρεν αἷμα,   280
αἰθὴρ παφλάζων καταΐσσεται οἴδματι μάργῳ,
εὖτε δ' ἀναθρῴσκῃ, πάλιν ἐκπνέει· ὥσπερ ὅταν
    παῖς,
295 κλεψύδρην παίζουσα διπετέος χαλκοῖο,
εὖτε μὲν αὐλοῦ πορθμὸν ἐπ' εὐειδεῖ χερὶ θεῖσα
εἰς ὕδατος βάπτῃσι τέρεν δέμας ἀργυφέοιο,   285
οὐ τότ' ἐς ἄγγοσδ' ὄμβρος ἐσέρχεται, ἀλλά μιν
    εἴργει
αἰθέρος ὄγχος ἔσωθε πεσὼν ἐπὶ τρήματα πυκνά,
300 εἰς ὅ κ' ἀποστεγάσῃ πυκινὸν ῥόον· αὐτὰρ ἔπειτα
πνεύματος ἐλλείποντος ἐσέρχεται αἴσιμον ὕδωρ.
ὣς δ' αὔτως ὅθ' ὕδωρ μὲν ἔχει κάτα βένθεα
    χαλκοῦ   300

284–285. Philop. on Arist. de gen. anim. 59 a.

284. MS. ὕδωρ οἴνῳ μᾶλλον ἐναρίθμιον. Text from Stein.

236. Plut. de déf. orac. 433 B.

MS. γλαυκῆς κρόκου, corr. Karst. and Xylander.

287–311. Arist. de respir. 7; 473 b 9.

287. Mil δίαιμοι. 289. MSS. ἐπιστομίοις, ZMil ἐπιστομίαις, corr. Stz. MSS. πυκναῖς or πυκίνοις, Mil δόναξι. 290. Some MSS. τέθρα, Mil φόνον, others φανὸν. 291. M μέν γ' ἐνθεῖναι θέρει, pr Z εὔπνοιαν. 292. Several MSS. ἐπάξῃ, ἐπαΐξῃ. 293. Bekker with majority of MSS. καταβήσεται. 294. MSS. ἀναθρώσκει, corr. Karst. 295. Several MSS. κλεψύδραις, il παίζησι, MZ παίζουσι, others παίζουσα, MZil διπετέος, others δι' εὐπετέος. 298. ilMZ οὐδ' ὅτ', οὐδέτ', Bk οὐδ' ὅγ', Stein οὐ τότ'. 299. MSS. ἀέρος, corr. Stein. 301. MSS. αὔξιμον, a few others αἴσιμον.

284. Water combines better with wine, but it is unwilling to combine with oil.

·

286. The bloom of the scarlet dye mingles with shining linen.

287. So all beings breathe in and out; all have bloodless tubes of flesh spread over the outside of the body, and at the openings of these the outer layers of skin are pierced all over with close-set ducts, so that the blood remains within, while a facile opening is cut for the air to pass through. Then whenever the soft blood speeds away from these, the air speeds bubbling in with impetuous wave, and whenever the blood leaps back the air is breathed out; as when a girl, playing with a klepsydra of shining brass, takes in her fair hand the narrow opening of the tube and dips it in the soft mass of silvery water, the water does not at once flow into the vessel, but the body of air within pressing on the close-set holes checks it till she uncovers the compressed stream; but then when the air gives way the determined amount of water enters. (302.) And so in the same way when the water occupies the depths of the bronze vessel, as long as the narrow opening and passage is blocked up by human flesh, the air outside striving eagerly to enter holds back the water inside behind the gates of the resounding tube, keeping control of its end, until she lets go with her hand.

πορθμοῦ χωσθέντος βροτέῳ χροὶ ἠδὲ πόροιο,
αἰθὴρ δ' ἐκτὸς ἔσω λελιημένος ὄμβρον ἐρύκει

305 ἀμφὶ πύλας ἰσθμοῖο δυσηχέος, ἄκρα κρατύνων,
εἰς ὅ κε χειρὶ μεθῇ · τότε δ' αὖ πάλιν, ἔμπαλιν ἢ
        πρίν,
πνεύματος ἐμπίπτοντος ὑπεκθέει αἴσιμον ὕδωρ.   295
ὣς δ' αὔτως τέρεν αἷμα κλαδασσόμενον διὰ γυίων
ὁππότε μὲν παλίνορσον ἀπαΐξειε μυχόνδε,

310 αἰθέρος εὐθὺς ῥεῦμα κατέρχεται οἴδματι θῦον,
εὖτε δ' ἀναθρῴσκῃ, πάλιν ἐκπνέει ἶσον ὀπίσσω.
κέρματα θηρείων μελέων μυκτῆρσιν ἐρευνῶν.   300
ὧδε μὲν οὖν πνοίης τε λελόγχασι πάντα καὶ
        ὀσμῶν.   301

315   σάρκινον ὄζον.

ὡς δ' ὅτε τις πρόοδον νοέων ὡπλίσσατο λύχνον
χειμερίην διὰ νύκτα, πυρὸς σέλας αἰθομένοιο
ἅψας, παντοίων ἀνέμων λαμπτῆρας ἀμοργούς,
οἵτ' ἀνέμων μὲν πνεῦμα διασκιδνᾶσιν ἀέντων,   305

320 φῶς δ' ἔξω διαθρῷσκον, ὅσον ταναώτερον ἦεν,
λάμπεσκεν κατὰ βηλὸν ἀτειρέσιν ἀκτίνεσσιν·
ὣς δὲ τότ' ἐν μήνιγξιν ἐεργμένον ὠγύγιον πῦρ

Cf. Simpl. *Phys.* 151 v.   303. Many MSS. χρωσθέντος.
307. MSS. αὔξιμον, Bk. αἴσιμον.   309. MSS. ἐπαΐξειε, corr.
Stein.   310. MZil αἰθέρος, others ἕτερον, MZil οἶδμα τιτα'νων.
311. l ἀναθρῴσκοι.
313.¹ Plut. *Quaest. nat.* 917 E ; *de curios.* 520 F.
MS. (Q.n.) κέμματα, (de c.) τέρματα, Buttmann κέρματα.
From Plutarch *Mor.* 917 E and Arist. *Problem. inedit.* II. 101,
(Didot, IV. p. 310) ; Diels *Hermes* xv. 176 restores the following
line after 313 :
        < ἐν δρίῳ > ὅσσ' ἀπέλειπε ποδῶν ἁπαλὴ περίπνοια.
314. Theophrast. *de sens.* § 22.
315. Theophr. *ibid.* § 9.   Diels *Dor.* 501 suggests ὀστοῦν.
316–325. Arist. *de sens. et sensib.* c. 2 ; 437 b 26.   Alex. Aphrod. on
this passage.
318. YE ἀμόργους, Ml ἀμουργούς.   320. Many MSS. πῦρ.   323. MSS.
λεπτῇσιν γ' ὀθόνῃσιν corr. Bekker : several MSS. ἐχεύατο,
λοχάζετο.   324. Several MSS. ἀμφιναέντος.

¹ Stein omits 312 from his numbering of the lines.

(306.) Then, on the other hand, the very opposite takes place to what happened before ; the determined amount of water runs off as the air enters. Thus in the same way when the soft blood, surging violently through the members, rushes back into the interior, a swift stream of air comes in with hurrying wave, and whenever it (the blood) leaps back, the air is breathed out again in equal quantity.

313. With its nostrils seeking out the fragments of animals' limbs, < as many as the delicate exhalation from their feet was leaving behind in the wood. >

314. So, then, all things have obtained their share of breathing and of smelling.

315. (The ear) an offshoot of flesh.

316. And as when one with a journey through a stormy night in prospect provides himself with a lamp and lights it at the bright-shining fire—with lanterns that drive back every sort of wind, for they scatter the breath of the winds as they blow—and the light darting out, inasmuch as it is finer (than the winds), shines across the threshold with untiring rays ; so then elemental fire, shut up in membranes, it entraps in fine coverings to be the round pupil, and the coverings protect it against the deep water which flows about it, but the fire darting forth, inasmuch as it is finer. . . .

λεπτῆς εἰν ὀθόνῃσι λοχάζετο κύκλοπα κούρην·
αἱ δ' ὕδατος μὲν βένθος ἀπέστεγον ἀμφινάοντος, 310
325 πῦρ δ' ἔξω διαθρῷσκον, ὅσον ταναώτερον ἦεν . . .

(ὀφθαλμῶν) μία γίγνεται ἀμφοτέρων ὄψ.   311

αἵματος ἐν πελάγεσσι τεθραμμένη ἀντιθορόντος, 315
τῇ τε νόημα μάλιστα κυκλίσκεται ἀνθρώποισιν·
αἷμα γὰρ ἀνθρώποις περικάρδιόν ἐστι νόημα.

330 πρὸς παρεὸν γὰρ μῆτις ἀέξεται ἀνθρώποισιν.   318

ὅσσον τ' ἀλλοῖοι μετέφυν, τόσον ἂρ σφίσιν αἰεὶ 319
καὶ φρονέειν ἀλλοῖα παρίστατο.

γαίῃ μὲν γὰρ γαῖαν ὀπώπαμεν, ὕδατι δ' ὕδωρ,   321
αἰθέρι δ' αἰθέρα δῖον, ἀτὰρ πυρὶ πῦρ ἀΐδηλον,
335 στοργῇ δὲ στοργήν, νεῖκος δέ τε νείκεϊ λυγρῷ.
ἐκ τούτων γὰρ πάντα πεπήγασιν ἁρμοσθέντα
καὶ τούτοις φρονέουσι καὶ ἥδοντ' ἠδὲ ἀνιῶνται.

---

326. Arist. *Poet.* c. 21 ; 1458 a 5.   Strabo, viii. 364.
327-329. Stob. *Ecl. Phys.* i. p. 1026.

327. MSS. τετραμένα, corr. Grot.   *ACt.* ἀντιθρῶντος, other MSS.
ἀντιθροῶντος, corr. Bergk.   328. *ACt.* κικλήσκεται   329. Cf.
Etym. M. and *Or.* under αἷμα ; Tertul. *de an.* xv. 576 ; Chalcid. on *Tim.* p. 305.

330-332. Arist. *de anim.* iii. 3 ; 427 a 23 ; and Philop. on this passage.
Arist. *Met.* iii. 5 ; 1009 b 18 ; Themist. on Arist. *de anima* 85 b.

330. Some MSS. ἐναύξεται.   330. MS. omits τ'.   331. MS. καὶ τὸ
φρονεῖν, corr. Karst.

333-335. Arist. *de anim.* i. 2 ; 404 b 12 ; *Met.* ii. 4 ; 1000 b 6 ; Sext.
Emp. *Math.* i. 303, vii. 92, 121.   Philop. on Arist. *de Gen. et corr.* 59 b ;
Hipp. *Ref. haer.* p. 165.   Single lines are mentioned elsewhere.

334. Sext. ἠέρι δ' ἠέρα.   335. Sometimes στοργὴν δὲ στοργῇ.

336-337. Theophr. *de sens.* § 10 ; *Dox.* 502.

336. MS. ὡς ἐκ τούτων π., corr. Karst.   337. MS. ἥδονται καὶ ἀ.,
corr. Karst.

326. There is one vision coming from both (eyes).

327. (The heart) lies in seas of blood which darts in opposite directions, and there most of all intelligence centres for men; for blood about the heart is intelligence in the case of men.

330. For men's wisdom increases with reference to what lies before them.

331. In so far as they change and become different, to this extent other sorts of things are ever present for them to think about.

333. For it is by earth that we see earth, and by water water, and by air glorious air; so, too, by fire we see destroying fire, and love by love, and strife by baneful strife. For out of these (elements) all things are fitted together and their form is fixed, and by these men think and feel both pleasure and pain.

ΠΕΡΙ ΦΥΣΕΩΣ ΤΡΙΤΟΣ.

Εἰ γὰρ ἐφημερίων ἕνεκέν τί σοι, ἄμβροτε Μοῦσα,
ἡμετέρης ἔμελεν μελέτης διὰ φροντίδας ἐλθεῖν,
340 εὐχομένῳ νῦν αὖτε παρίστασο, Καλλιόπεια,
ἀμφὶ θεῶν μακάρων ἀγαθὸν λόγον ἐμφαίνοντι.

ὄλβιος ὃς θείων πραπίδων ἐκτήσατο πλοῦτον,   354
δειλὸς δ᾽ ᾧ σκοτόεσσα θεῶν πέρι δόξα μέμηλεν.

οὐκ ἔστιν πελάσασθ᾽ οὐδ᾽ ὀφθαλμοῖσιν ἐφικτὸν   356
345 ἡμετέροις ἢ χερσὶ λαβεῖν, ἥπερ τε μεγίστη
πειθοῦς ἀνθρώποισιν ἁμαξιτὸς εἰς φρένα πίπτει.
οὐ μὲν γὰρ βροτέῃ κεφαλῇ κατὰ γυῖα κέκασται,
οὐ μὲν ἀπαὶ νώτοιο δύο κλάδοι ἀίσσονται,   360
οὐ πόδες, οὐ θοὰ γοῦν᾽, οὐ μήδεα λαχνήεντα,
350 ἀλλὰ φρὴν ἱερὴ καὶ ἀθέσφατος ἔπλετο μοῦνον,
φροντίσι κόσμον ἅπαντα καταΐσσουσα θοῇσιν.

338–341. Hipp. *Ref. haer.* vii. 31 ; 254.   Cf. Schneid. *Philol.* vi. 167.

338. MS. εἰκάφαι φημερίων, corr. Mill.   MS. τινὸς, corr. Schneid.
339. MS. ἡμετέρας μελέτας, corr. Schn.   340. MS. εὐχομένων,
corr. Schn.   341. MS. μακάρων, corr. Mill.   Schn. καθαρὸν
λόγον.

342–343. Clem. Al. *Strom.* 733.
344–346. Clem. Al. *Strom.* 694 ; Theodor. Ther. i. 476 D.

344. Theod. πελάσασθ᾽ οὐδ᾽, Clem. πελάσασθαι ἐν.

347–351. Ammon. on Arist. *de interpret.* 199 b ; Schol. Arist. i. 35 b.
Tzet. *Chiliad.* xiii. 79.   348–349. Hippol. *Ref. haer.* p. 248.   350–351.
Tzet. vii. 522.

347. Ammon. οὔτε γὰρ ἀνδρομέῃ κεφαλῇ, Tzt. οὐ μὲν γὰρ βροτέῃ
κεφαλῇ.   348. Tzt. οὐ μὲν ἀπαὶ, Hippol. οὐ γὰρ ἀπὸ, Ammon.
Tzt. νώτων γε . . . ἀίσσουσιν.   Text from Hippol.   349.
Hippol. γούνατ᾽ οὐ μήδεα γενήεντα.   (349a. Hippol. adds after
349 the following ἀλλὰ σφαῖρος ἔην καὶ ἴσος ἐστὶν αὑτῷ, Schneid.
ἀλλὰ σφαῖρος ἔεις καὶ πάντοθεν ἴσος ἑαυτῷ.)

Book III.

338. Would that in behalf of perishable beings thou, immortal Muse, mightest take thought at all for our thought to come by reason of our cares! Hear me now and be present again by my side, Kalliopeia, as I utter noble discourse about the blessed gods.

342. Blessed is he who has acquired a wealth of divine wisdom, but miserable he in whom there rests a dim opinion concerning the gods.

344. It is not possible to draw near (to god) even with the eyes, or to take hold of him with our hands, which in truth is the best highway of persuasion into the mind of man; for he has no human head fitted to a body, nor do two shoots branch out from the trunk, nor has he feet, nor swift legs, nor hairy parts, but he is sacred and ineffable mind alone, darting through the whole world with swift thoughts.

ΚΑΘΑΡΜΟΙ

'Ω φίλοι, οἳ μέγα ἄστυ κατὰ ζαθέου Ἀκράγαντος 389
ναίετ' ἀν' ἄκρα πόλευς, ἀγαθῶν μελεδήμονες
ἔργων,
ξείνων αἰδοίων λιμένες, κακότητος ἄπειροι,
355 χαίρετ'· ἐγὼ δ' ὕμμιν θεὸς ἄμβροτος, οὐκέτι
θνητὸς,
πωλεῦμαι μετὰ πᾶσι τετιμένος, ὥσπερ ἔοικε,
ταινίαις τε περίστεπτος στέφεσίν τε θαλείοις.
τοῖσιν ἅμ' εὖτ' ἂν ἴκωμαι ἐς ἄστεα τηλεθόωντα, 395
ἀνδράσιν ἠδὲ γυναιξὶ σεβίζομαι· οἱ δ' ἅμ'
ἕπονται
360 μυρίοι, ἐξερέοντες ὅπη πρὸς κέρδος ἀταρπός,
οἱ μὲν μαντοσυνέων κεχρημένοι, οἱ δ' ἐπὶ
νούσων,
δηρὸν δὴ χαλεπῇσι πεπαρμένοι ἀμφ' ὀδύνῃσι,
παντοίων ἐπύθοντο κλύειν εὐηκέα βάξιν. 400
ἀλλὰ τί τοῖσδ' ἐπίκειμ', ὡσεὶ μέγα χρῆμά τι
πράσσων,
365 εἰ θνητῶν περίειμι πολυφθερέων ἀνθρώπων;

352–363. Diog. Laer. viii. 62. Omitting 354, 362, *Anthol.* Bosch. i.
86. 352–353, 355–356. *Anth. gr.* Jacobs ix. 569. 352–353. Diog. Laer.
viii. 54 (cited as beginning of Book on Purifications). 354 inserted by
Stz. from Diod. Sic. xiii. 83. 355. Diog. Laer. viii. 66 ; Sext. Emp. *Math.*
i. 302 ; Philost. *vit. Apoll.* i. 1.; Lucian, *pro laps. inter salut.* i. 496 ;
Cedren. *chron.* i. 157.

352. MS. ξανθοῦ, Bergk ζαθέου. 353. variant ναίετε ἄκρην : variants
ἀν, ἀν', ἀν. Anth. πόληος, Bergk πόλεως, Steph. πόλευς. 354. MS.
αἰδοῖοι, Bergk αἰδοίων. 355. Vulg. ὑμῖν, Bergk ὕμμιν. 356. Cd.
Vind. τετιμημένος . . . ἔοικα. 357. Vulg. θαλείης, corr. Karst.
361. MS. δέ τι, corr. Stz. Clem. Al. *Strom.* 754 παρακο-
λουθεῖν . . . τοὺς μὲν μαντοσυνῶν κεχρημένους, τοὺς δ' ἐπὶ νοῦσον
σίδηρὸν δὴ χαλεποῖσι πεπαρμένους. 363. Platt, *Journ. Philol.*
48 p. 247 ἐβόλοντο : MS. εὐηκέα, Scal. εὐήχεα.

364–365. Sext. Emp. *Math.* i. 302.

365. Some MSS. πολυφθορέων. Cf. 163.

On Purifications.

352. O friends, ye who inhabit the great city of sacred Akragas up to the acropolis, whose care is good deeds, who harbour strangers deserving of respect, who know not how to do baseness, hail! I go about among you an immortal god, no longer a mortal, honoured by all, as is fitting, crowned with fillets and luxuriant garlands. With these on my head, so soon as I come to flourishing cities I am reverenced by men and by women; and they follow after me in countless numbers, inquiring of me what is the way to gain, some in want of oracles, others of help in diseases, long time in truth pierced with grievous pains, they seek to hear from me keen-edged account of all sorts of things.

364. But why do I lay weight on these things, as though I were doing some great thing, if I be superior to mortal, perishing men?

ὦ φίλοι, οἶδα μὲν οὖν ὅτ᾽ ἀληθείη παρὰ μύθοις,   407
οὓς ἐγὼ ἐξερέω · μάλα δ᾽ ἀργαλέη γε τέτυκται
ἀνδράσι καὶ δύσζηλος ἐπὶ φρένα πίστιος ὅρμη.

ἔστιν ἀνάγκης χρῆμα, θεῶν ψήφισμα παλαιόν,   1
370 ἀΐδιον, πλατέεσσι κατεσφρηγισμένον ὅρκοις.

εὖτέ τις ἀμπλακίῃσι φόνῳ φίλα γυῖα μιήνῃ   3
αἵματος ἢ ἐπίορκον ἁμαρτήσας ἐπομόσσῃ
δαίμων, οἵτε μακραίωνος λελάχασι βιοῖο,   4
τρίς μιν μυρίας ὥρας ἀπὸ μακάρων ἀλάλησθαι,
375 φυόμενον παντοῖα διὰ χρόνου εἴδεα θνητῶν,   6
ἀργαλέας βιότοιο μεταλλάσσοντα κελεύθους.

αἰθέριον μὲν γάρ σφε μένος πόντονδε διώκει,   16
πόντος δ᾽ ἐς χθονὸς οὖδας ἀπέπτυσε, γαῖα δ᾽ ἐς
  αὐγὰς
ἠελίου ἀκάμαντος, ὁ δ᾽ αἰθέρος ἔμβαλε δίναις.
380 ἄλλος δ᾽ ἐξ ἄλλου δέχεται, στυγέουσι δὲ πάντες.
τῶν καὶ ἐγὼ νῦν εἰμί, φυγὰς θεόθεν καὶ ἀλήτης,   7
νείκεϊ μαινομένῳ πίσυνος.

366-368. Clem. Al. *Strom.* 648.

366. *AH* ὅτ᾽ ἀληθείη, Cd. Paris. ἐκ τ᾽ ἀληθείη. 367. Diels οὓς ἐρέω · μάλα δ᾽ ἀργαλέη πάντεσσι τέτυκται.

369-382. 369, 371, 373-374, 381 Plut. *de exil.* 607 c. 369-370, 372-383. Hippol. *Ref. haer.* 249-251 (scattered through the text). 369-370. Simpl. *Phys.* 272 v; Stob. *Ecl.* ii. 7; 384. 374-375. Origen *c. Cels.* viii. 53 p. 780. 377-380. Plut. *de Is. et Os.* 361 c (Euseb. *Praep. Ev.* v. 5; 187). 377-379. Plut. *de vit. alien.* 830 F. 381-382. Asclep. in Brand. Schol. Arist. 629 a; Hierokl. *carm. aur.* 254; Plotin. *Enn.* iv. 81; 468 c.

369. Plut. ἔστι τῆς (τι), Hippol. ἔστι τί : Simpl. σφράγισμα. 371. Panz. Schneid. φρενῶν. 372. MS. ὃς καὶ ἐπιορκον ἁμαρτήσας ἐπομώσει, corr. Schneid. Schneid. αἵμασιν, Stein αἵματος. Knatz rejects 372 as a gloss from Hesiod *Theog.* 793. 373. Plut. δαίμονες οἵτε μακραίωνες λελόγχασι βίοιο, Hippol. δαιμόνιοί τε (remainder as in text), Heeren δαίμων., Orig. Hipp. μὲν ἀπὸ. Cf. ἀπαὶ v. 348. 375. Orig. γιγνομένην παντοίαν διὰ χρόνου ἰδέαν, Hippol. φυομένους παντοῖα διὰ χρόνου εἴδεα. 377. Hippol. μέν γε. 378. Plut. *de vit. alien.* δὲ χθονὸς . . . ἀνέπτυσε. Plut. *de Is.* ἐσαῦθις. 378. Hipp. φαέθοντος. 381. MSS. ἄς, τὴν, τὼς, corr. Scal.; Hippol. confirms correction. Hippol. omits νῦν. Asclep. δεῦρ᾽. 382. Asclep. αἰθομένῳ.

366. Friends, I know indeed when truth lies in the discourses that I utter ; but truly the entrance of assurance into the mind of man is difficult and hindered by jealousy.

369. There is an utterance of Necessity, an ancient decree of the gods, eternal, sealed fast with broad oaths : whenever any one defiles his body sinfully with bloody gore or perjures himself in regard to wrong-doing, one of those spirits who are heir to long life, thrice ten thousand seasons shall he wander apart from the blessed, being born meantime in all sorts of mortal forms, changing one bitter path of life for another. For mighty Air pursues him Seaward, and Sea spews him forth on the threshold of Earth, and Earth casts him into the rays of the unwearying Sun, and Sun into the eddies of Air ; one receives him from the other, and all hate him. One of these now am I too, a fugitive from the gods and a wanderer, at the mercy of raging Strife.

ἤδη γάρ ποτ' ἐγὼ γενόμην κοῦρός τε κόρη τε   380
θάμνος τ' οἰωνός τε καὶ εἰν ἅλι ἔλλοπος ἰχθύς.

385 κλαῦσά τε καὶ κώκυσα, ἰδὼν ἀσυνήθεα χῶρον,   13
ἔνθα Φόνος τε Κότος τε καὶ ἄλλων ἔθνεα Κηρῶν   21
αὐχμηραί τε νόσοι καὶ σήψιες ἔργα τε ρευστά.
'Ατῆς ἀν λειμῶνα κατὰ σκότος ἠλάσκουσιν.   23

αἰῶνος ἀμερθείς.

390 ἐξ οἵης τιμῆς τε καὶ ὅσσου μήκεος ὄλβου   11
ὧδε πεσὼν κατὰ γαῖαν ἀναστρέφομαι μετὰ
θνητοῖς.

ἠλύθομεν τόδ' ὑπ' ἄντρον ὑπόστεγον.   31

ἔνθ' ἦσαν Χθονίη τε καὶ 'Ηλιόπη ταναῶπις,   24
Δῆρις θ' αἱματόεσσα καὶ 'Αρμονίη θεμερῶπις,

383-384. Clem. Al. *Strom.* 750; Diog. Laer. viii. 77; Athen. viii.
365; Philostr. *vit. Apoll.* i. 1; 2, and often.

383. Hippol. *Philos.* 3 ἤτοι μὲν γὰρ, *Cedren. Chron.* i. 157 ἤτοι μὲν
πρῶτα. Often κούρη τε κόρος τε. 384. Cedren. καὶ θὴρ κ.θ. ἐξ ἁλὸς
ἔμπνους ἰχθὺς καὶ ἐν 'Ολυμπίᾳ βοῦς, Diog. Laer. ἔμπυρος, Athen.
ἔμπορος, Clem. ἔλλοπος. Others ἄμφορος, νήχυτος, φαίδιμος.

385-388. 385. Clem. Al. *Strom.* 516. 385b-386. Hierocl. *carm. aur.*
254. 386, 388. Synesius *de prov.* i. 89 D. 386-387. Prokl. on *Kratyl.*
103; 386. Philo vol. ii. 638 Mang. 388. Synes. *epist.* 147; Julian. Imp.
orat. &c.

385. Clem. ἀσυνήθεα, Hierocl. ἀτέρπεα 386. Synes. φθόνος, Philo
φόνοι τε λίμοι τε. 388. Syn. Iul. ἐν λειμῶνι, Hier. ἀνὰ λειμῶνα,
corr. Bentl.

389. Hierocl., as just cited; λειμῶνα ὃν ἀπολιπὼν . . . εἰς γήινον
ἔρχεται σῶμα ὀλβίου αἰῶνος ἀμερθείς.

390-391. Clem. Al. *Strom.* 516. 390. Plut. *de exil.* 607 E; Stob.
Flor. ii. 80 Gais.

390. Clem. καὶ οἶον. 391. Clem. λιπών.

392. Porphyr. *de ant. nymph.* c. viii.

393-399. (United by Bergk.) 393-396. Plut. *de tranquil. an.* 474 B.
394. Plut. *de Is. Os.* 370 E. 396. Tztz. *Chiliad.* xii. 575. 397-
399. Cornut. *de nat. deor.* chap. xvii.

394. Plut. *Is. Os.* μέροπι. 395. MS. Δειναίη, corr. Bentl. 396. Tzt.

383. For before this I was born once a boy, and a maiden, and a plant, and a bird, and a darting fish in the sea. **385.** And I wept and shrieked on beholding the unwonted land where are Murder and Wrath, and other species of Fates, and wasting diseases, and putrefaction and fluxes.

388. In darkness they roam over the meadow of Ate.

389. Deprived of life.

390. From what honour and how great a degree of blessedness have I fallen here on the earth to consort with mortal beings !

392. We enter beneath this over-roofed cave.

393. Where were Chthonie and far-seeing Heliope (*i.e.* Earth and Sun ?), bloody Contention and Harmony of sedate face, Beauty and Ugliness, Speed and Loitering, lovely Truth and dark-eyed Obscurity, Birth and Death, and Sleep and Waking, Motion and Stability, many-crowned Greatness and Lowness, and Silence and Voice.

395 Καλλιστώ τ' Αἰσχρή τε, Θόωσά τε Δηναίη τε,
Νημερτής τ' ἐρόεσσα μελάγκουρός τ' Ἀσάφεια,
Φυσώ τε Φθιμένη τε, καὶ Εὐναίη καὶ Ἔγερσις,
Κινώ τ' Ἀστεμφής τε, πολυστέφανός τε Μεγιστὼ
†καὶ Φορύη, Σιωπή τε καὶ Ὀμφαίη.†

400 ὦ πόποι, ὦ δειλὸν θνητῶν γένος, ὦ δυσάνολβον,   14
τοίων ἔκ τ' ἐρίδων ἔκ τε στοναχῶν ἐγένεσθε.

σαρκῶν αἰολόχρωτι περιστέλλουσα χιτῶνι.   379

ἀμφιβρότην χθόνα.

ἐκ μὲν γὰρ ζώων ἐτίθει νεκροείδε' ἀμείβων.   378

405 οὐδέ τις ἦν κείνοισιν Ἄρης θεὸς οὐδὲ Κυδοιμὸς,   368
οὐδὲ Ζεὺς βασιλεὺς οὐδὲ Κρόνος οὐδὲ Ποσειδῶν,
ἀλλὰ Κύπρις βασίλεια.   370
τὴν οἵγ' εὐσεβέεσσιν ἀγάλμασιν ἱλάσκοντο
γραπτοῖς τε ζώοισι μύριοισί τε δαιδαλεόδμοις
410 σμύρνης τε ἀκρήτου θυσίαις λιβάνου τε θυώδους,

μελάγκο(υ)ρος, Plut. μελάγκαρπος. MSS. φορίη, σόφη. Mullach
Σιωπή.

400-401. Clem. Al. *Strom.* 516-517.   Timon Phlias. in Euseb. *Pr. ev.*
xiv. 18.

    400. MS. ἢ δ, corr. Scalig.   401. MS. οἴων, corr. Stein.   Cf. Timon
and Porphyr. *de abstin.* ii. 27.

402. Stob. *Ecl.* i. 1050; Plut. *de esu car.* 998 c.
    Plut. ἀλλογνῶτι, Stob. V ἀλλοιχᾶτι, A ἀλλογλῶτι.

403. Plut. *Quaest. conv.* 683 E.

404. Clem. Al. *Strom.* 516.

    MS. νεκρὰ, εἶδε', Flor. ἠδὲ, corr.

405-414. Porphyr. *de abstin.* ii. 21 (405-412), 27 (413-414).   405-
411. Athen. xii. 510 D.   405-407. Eustath. *Iliad.* x. p. 1261, 44.   412-
414. Euseb. *Pr. ev.* iv. 14 from Porphyry ; Cyrill. *adv. Julian.* ix. 307.
    406. Porphyr. οὐδ' ὁ Κρόνος, Eustath. omits.   407. Porphyr. adds
ἤ ἐστιν ἡ φιλία.   408. Cf. Plato *Legg.* vi. 782 D and Iamblich.
Vit. Pyth. 151.   409. Athen. γρ. δὲ, Burnett μακτοῖς :
Porphyr. δαιδαλεόσμοις.   410. Porphyr. ἀκράτου.   411. Athen.

400. Alas, ye wretched, ye unblessed race of mortal beings, of what strifes and of what groans were ye born !

402. She wraps about them a strange garment of flesh.

403. Man-surrounding earth.

404. For from being living he made them assume the form of death by a change. . . .

405. Nor had they any god Ares, nor Kydoimos (Uproar), nor king Zeus, nor Kronos, nor Poseidon, but queen Kypris.   Her they worshipped with hallowed offerings, with painted figures, and perfumes of skilfully made odour, and sacrifices of unmixed myrrh and fragrant frankincense, casting on the ground libations from tawny bees. And her altar was not moistened with pure blood of bulls, but it was the greatest defilement among men, to deprive animals of life and to eat their goodly bodies.

ξουθῶν τε σπονδὰς μελιτῶν ῥιπτοῦντες ἐς οὖδας,
ταύρων δ' ἀκρήτοισι φόνοις οὐ δεύετο βωμός.   375
ἀλλὰ μύσος τοῦτ' ἔσκεν ἐν ἀνθρώποισι μέγιστον,
θυμὸν ἀπορραίσαντας ἐέδμεναι ἠέα γυῖα.

415 ἦν δέ τις ἐν κείνοισιν ἀνὴρ περιούσια εἰδὼς   440
παντοίων τε μάλιστα σοφῶν ἐπιήρανος ἔργων,   442
ὃς δὴ μήκιστον πραπίδων ἐκτήσατο πλοῦτον.   441
ὁππότε γὰρ πάσῃσιν ὀρέξαιτο πραπίδεσσιν,
ῥεῖά γε τῶν ὄντων πάντων λεύσσεσκεν ἕκαστον,
420 καί τε δέκ' ἀνθρώπων καί τ' εἴκοσιν αἰώνεσσιν... 445

ἦσαν γὰρ κτίλα πάντα καὶ ἀνθρώποισι προσηνῆ, 364
φῆρές τ' οἰωνοί τε, φιλοφροσύνῃ τε δεδήει,
δένδρεα δ' ἐμπεδόφυλλα καὶ ἐμπεδόκαρπα
    τεθήλει,
καρπῶν ἀφθονίῃσι κατήορα πάντ' ἐνιαυτόν.

425 οὐ πέλεται τοῖς μὲν θεμιτὸν τόδε, τοῖς δ'
    ἀθέμιστον,   403
ἀλλὰ τὸ μὲν πάντων νόμιμον διά τ' εὐρυμέδοντος
αἰθέρος ἠνεκέως τέταται διά τ' ἀπλέτου αὐγῆς.

ξανθῶν . . . ῥίπτοντες. 412. Porphyr. Cyrill. ἀκρίτοισι, Euseb.
ἀκράτοισι, corr. Scalig. Porphyr. δεύεται.   413. Cyrill. ἔσχον.
414. Porphyr. ἀπορρέσαντες . . . ἐέλμεναι, corr. Stein and Viger.
415-420. Iamblich. Vit. Pyth. 67.   Porphyr. Vit. Pyth. 30.   415,
417. Diog. Laer. viii. 54.
    Order of verses in MS. 415, 17, 16.
421-424. 421-422. Schol. Nicand. Theriac. p. 81 Schn.   423-424.
Theophrast. de caus. plant. i. 13, 2.   Cf. Plut. Quaest. conv. 649 c.
    422. MS. φιλοφροσύνη, corr. Stz.   423-424. ἀείφυλλα καὶ ἐμπεδό-
κάρπά φησι θάλλειν καρπῶν ἀφθονίῃσι κατ' ἠέρα πάντ' ἐνιαυτὸν
restored by Hermann.   Herm. αἰείφυλλα, corr. Karst. from
Plutarch.   Stz. κατ' ἠέρα, Lobeck. κατήορα.
425-427. Arist. Rhet. i. 13 1373 b 15.
    425. Arist. τοῦτο γὰρ οὐ τισὶ μὲν δίκαιον, τισὶ δ' οὐ δίκαιον, Karst.
θεμιτὸν . . . ἀθέμιστον.   427. ϔbZbAc αὐγῆς, Bekker from one
MS. αὖ γῆς.

415. And there was among them a man of unusual knowledge, and master especially of all sorts of wise deeds, who in truth possessed greatest wealth of mind; for whenever he reached out with all his mind, easily he beheld each one of all the things that are, even for ten and twenty generations of men.

421. For all were gentle and obedient toward men, both animals and birds, and they burned with kindly love; and trees grew with leaves and fruit ever on them, burdened with abundant fruit all the year.

425. This is not lawful for some and unlawful for others, but what is lawful for all extends on continuously through the wide-ruling air and the boundless light.

427. Will ye not cease from evil slaughter? See ye not that ye are devouring each other in heedlessness of mind?

οὐ παύσεσθε φόνοιο δυσηχέος ; οὐκ ἐσορᾶτε   416
ἀλλήλους δάπτοντες ἀκηδείῃσι νόοιο ;
430 μορφὴν δ' ἀλλάξαντα πατὴρ φίλον υἱὸν ἀείρας   410
σφάζει ἐπευχόμενος, μέγα νήπιος· οἱ δὲ φορεῦνται
λισσόμενοι θύοντος· ὁ δ' ἀρ νήκουστος ὁμοκλέων
σφάξας ἐν μεγάροισι κακὴν ἀλεγύνατο δαῖτα.
ὣς δ' αὕτως πατέρ' υἱὸς ἑλὼν καὶ μητέρα παῖδες
435 θυμὸν ἀπορραίσαντε φίλας κατὰ σάρκας ἔδουσιν.

οἴμοι ὅτ' οὐ πρόσθεν με διώλεσε νηλεὲς ἦμαρ,   9
πρὶν σχέτλ' ἔργα βορᾶς περὶ χείλεσι μητί-
σασθαι.

ἐν θήρεσσι λέοντες ὀρειλεχέες χαμαιεῦναι   382
γίγνονται, δάφναι δ' ἐνὶ δένδρεσσιν ἠυκόμοισιν.
440   δαφναίων φύλλων ἀπὸ πάμπαν ἔχεσθαι.   419
δειλοί, πανδειλοί, κυάμων ἄπο χεῖρας ἔχεσθαι.   418
κρηνάων ἄπο πέντε ταμὼν ἐν ἀτειρέι χαλκῷ   422
χεῖρας ἀπόρρυψαι.

        νηστεῦσαι κακότητος.   406

428-429. Sext. E. *Math.* ix. 129.

430-435. Sext. following the last verses. 430-431. Plut. *de super-stitione* 171 c.

431. MSS. οἱ δὲ πορεῦνται, Scalig. ὃς . . . πορεῦται, Diels φορεῦνται. 432. MSS. θύοντες ὅδ' ἀνήκουστος, corr. Hermann. 435. MSS. ἀπορραίσαντα, corr. Karst.

436-437. Porphyr. *de abst.* ii. 31.

438-439. Aelian, *Hist. An.* xii. 7 ; *Orphic. Frag.* p. 511 Herm.

438. Ael. ἐν θηρσὶ δὲ.

440. Plut. *Quaest. conv.* 646 D.

MSS. τῆς δάφνης τῶν φύλλων ἀπὸ πάμπαν ἔχεσθαι χρή, corr. Stein.

441. Aul. Gell. *N.A.* iv. 11 ; Didym. *Geopon.* ii. 35, 8.

442-443. Theo. Smyrn. *Arith.* i. 19 Bull, p. 15, 9 Hill.

MS. κρηνάων ἀπὸ πεντ' ἀνιμῶντα, φησίν, ἀτείρει χαλκῷ δεῖν ἀπορρύπτεσθαι, Arist. *poet.* xxi. ; 1457 b 13 ταμὼν ἀτειρέι χαλκῷ. Text from Diels.

444. Plut. *de ira* 464 B.

430. A father takes up his dear son who has changed his form and slays him with a prayer, so great is his folly ! They are borne along beseeching the sacrificer ; but he does not hear their cries of reproach, but slays them and makes ready the evil feast. Then in the same manner son takes father and daughters their mother, and devour the dear flesh when they have deprived them of life.

436. Alas that no ruthless day destroyed me before I devised base deeds of devouring with the lips !

438. Among beasts they become lions haunting the mountains, whose couch is the ground, and among fair-foliaged trees they become laurels.

440. Refrain entirely from laurel leaves.

441. Miserable men, wholly miserable, restrain your hands from beans.

442. Compounding the water from five springs in unyielding brass, cleanse the hands.

444. Fast from evil.

445. Accordingly ye are frantic with evils hard to bear, nor ever shall ye ease your soul from bitter woes.

447. But at last are they prophets and hymn-writers and physicians and chieftains among men dwelling on the earth ; and from this they grow to be gods, receiving the greatest honours, sharing the same hearth with the other immortals, their table companions, free from human woes, beyond the power of death and harm.

445 τοιγάρτοι χαλεπῇσιν ἀλύοντες κακότησιν   420
οὔποτε δειλαίων ἀχέων λωφήσετε θυμόν.

εἰς δὲ τελὸς μάντεις τε καὶ ὑμνοπόλοι καὶ ἰητροὶ 384
καὶ πρόμοι ἀνθρώποισιν ἐπιχθονίοισι πέλονται,
ἔνθεν ἀναβλαστοῦσι θεοὶ τιμῇσι φέριστοι,
450 ἀθανάτοις ἄλλοισιν ὁμέστιοι, αὐτοτράπεζοι,
εὔνιες ἀνδρείων ἀχέων, ἀπόκηροι, ἀτειρεῖς.

445-446. Clem. Al. Protr. p. 23. Cf. Carmen aureum v. 54 f.
447-449. Clem. Al. Strom. p. 632 ; Theod. Therap. viii. p. 599.
450-451. Clem. Al. Strom. p. 722; Euseb. Praep. evang. xiii. 13.
    MSS. ἐόντες d. Ἀχαιῶν ἀπόκληροι ἀπηρεῖς corr. Scaliger.

PASSAGES FROM PLATO RELATING TO EMPEDOKLES.

Phaed. 96 B. Is blood that with which we think, or
air, or fire . . .?[1]

Gorg. 493 A. And perhaps we really are dead, as I
once before heard one of the wise men say : that now we
are dead, and the body our tomb, and that that part of the
soul, it so happens, in which desires are, is open to persuasion and moves upward and downward. And indeed
a clever man—perhaps some inhabitant of Sicily or
Italy—speaking allegorically, and taking the word from
'credible' (πιθανός) and 'persuadable' (πιστικός), called
it a jar (πίθος). And those without intelligence he called
uninitiated, and that part of the soul of the uninitiated
where the desires are, he called its intemperateness, and
said it was not watertight, as a jar might be pierced with
holes—using the simile because of its insatiate desires.

Meno 76 C. Do you say, with Empedokles, that there
are certain effluences from things ?—Certainly.

And pores, into which and through which the
effluences go ?—Yes indeed.

[1] Cf. Cicero, Tusc. I. 9: 'Empedocles animum esse censet cordi
suffusum sanguinem.'

And that some of the effluences match certain of the pores, and others are smaller or larger ?—It is true.

And there is such a thing as vision ?—Yes.

And . . . colour is the effluence of forms in agreement with vision and perceptible by that sense ?—It is.

Sophist. 242 D. And certain Ionian and Sicilian Muses agreed later that it is safest to weave together both opinions and to say that Being is many and one [πολλά τε καὶ ἕν], and that it is controlled by hate and love. Borne apart it is always borne together, say the more severe of the Muses. But the gentler concede that these things are always thus, and they say, in part, that sometimes all is one and rendered loving by Aphrodite, while at other times it is many and at enmity with itself by reason of a sort of strife.

PASSAGES IN ARISTOTLE REFERRING TO EMPEDOKLES.

Phys. i. 3 ; 187 a 20. And others say that the opposites existing in the unity are separated out of it, as Anaximandros says, and as those say who hold that things are both one and many, as Empedokles and Anaxagoras.

i. 4 ; 188 a 18. But it is better to assume elements fewer in number and limited, as Empedokles does.

ii. 4 ; 196 a 20. Empedokles says that the air is not always separated upwards, but as it happens.

viii. 1 ; 250 b 27. Empedokles says that things are in motion part of the time and again they are at rest; they are in motion when Love tends to make one out of many, or Strife tends to make many out of one, and in the intervening time they are at rest (Vv. 69–73).

viii. 1 ; 252 a 6. So it is necessary to consider this (motion) a first principle, which it seems Empedokles means in saying that of necessity Love and Strife control things and move them part of the time, and that they are at rest during the intervening time.

De Caelo 279 b 14. Some say that alternately at one time there is coming into being, at another time there is perishing, and that this always continues to be the case; so say Empedokles of Agrigentum and Herakleitos of Ephesus.

ii. 1; 284 a 24. Neither can we assume that it is after this manner nor that, getting a slower motion than its own downward momentum on account of rotation, it still is preserved so long a time, as Empedokles says.

ii. 13; 295 a 15. But they seek the cause why it remains, and some say after this manner, that its breadth or size is the cause; but others, as Empedokles, that the movement of the heavens revolving in a circle and moving more slowly, hinders the motion of the earth, like water in vessels. . . .

iii. 2; 301 a 14. It is not right to make genesis take place out of what is separated and in motion. Wherefore Empedokles passes over genesis in the case of Love; for he could not put the heaven together preparing it out of parts that had been separated, and making the combination by means of Love; for the order of the elements has been established out of parts that had been separated, so that necessarily it arose out of what is one and compounded.

iii. 2; 302 a 28. Empedokles says that fire and earth and associated elements are the elements of bodies, and that all things are composed of these.

iii. 6; 305 a 1. But if separation shall in some way be stopped, either the body in which it is stopped will be indivisible, or being separable it is one that will never be divided, as Empedokles seems to mean.

iv. 2; 309 a 19. Some who deny that a void exists, do not define carefully light and heavy, as Anaxagoras and Empedokles.

Gen. corr. i. 1 ; 314 b 7. Wherefore Empedokles speaks after this manner, saying that nothing comes into being, but there is only mixture and separation of the mixed.

i. 1 ; 315 a 3. Empedokles seemed both to contradict things as they appear, and to contradict himself. For at one time he says that no one of the elements arises from another, but that all other things arise from these ; and at another time he brings all of nature together into one, except Strife, and says that each thing arises from the one.

i. 8; 324 b 26. Some thought that each sense impression was received through certain pores from the last and strongest agent which entered, and they say that after this manner we see and hear and perceive by all the other senses, and further that we see through air and water and transparent substances because they have pores that are invisible by reason of their littleness, and are close together in series ; and the more transparent substances have more pores. Many made definite statements after this manner in regard to certain things, as did Empedokles, not only in regard to active and passive bodies, but he also says that those bodies are mingled, the pores of which agree with each other. . . .

i. 8 ; 325 a 34. From what is truly *one* multiplicity could not arise, nor yet could unity arise from what is truly manifold, for this is impossible ; but as Empedokles and some others say, beings are affected through pores, so all change and all happening arises after this manner, separation and destruction taking place through the void, and in like manner growth, solid bodies coming in gradually. For it is almost necessary for Empedokles to say as Leukippos does ; for there are some solid and indivisible bodies, unless pores are absolutely contiguous.

325 b 19. But as for Empedokles, it is evident that he

holds to genesis and destruction as far as the elements
are concerned, but how the aggregate mass of these
arises and perishes, it is not evident, nor is it possible
for one to say who denies that there is an element of
fire, and in like manner an element of each other thing—
as Plato wrote in the Timaeos.

ii. 3 ; 330 b 19. And some say at once that there are
four elements, as Empedokles. But he combines them
into two ; for he sets all the rest over against fire.

ii. 6 ; 333 b 20. Strife then does not separate the
elements, but Love separates those which in their origin
are before god ; and these are gods.

Meteor. 357 a 24. In like manner it would be absurd
if any one, saying that the sea is the sweat of the earth,
thought he was saying anything distinct and clear, as
for instance Empedokles ; for such a statement might
perhaps be sufficient for the purposes of poetry (for the
metaphor is poetical), but not at all for the knowledge of
nature.

369 b 11. Some say that fire originates in the clouds ;
and Empedokles says that this is what is encompassed
by the rays of the sun.

De anim. i. 2 ; 404 b 7. As many as pay careful
attention to the fact that what has soul is in motion,
these assume that soul is the most important source of
motion ; and as many as consider that it knows and
perceives beings, these say that the first principle is
soul, some making more than one first principle and
others making one, as Empedokles says the first principle is the product of all the elements, and each of these
is soul, saying (Vv. 333–335).

i. 4 ; 408 a 14. And in like manner it is strange that
soul should be the cause of the mixture ; for the mixture
of the elements does not have the same cause as flesh
and bone. The result then will be that there are many

souls through the whole body, if all things arise out of the elements that have been mingled together; and the cause of the mixture is harmony and soul.

i. 5 ; 410 a 28. For it involves many perplexities to say, as Empedokles does, that each thing is known by the material elements, and like by like. . . . And it turns out that Empedokles regards god as most lacking in the power of perception ; for he alone does not know one of the elements, Strife, and (hence) all perishable things ; for each of these is from all (the elements).

ii. 4 ; 415 b 28. And Empedokles was incorrect when he went on to say that plants grew downwards with their roots together because the earth goes in this direction naturally, and that they grew upwards because fire goes in this direction.

ii. 7 ; 418 b 20. So it is evident that light is the presence of this (fire). And Empedokles was wrong, and any one else who may have agreed with him, in saying that the light moves and arises between earth and what surrounds the earth, though it escapes our notice.

De sens. 441 a 4. It is necessary that the water in it should have the form of a fluid that is invisible by reason of its smallness, as Empedokles says.

446 a 26. Empedokles says that the light from the sun first enters the intermediate space before it comes to vision or to the earth.

· *De respir.* 477 a 32. Empedokles was incorrect in saying that the warmest animals having the most fire were aquatic, avoiding the excess of warmth in their nature, in order that since there was a lack of cold and wet in them, they might be preserved by their position.

Pneumat. 482 a 29. With reference to breathing some do not say what it is for, but only describe the manner in which it takes place, as Empedokles and Demokritos.

484 a 38. Empedokles says that fingernails arise from sinew by hardening.

Part. anim. i. 1 ; 640 a 19. So Empedokles was wrong in saying that many characteristics appear in animals because it happened to be thus in their birth, as that they have such a spine because they happen to be descended from one that bent itself back. . . .

i. 1 ; 642 a 18. And from time to time Empedokles chances on this, guided by the truth itself, and is compelled to say that *being* and *nature* are reason, just as when he is declaring what a bone is ; for he does not say it is one of the elements, nor two or three, nor all of them, but it is the reason of the mixture of these.

De Plant. i. ; 815 a 16. Anaxagoras and Empedokles say that plants are moved by desire, and assert that they have perception and feel pleasure and pain. . . . Empedokles thought that sex had been mixed in them. (Note 817 a 1, 10, and 36.)

i. ; 815 b 12. Empedokles *et al.* said that plants have intelligence and knowledge.

i. ; 817 b 35. Empedokles said again that plants have their birth in an inferior world which is not perfect in its fulfilment, and that when it is fulfilled an animal is generated.

i. 3 ; 984 a 8. Empedokles assumes four elements, adding earth as a fourth to those that have been mentioned ; for these always abide and do not come into being, but in greatness and smallness they are compounded and separated out of one and into one.

i. 3 ; 984 b 32. And since the opposite to the good appeared to exist in nature, and not only order and beauty but also disorder and ugliness, and the bad appeared to be more than the good and the ugly more than the beautiful, so some one else introduced Love and Strife, each the cause of one of these. For if one were to follow and make the assumption in accordance with reason and not in accordance with what Empedokles foolishly says, he will find Love to be the cause of what is good, and Strife of what is bad; so that if one were to say that Empedokles spoke after a certain manner and was the first to call the bad and the good first principles, perhaps he would speak rightly, if the good itself were the cause of all good things, and the bad of all bad things.

Met. i. 4; 915 a 21. And Empedokles makes more use of causes than Anaxagoras, but not indeed sufficiently; nor does he find in them what has been agreed upon. At any rate love for him is often a separating cause and strife a uniting cause. For whenever the all is separated into the elements by strife, fire and each of the other elements are collected into one; and again, whenever they all are brought together into one by love, parts are necessarily separated again from each thing. Empedokles moreover differed from those who went before, in that he discriminated this cause and introduced it, not making the cause of motion one, but different and opposite. Further, he first described the four elements spoken of as in the form of matter; but he did not use them as four but only as two, fire by itself, and the rest opposed to fire as being one in nature, earth and air and water.

i. 8; 989 a 20. And the same thing is true if one asserts that these are more numerous than one, as Empedokles says that matter is four substances. For it is necessary that the same peculiar results should hold good with reference to him. For we see the elements arising from each other inasmuch as fire and earth do not continue the same substance (for so it is said of them in the verses on nature); and with reference to the cause of their motion, whether it is necessary to assume one or two, we must think that he certainly did not speak either in a correct or praiseworthy manner.

i. 9 ; 993 a 15.   For the first philosophy seems to speak inarticulately in regard to all things, as though it were childish in its causes and first principle, when even Empedokles says that a bone exists by reason, that is, that it was what it was and what the essence of the matter was.

Meta. ii. 4 ; 1000 a 25.   And Empedokles who, one might think, spoke most consistently, even he had the same experience, for he asserts that a certain first principle, Strife, is the cause of destruction ; but one might think none the less that even this causes generation out of the unity ; for all other things are from this as their source, except god.

Meta. ii. 4 ; 1000 a 32.   And apart from these verses (vv. 104–107) it would be evident, for if strife were not existing in things, all would be one, as he says; for when they come together, strife comes to a stand last of all. Wherefore it results that for him the most blessed God has less intelligence than other beings ; for he does not know all the elements ; for he does not have strife, and knowledge of the like is by the like.

Meta. ii. 4 ; 1000 b 16.   He does not make clear any cause of necessity.   But, nevertheless, he says thus much alone consistently, for he does not make some beings perishable and others imperishable, but he makes all perishable except the elements.   And the problem now under discussion is why some things exist and others do not, if they are from the same (elements).

Meta. xi. 10; 1075 b 2.   And Empedokles speaks in a manner, for he makes friendship the good.   And this is the first principle, both as the moving cause, for it brings things together ; and as matter, for it is part of the mixture.

Ethic. vii. 5 ; 1147 b 12.   He has the power to speak

but not to understand, as a drunken man repeating verses of Empedokles.

Ethic. viii. 2 ; 1155 b 7.   Others, including Empedokles, say the opposite, that the like seeks the like.

Moral. ii. 11 ; 1208 b 11.   And he says that when a dog was accustomed always to sleep on the same tile, Empedokles was asked why the dog always sleeps on the same tile, and he answered that the dog had some likeness to the tile, so that the likeness is the reason for its frequenting it.

Poet. 1; 1447 b 16.   Homer and Empedokles have nothing in common but the metre, so that the former should be called a poet, the latter should rather be called a student of nature.

Fr. 65 ; Diog. Laer. viii. 57.   Aristotle, in the *Sophist,* says that Empedokles first discovered rhetoric and Zeon dialectic.

Fr. 66; Diog. Laer. viii. 63.   Aristotle says that (Empedokles) became free and estranged from every form of rule, if indeed he refused the royal power that was granted to him, as Xanthos says in his account of him, evidently much preferring his simplicity.

PASSAGES IN DIELS' 'DOXOGRAPHI GRAECI' RELATING TO
EMPEDOKLES.

Aet. Plac. i. 3 ; *Dox.* 287.   Empedokles of Akragas, son of Meton, says that there are four elements, fire, air, water, earth ; and two dynamic first principles, love and strife ; one of these tends to unite, the other to separate. And he speaks as follows :—Hear first the four roots of all things, bright Zeus and life-bearing Hera and Aidoneus, and Nestis, who moistens the springs of men with her tears.   Now by Zeus he means the seething and the aether, by life-bearing Hera the moist air,

and by Aidoneus the earth; and by Nestis, spring
of men, he means as it were moist seed and water.
i. 4; 291. Empedokles: The universe is one; not
however that the universe is the all, but some little
part of the all, and the rest is matter. i. 7; 303. And
he holds that the one is necessity, and that its matter
consists of the four elements, and its forms are strife and
love. And he calls the elements gods, and the mixture
of these the universe. And its uniformity will be resolved into them;[1] and he thinks souls are divine, and
that pure men who in a pure way have a share of them
(the elements) are divine. i. 13; 312. Empedokles:
Back of the four elements there are smallest particles,
as it were elements before elements, homoeomeries (that
is, rounded bits). i. 15; 313. Empedokles declared that
colour is the harmonious agreement of vision with the
pores. And there are four equivalents of the elements
—white, black, red, yellow. i. 16; 315. Empedokles (and
Xenokrates): The elements are composed of very small
masses which are the most minute possible, and as it
were elements of elements. i. 24; 320. Empedokles et al.
and all who make the universe by putting together bodies
of small parts, introduce combinations and separations,
but not genesis and destruction absolutely; for these
changes take place not in respect to quality by transformation, but in respect to quantity by putting together.
i. 26; 321. Empedokles: The essence of necessity is the
effective cause of the first principles and of the elements.

Aet. *Plac.* ii. 1; *Dox.* 328. Empedokles: The course
of the sun is the outline of the limit of the universe.
ii. 4; 331. Empedokles: The universe <arises and>
perishes according to the alternating rule of Love and
Strife. ii. 6; 334. Empedokles: The aether was first
separated, and secondly fire, and then earth, from which,

[1] Cf. p. 119, note 1.

as it was compressed tightly by the force of its rotation, water gushed forth; and from this the air arose as vapour, and the heavens arose from the aether, the sun from the fire, and bodies on the earth were compressed out of the others. ii. 7; 336. Empedokles: Things are not in fixed position throughout the all, nor yet are the places of the elements defined, but all things partake of one another. ii. 8; 338. Empedokles: When the air gives way at the rapid motion of the sun, the north pole is bent so that the regions of the north are elevated and the regions of the south depressed in respect to the whole universe. ii. 10; 339. Empedokles: The right side is toward the summer solstice, and the left toward the winter solstice. ii. 11; 339. Empedokles: The heaven is solidified from air that is fixed in crystalline form by fire, and embraces what partakes of the nature of fire and of the nature of air in each of the hemispheres. ii. 13; 341. Empedokles: The stars are fiery bodies formed of fiery matter, which the air embracing in itself pressed forth at the first separation. 342. The fixed stars are bound up with the crystalline (vault), but the planets are set free. ii. 20; 350. Empedokles: There are two suns; the one is the archetype, fire in the one hemisphere of the universe, which has filled that hemisphere, always set facing the brightness which corresponds to itself; the other is the sun that appears, the corresponding brightness in the other hemisphere that has been filled with air mixed with heat, becoming the crystalline sun by reflection from the rounded earth, and dragged along with the motion of the fiery hemisphere; to speak briefly, the sun is the brightness corresponding to the fire that surrounds the earth. ii. 21; 351. The sun which faces the opposite brightness, is of the same size as the earth. ii. 23; 353. Empedokles: The solstices are due to the fact that the sun is hindered from moving

always in a straight line by the sphere enclosing it, and
by the tropic circles. ii. 24 ; 354. The sun is eclipsed
when the moon passes before it. ii. 25 ; 357. Empedokles : The moon is air rolled together, cloudlike, its fixed
form due to fire, so that it is a mixture. ii. 27 ; 358. The
moon has the form of a disk. ii. 28 ; 358. The moon
has its light from the sun. ii. 31 ; 362. Empedokles :
The moon is twice as far from the sun as it is from the
earth (?) 363. The distance across the heavens is greater
than the height from earth to heaven, which is the distance of the moon from us ; according to this the heaven
is more spread out, because the universe is disposed in
the shape of an egg.

Aet. *Plac.* iii. 3 ; *Dox.* 368. Empedokles : (Thunder
and lightning are) the impact of light on a cloud so that
the light thrusts out the air which hinders it ; the ex-
tinguishing of the light and the breaking up of the cloud
produces a crash, and the kindling of it produces lightning, and the thunderbolt is the sound of the lightning.
iii. 8 ; 375. Empedokles and the Stoics : Winter comes
when the air is master, being forced up by condensation ;
and summer when fire is master, when it is forced downwards. iii. 16 ; 381. The sea is the sweat of the earth,
brought out by the heat of the sun on account of
increased pressure.

Aet. *Plac.* iv. 3 ; Theod. v. 18 ; *Dox.* 389. Empedokles : The soul is a mixture of what is air and aether
in essence. iv. 5 ; 392. Empedokles et al. : Mind and
soul are the same, so that in their opinion no animal
would be absolutely devoid of reason. Theod. v. 23 ; 392.
Empedokles et al. : The soul is imperishable. Aet. iv. 9 ;
396. Empedokles et al. : Sensations are deceptive.
397. Sensations arise part by part according to the symmetry of the pores, each particular object of sense being
adapted to some sense (organ). iv. 13 ; 403. Empe-

dokles: Vision receives impressions both by means of rays and by means of images. But more by the second method; for it receives effluences. iv. 14; 405. (Reflections from mirrors) take place by means of effluences that arise on the surface of the mirror, and they are completed by means of the fiery matter that is separated from the mirror, and that bears along the air which lies before them into which the streams flow. iv. 6; 406. Empedokles: Hearing takes place by the impact of wind on the cartilage of the ear, which, he says, is hung up inside the ear so as to swing and be struck after the manner of a bell. iv. 17; 407. Empedokles: Smell is introduced with breathings of the lungs; whenever the breathing becomes heavy, it does not join in the perception on account of roughness, as in the case of those who suffer from a flux. iv. 22; 411. Empedokles: The first breath of the animal takes place when the moisture in infants gives way, and the outside air comes to the void to enter the opening of the lungs at the side; and after this the implanted warmth at the onset from without presses out from below the airy matter, the breathing out; and at the corresponding return into the outer air it occasions a corresponding entering of the air, the breathing in. And that which now controls the blood as it goes to the surface and as it presses out the airy matter through the nostrils by its own currents on its outward passage, becomes the breathing out; and when the air runs back and enters into the fine openings that are scattered through the blood, it is the breathing in. And he mentions the instance of the clepsydra.

Act. *Plac.* v. 7; 419. Empedokles: Male or female are born according to warmth and coldness; whence he records that the first males were born to the east and south from the earth, and the females to the north. v. 8; 420. Empedokles: Monstrosities are due to too much or too little seed (*semen*), or to disturbance of motion, or to division into several parts, or to a bending aside. v. 10; 421. Empedokles: Twins and triplets are due to excess of seed and division of it. v. 11; 422. Empedokles: Likenesses (of children to parents) are due to power of the fruitful seed, and differences occur when the warmth in the seed is dissipated.[1] v. 12; 423. Empedokles: Offspring are formed according to the fancy of the woman at the time of conception; for oftentimes women fall in love with images and statues, and bring forth offspring like these. v. 14; 425. Empedokles: (Mules are not fertile) because the womb is small and low and narrow, and attached to the belly in a reverse manner, so that the seed does not go into it straight, nor would it receive the seed even if it should reach it. v. 15; 425. Empedokles: The embryo is [not] alive, but exists without breathing in the belly; and the first breath of the animal takes place at birth, when the moisture in infants gives way, and when the airy matter from without comes to the void, to enter into the openings of the lungs. v. 19; 430. Empedokles: The first generations of animals and plants were never complete, but were yoked with incongruous parts; and the second were forms of parts that belong together; and the third, of parts grown into one whole; and the fourth were no longer from like parts, as for instance from earth and water, but from elements already permeating each other; for some the food being condensed, for others the fairness of the females causing an excitement of the motion of the seed. And the classes of all the animals were separated on account of such mixings; those more adapted to the water rushed into this, others sailed up into the air as many as had the more of fiery matter, and the heavier remained on the earth, and equal portions in the mixture spoke in

[1] Cf. Galen, *Hist. Phil.* 118; *Dox.* 642.

the breasts of all. v. 22; 434. Empedokles: Flesh is
the product of equal parts of the four elements mixed
together, and sinews of double portions of fire and earth
mixed together, and the claws of animals are the product
of sinews chilled by contact with the air, and bones of two
equal parts of water and of earth and four parts of fire
mingled together. And sweat and tears come from blood
as it wastes away, and flows out because it has become
rarefied. v. 24; 435. Empedokles: Sleep is a moderate
cooling of the warmth in the blood, death a complete cooling. v. 25; 437. Empedokles: Death is a separation of
the fiery matter out of the mixture of which the man
is composed; so that from this standpoint death of the
body and of the soul happens together; and sleep is a
separating of the fiery matter. v. 26; 438. Empedokles:
Trees first of living beings sprang from the earth, before
the sun was unfolded in the heavens and before day and
night were separated; and by reason of the symmetry
of their mixture they contain the principle of male and
female; and they grow, being raised by the warmth that
is in the earth, so that they are parts of the earth, just
as the fœtus in the belly is part of the womb; and
the fruits are secretions of the water and fire in the
plants; and those which lack (sufficient) moisture shed
their leaves in summer when it is evaporated, but those
which have more moisture keep their leaves, as in the
case of the laurel and the olive and the date-palm;
and differences in their juices are (due to) variations in
the number of their component parts, and the differences
in plants arise because they derive their homoeomeries
from (the earth which) nourishes them, as in the case
of grape-vines; for it is not the kind of vine which
makes wine good, but the kind of soil which nurtures
it. v. 26; 440: Empedokles: Animals are nurtured by
the substance of what is akin to them [moisture], and

they grow with the presence of warmth, and grow smaller
and die when either of these is absent; and men of the
present time, as compared with the first living beings,
have been reduced to the size of infants (?). v. 28 ; 440.
Empedokles : Desires arise in animals from a lack of the
elements that would render each one complete, and
pleasures . . .

Theophr. *Phys. opin.* 3 ; *Dox.* 478.   Empedokles of
Agrigentum makes the material elements four : fire and
air and water and earth, all of them eternal, and
changing in amount and smallness by composition and
separation ; and the absolute first principles by which
these four are set in motion, are Love and Strife ; for the
elements must continue to be moved in turn, at one
time being brought together by Love and at another
separated by Strife ; so that in his view there are six
first principles ; for sometimes he gives the active power
to Love and Strife, when he says (vv. 67–68) : 'Now
being all united by Love into one, now each borne apart
by hatred engendered of Strife ;' and again he ranks
these as elements along with the four when he says
(vv. 77–80) : 'And at another time it separated so that
there were many out of the one ; fire and water and
earth and boundless height of air, and baneful Strife
apart from these, balancing each of them, and Love
among them, their equal in length and breadth.'

Fr. 23 ; *Dox.* 495.   Some say that the sea is as it
were a sort of sweat from the earth ; for when the earth
is warmed by the sun it gives forth moisture ; accordingly it is salt, for sweat is salt.   Such was the opinion
of Empedokles.

Theophr. *de sens.* 7 ; *Dox.* 500.   Empedokles speaks in
like manner concerning all the senses, and says that we
perceive by a fitting into the pores of each sense.   So they

are not able to discern one another's objects, for the
pores of some are too wide and of others too narrow for
the object of sensation, so that some things go right
through untouched, and others are unable to enter completely. And he attempts to describe what vision is ; and
he says that what is in the eye is fire and water, and
what surrounds it is earth and air, through which light
being fine enters, as the light in lanterns.   Pores of fire
and water are set alternately, and the fire-pores recognise white objects, the water-pores black objects ; for
the colours harmonise with the pores.   And the colours
move into vision by means of effluences.   And they are
not composed alike . . . and some of opposite elements ;
for some the fire is within and for others it is on the outside, so some animals see better in the daytime and
others at night ; those that have less fire see better
by day, for the light inside them is balanced by the
light outside them ; and those that have less water
see better at night, for what is lacking is made up for
them.   And in the opposite case the contrary is true ;
for those that have the more fire are dim-sighted, since
the fire increasing plasters up and covers the pores
of water in the daytime ; and for those that have
water in excess, the same thing happens at night ; for
the fire is covered up by the water. . . . Until in the
case of some the water is separated by the outside light,
and in the case of others the fire by the air ; for the cure
of each is its opposite.   That which is composed of both
in equal parts is the best tempered and most excellent
vision.   This, approximately, is what he says concerning vision.   And hearing is the result of noises
coming from outside.   For when (the air) is set in motion
by a sound, there is an echo within ; for the hearing is
as it were a bell echoing within, and the ear he calls an
' offshoot of flesh ' (v. 315) : and the air when it is set

in motion strikes on something hard and makes an
echo.[1]   And smell is connected with breathing, so those
have the keenest smell whose breath moves most quickly ;
and the strongest odour arises as an effluence from fine
and light bodies.   But he makes no careful discrimina-
tion with reference to taste and touch separately, either
how or by what means they take place, except the
general statement that sensation takes place by a fitting
into the pores ; and pleasure is due to likenesses in the
elements and in their mixture, and pain to the opposite.
And he speaks similarly concerning thought and ignorance: Thinking is by what is like, and not perceiving
is by what is unlike, since thought is the same thing as,
or something like, sensation.   For recounting how we
recognise each thing by each, he said at length (vv.
336–337) : Now out of these (elements) all things are fitted
together and their form is fixed, and by these men think
and feel pleasure and pain.   So it is by blood especially
that we think ; for in this especially are mingled <all>
the elements of things.   And those in whom equal and
like parts have been mixed, not too far apart, nor
yet small parts, nor exceeding great, these have the
most intelligence and the most accurate senses; and
those who approximate to this come next; and those
who have the opposite qualities are the most lacking in
intelligence.   And those in whom the elements are
scattered and rarefied, are torpid and easily fatigued ;
and those in whom the elements are small and thrown
close together, move so rapidly and meet with so many
things that they accomplish but little by reason of the
swiftness of the motion of the blood.   And those in
whom there is a well-tempered mixture in some one
part, are wise at this point ; so some are good orators,
others good artisans, according as the mixture is in the

---

[1] Reading κινούμενον with Diels.

hands or in the tongue ; and the same is true of the other powers.

Theophr. *de sens.* 59 ; *Dox.* 516. And Empedokles says of colours that white is due to fire, and black to water.

Cic. *De nat. deor.* xii. ; *Dox.* 535. Empedokles, along with many other mistakes, makes his worst error in his conception of the gods. For the four beings of which he holds that all things consist, he considers divine ; but it is clear that these are born and die and are devoid of all sense.

Hipp. *Phil.* 3 ; *Dox.* 558. And Empedokles, who lived later, said much concerning the nature of the divinities, how they live in great numbers beneath the earth and manage things there. He said that Love and Strife were the first principle of the all, and that the intelligent fire of the monad is god, and that all things are formed from fire and are resolved into fire ; and the Stoics agree closely with his teaching, in that they expect a general conflagration. And he believed most fully in transmigration, for he said : 'For in truth I was born a boy and a maiden, and a plant and a bird, and a fish whose course lies in the sea.' He said that all souls went at death into all sorts of animals.

Hipp. *Phil.* 4 ; *Dox.* 559. See Herakleitos, p. 64.

Plut. *Strom.* 10 ; *Dox.* 582. Empedokles of Agrigentum : The elements are four—fire, water, aether, earth. And the cause of these is Love and Strife. From the first mixture of the elements he says that the air was separated and poured around in a circle ; and after the air the fire ran off, and not having any other place to go to, it ran up from under the ice that was around the air. And there are two hemispheres moving in a circle around the earth, the one of pure fire, the other of air and a little fire mixed, which he thinks is night. And motion began as a result of the weight of the fire when it was collected. And the sun is not fire in its nature, but a reflection of fire, like that which takes place in water. And he says the moon consists of air that has been shut up by fire, for this becomes solid like hail; and its light it gets from the sun. The ruling part is not in the head or in the breast, but in the blood; wherefore in whatever part of the body the more of this is spread, in that part men excel.

Epiph. *adv. Haer.* iii. 19; *Dox.* 591. Empedokles of Agrigentum, son of Meton, regarded fire and earth and water and air as the four first elements, and he said that enmity is the first of the elements. For, he says, they were separated at first, but now they are united into one, becoming loved by each other. So in his view the first principles and powers are two, Enmity and Love, of which the one tends to bring things together and the other to separate them.

235

XI.

ANAXAGORAS.

ANAXAGORAS of Klazomenae, son of Hegesiboulos, was born in the seventieth Olympiad (500–497) and died in the first year of the eighty-eighth Olympiad (428), according to the chronicles of Apollodoros. It is said that he neglected his possessions in his pursuit of philosophy; he began to teach philosophy in the archonship of Kallias at Athens (480). The fall of a meteoric stone at Aegos Potamoi (467 or 469) influenced profoundly his views of the heavenly bodies. Perikles brought him to Athens, and tradition says he remained there thirty years. His exile (434–432) was brought about by the enemies of Perikles, and he died at Lampsakos. He wrote but one book, according to Diogenes, and the same authority says this was written in a pleasing and lofty style.

Literature :—Schaubach, *Anax. Claz. Frag.* Lips. 1827 ; W. Schorn, *Anax. Claz. et Diog. Apoll. Frag.* Bonn 1829 ; Panzerbieter, *De frag. Anax. ord.* Meining. 1836 ; Fr. Breier, *Die Philosophie des Anax. nach Arist.* Berl. 1840. Cf. Diels, *Hermes* xiii. 4.

Fragments of Anaxagoras.

1. ὁμοῦ χρήματα πάντα ἦν ἄπειρα καὶ πλῆθος καὶ σμικρότητα· καὶ γὰρ τὸ σμικρὸν ἄπειρον ἦν. καὶ πάντων ὁμοῦ ἐόντων οὐδὲν ἔνδηλον ἦν ὑπὸ σμικρότητος· πάντα γὰρ ἀήρ τε καὶ αἰθὴρ κατεῖχεν ἀμφότερα ἄπειρα ἐόντα· ταῦτα γὰρ μέγιστα ἔνεστιν ἐν τοῖς σύμπασι καὶ πλήθει καὶ μεγέθει.

2. καὶ γὰρ ἀήρ τε καὶ αἰθὴρ ἀποκρίνονται ἀπὸ τοῦ πολλοῦ τοῦ περιέχοντος. καὶ τό γε περιέχον ἄπειρόν ἐστι τὸ πλῆθος.

4. πρὶν δὲ ἀποκριθῆναι ... πάντων ὁμοῦ ἐόντων οὐδὲ χροιὴ ἔνδηλος ἦν οὐδεμία· ἀπεκώλυε γὰρ ἡ σύμμιξις πάντων χρημάτων τοῦ τε διεροῦ καὶ τοῦ ξηροῦ καὶ τοῦ θερμοῦ καὶ τοῦ ψυχροῦ καὶ τοῦ λαμπροῦ καὶ τοῦ ζοφεροῦ καὶ γῆς πολλῆς ἐνεούσης καὶ σπερμάτων ἀπείρων πλήθους οὐδὲν ἐοικότων ἀλλήλοις. οὐδὲ γὰρ τῶν ἄλλων οὐδὲν ἔοικε τὸ ἕτερον τῷ ἑτέρῳ.

3. τούτων δὲ οὕτως ἐχόντων, χρὴ δοκεῖν ἐνεῖναι πολλά τε καὶ παντοῖα ἐν πᾶσι τοῖς συγκρινομένοις καὶ σπέρματα πάντων χρημάτων καὶ ἰδέας παντοίας ἔχοντα καὶ χροιὰς καὶ ἡδονάς.

Sources and Critical Notes.

1. Simpl. *Phys.* 33 v 155, 26.   (First clause 8 r 34, 20, and 37 r 172, 2.)

34, 20 and 172, 2 πάντα χρήματα. 155, 28. aD εὔδηλον, Text from *DE*.

2. Simpl. *Phys.* 33 v 155, 31.

155, 31. aD ὁ ἀήρ τε καὶ ὁ αἰθὴρ, Text follows *EF*.

4. Simpl. *Phys.* 33 v 156, 4.   (8 r 34, 21 substitutes for the last line a paraphrase of Fr. 3.)

34, 21 inserts ταῦτα after ἀποκριθῆναι. 34, 24 καὶ τῆς, Text from 156, 7.

3. Simpl. *Phys.* 8 r 34, 29.   33 v 156, 2.   33 v 157, 9.   (Cf. p. 34, 25 at end of Fr. 4.)

TRANSLATION.

1. All things were together, infinite both in number and in smallness ; for the small also was infinite. And when they were all together, nothing was clear and distinct because of their smallness; for air and aether comprehended all things, both being infinite ; for these are present in everything, and are greatest both as to number and as to greatness.

2. For air and aether are separated from the surrounding mass ; and the surrounding (mass) is infinite in quantity.

4. But before these were separated, when all things were together, not even was any colour clear and distinct ; for the mixture of all things prevented it, the mixture of moist and dry, of the warm and the cold, and of the bright and the dark (since much earth was present), and of germs infinite in number, in no way like each other ; for none of the other things at all resembles the one the other.

3. And since these things are so, it is necessary to think that in all the objects that are compound there existed many things of all sorts, and germs of all objects, having all sorts of forms and colours and tastes.

10. καὶ ἀνθρώπους τε συμπαγῆναι καὶ τὰ ἄλλα ζῷα
ὅσα ψυχὴν ἔχει. καὶ τοῖς γε ἀνθρώποισιν εἶναι καὶ
πόλεις συνῳκημένας καὶ ἔργα κατεσκευασμένα, ὥσπερ
παρ' ἡμῖν, καὶ ἠέλιόν τε αὐτοῖσιν εἶναι καὶ σελήνην καὶ
τὰ ἄλλα, ὥσπερ παρ' ἡμῖν, καὶ τὴν γῆν αὐτοῖσι φύειν
πολλά τε καὶ παντοῖα, ὧν ἐκεῖνοι τὰ ὀνήιστα συνενεγ-
κάμενοι εἰς τὴν οἴκησιν χρῶνται. ταῦτα μὲν οὖν μοι
λέλεκται περὶ τῆς ἀποκρίσιος, ὅτι οὐκ ἂν παρ' ἡμῖν μόνον
ἀποκριθείη, ἀλλὰ καὶ ἄλλῃ.

11. οὕτω τούτων περιχωρούντων τε καὶ ἀποκρινομένων ὑπὸ βίης τε καὶ ταχυτῆτος. βίην δὲ ἡ ταχυτὴς
ποιεῖ. ἡ δὲ ταχυτὴς αὐτῶν οὐδενὶ ἔοικε χρήματι τὴν
ταχυτῆτα τῶν νῦν ἐόντων χρημάτων ἐν ἀνθρώποις, ἀλλὰ
πάντως πολλαπλασίως ταχύ ἐστι.

14. τούτων δὲ οὕτω διακεκριμένων γινώσκειν χρὴ, ὅτι
πάντα οὐδὲν ἐλάσσω ἐστὶν οὐδὲ πλείω. οὐ γὰρ ἀνυστὸν
πάντων πλείω εἶναι, ἀλλὰ πάντα ἴσα ἀεί.

5. ἐν παντὶ παντὸς μοῖρα ἔνεστιν πλὴν νοῦ, ἔστιν
οἷσι δὲ καὶ νοῦς ἔνι.

6. τὰ μὲν ἄλλα παντὸς μοῖραν μετέχει, νοῦς δέ ἐστιν
ἄπειρον καὶ αὐτοκρατὲς καὶ μέμικται οὐδενὶ χρήματι, ἀλλὰ
μόνος αὐτὸς ἐφ' ἑαυτοῦ ἐστιν. εἰ μὴ γὰρ ἐφ' ἑαυτοῦ ἦν,

---

10. Simpl. *Phys.* 8 r 35, 3. 33 v 157, 9 (continuing Fr. 3).
Simpl. *de coelo.*

    157, 12. συνημμένας, Text from 35, 4. 157, 13. ἤλιον . . . αὐτοῖς
ἐνεῖναι. 35, 7. E τάσωνήιστα, aF τὰ ὀνιστὰ, Text from 157, 15.
    35, 8. (ταῦτα . . . ἄλλῃ) is omitted at 157, 16.

11. Simpl. *Phys.* 8 r 35, 14.

    35, 16. DE χρήματα. 17. DE νοῦν.

14. Simpl. *Phys.* 33 v 156, 10.

    DE τὰ πάντα, Text from aF.

5. Simpl. *Phys.* 35 r 164, 23.

6. Simpl. *Phys.* 35 v 164, 24 τὰ μὲν . . . μέμικται οὐδεν', and 33 r 156,
13, beginning νοῦς δέ ἐστιν. *Phys.* 156, 13 cf. 67 v 301, 5, and 38 v
176, 32 (37 r 174, 16). *Phys.* 156, 19 cf. 38 v 176, 34. *Phys.* 156, 24
cf. 35 v 165, 31 and 37 r 174, 7. *Phys.* 157, 2 cf. 37 r 175. 11 and 38

10. And men were constituted, and the other animals, as many as have life. And the men have inhabited cities and works constructed as among us, and they have sun and moon and other things as among us; and the earth brings forth for them many things of all sorts, of which they carry the most serviceable into the house and use them. These things then I have said concerning the separation, that not only among us would the separation take place, but elsewhere too.

11. So these things rotate and are separated by force and swiftness. And the swiftness produces force; and their swiftness is in no way like the swiftness of the things now existing among men, but it is certainly many times as swift.

14. When they are thus distinguished, it is necessary to recognise that they all become no fewer and no more. For it is impossible that more than all should exist, but all are always equal.

5. In all things there is a portion of everything except mind; and there are things in which there is mind also.

6. Other things include a portion of everything, but mind is infinite and self-powerful and mixed with nothing, but it exists alone itself by itself. For if it were

ἀλλά τεῳ ἐμέμικτο ἄλλῳ, μετεῖχεν ἂν ἁπάντων χρημάτων,
εἰ ἐμέμικτό τεῳ. ἐν παντὶ γὰρ παντὸς μοῖρα ἔνεστιν, ὥσπερ
ἐν τοῖς πρόσθεν μοι λέλεκται, καὶ ἂν ἐκώλυεν αὐτὸν τὰ
συμμεμιγμένα, ὥστε μηδενὸς χρήματος κρατεῖν ὁμοίως ὡς
καὶ μόνον ἐόντα ἐφ' ἑαυτοῦ. ἔστι γὰρ λεπτότατόν τε
πάντων χρημάτων καὶ καθαρώτατον καὶ γνώμην γε περὶ
παντὸς πᾶσαν ἴσχει καὶ ἰσχύει μέγιστον, καὶ ὅσα γε ψυχὴν
ἔχει καὶ μείζω καὶ ἐλάσσω, πάντων νοῦς κρατεῖ. καὶ τῆς
περιχωρήσιος τῆς συμπάσης νοῦς ἐκράτησεν, ὥστε περιχωρῆσαι τὴν ἀρχήν. καὶ πρῶτον ἀπὸ τοῦ σμικροῦ ἤρξατο
περιχωρεῖν, ἐπεὶ δὲ πλεῖον περιχωρεῖ, καὶ περιχωρήσει
ἐπὶ πλέον. καὶ τὰ συμμισγόμενά τε καὶ ἀποκρινόμενα καὶ
διακρινόμενα, πάντα ἔγνω νοῦς. καὶ ὁποῖα ἔμελλεν ἔσεσθαι καὶ ὁποῖα ἦν, καὶ ὅσα νῦν ἐστι καὶ ὁποῖα ἔσται,
πάντα διεκόσμησε νοῦς, καὶ τὴν περιχώρησιν ταύτην ἣν
νῦν περιχωρέει τά τε ἄστρα καὶ ὁ ἥλιος καὶ ἡ σελήνη καὶ
ὁ ἀὴρ καὶ ὁ αἰθὴρ οἱ ἀποκρινόμενοι. ἡ δὲ περιχώρησις
αὕτη ἐποίησεν ἀποκρίνεσθαι. καὶ ἀποκρίνεται ἀπό τε
τοῦ ἀραιοῦ τὸ πυκνὸν καὶ ἀπὸ τοῦ ψυχροῦ τὸ θερμὸν καὶ
ἀπὸ τοῦ ζοφεροῦ τὸ λαμπρὸν καὶ ἀπὸ τοῦ διεροῦ τὸ ξηρόν.
μοῖραι δὲ πολλαὶ πολλῶν εἰσι. παντάπασι δὲ οὐδὲν
ἀποκρίνεται οὐδὲ διακρίνεται ἕτερον ἀπὸ τοῦ ἑτέρου πλὴν
νοῦ. νοῦς δὲ πᾶς ὅμοιός ἐστι καὶ ὁ μείζων καὶ ὁ ἐλάττων.

v 176, 24. *Phys.* 157, 3 cf. 35 v 165, 14. *Phys.* 157, 4 cf. 35 v
165, 3.

   156, 15. 176, 34 ἐπ' ἑωυτοῦ: D ἀλλὰ τέῳ, E ἀλλὰ τέως, F ἀλλ'. Text
from a. 156, 16. DEF μετεῖχε μὲν, Text from a. 156, 17.
Refers to Fr. 5. aEF ἀνεκώλυεν, Text from D. 156, 20. ἴσχει.
177, 1 ἔχει. 156, 21. aDF omit καὶ before ὅσα, Text from E
and 177, 2. 177, 2 τὰ μείζω καὶ τὰ ἐλάσσω. 156, 22. ED¹
περιχωρήσεως, Text from aD²F. 177, 3 omits ὥστε—ἐπὶ
πλέον. 156, 23. E omits τοῦ before σμικροῦ. aF περιχωρῆσαι,
Text from DE. 156, 26. 165, 33 καὶ ὁπόσα νῦν ἐστι καὶ
ἔσται, 177, 5. ἄσσα νῦν μὴ ἐστι. 157, 3. 165, 15. After ὅμοιον
οὐδενὶ the words ἑτέρῳ ἀπείρων ὄντων should probably be
ascribed to Simpl. 157, 4. DE ἀλλ' ὅτῳ, F ἄλλῳ τῷ: F τὰ
πλεῖστα (also 165, 3), Text from aDE.

not by itself, but were mixed with anything else, it would include parts of all things, if it were mixed with anything; for a portion of everything exists in everything, as has been said by me before, and things mingled with it would prevent it from having power over anything in the same way that it does now that it is alone by itself. For it is the most rarefied of all things and the purest, and it has all knowledge in regard to everything and the greatest power; over all that has life, both greater and less, mind rules. And mind ruled the rotation of the whole, so that it set it in rotation in the beginning. First it began the rotation from a small beginning, then more and more was included in the motion, and yet more will be included. Both the mixed and the separated and distinct, all things mind recognised. And whatever things were to be, and whatever things were, as many as are now, and whatever things shall be, all these mind arranged in order; and it arranged that rotation, according to which now rotate stars and sun and moon and air and aether, now that they are separated. Rotation itself caused the separation, and the dense is separated from the rare, the warm from the cold, the bright from the dark, the dry from the moist. And there are many portions of many things. Nothing is absolutely separated nor distinct, one thing from another, except mind. All mind is of like character, both the greater and the smaller. But nothing different is like anything else, but

R

ἕτερον δὲ οὐδέν ἐστιν ὅμοιον οὐδένι, ἀλλ' ὅτῳ πλεῖστα ἔνι, ταῦτα ἐνδηλότητα ἐν ἕκαστόν ἐστι καὶ ἦν.

7. καὶ ἐπεὶ ἤρξατο ὁ νοῦς κινεῖν, ἀπὸ τοῦ κινουμένου παντὸς ἀπεκρίνετο, καὶ ὅσον ἐκίνησεν ὁ νοῦς, πᾶν τοῦτο διεκρίθη. κινουμένων δὲ καὶ διακρινομένων ἡ περιχώρησις πολλῷ μᾶλλον ἐποίει διακρίνεσθαι.

8. τὸ μὲν πυκνὸν καὶ διερὸν καὶ ψυχρὸν καὶ τὸ ζοφερὸν ἐνθάδε συνεχώρησεν ἔνθα νῦν <ἡ γῆ>· τὸ δὲ ἀραιὸν καὶ τὸ θερμὸν καὶ τὸ ξηρὸν <καὶ τὸ λαμπρὸν> ἐξεχώρησεν εἰς τὸ πρόσω τοῦ αἰθέρος.

9. ἀπὸ τουτέων ἀποκρινομένων συμπήγνυται γῆ· ἐκ μὲν γὰρ τῶν νεφελῶν ὕδωρ ἀποκρίνεται, ἐκ δὲ τοῦ ὕδατος γῆ, ἐκ δὲ τῆς γῆς λίθοι συμπήγνυνται ὑπὸ τοῦ ψυχροῦ, οὗτοι δὲ ἐκχωρέουσι μᾶλλον τοῦ ὕδατος.

12. ὁ δὲ νοῦς, ὡς ἀεί ποτε, κάρτα καὶ νῦν ἐστιν, ἵνα καὶ τὰ ἄλλα πάντα, ἐν τῷ πολλῷ περιέχοντι καὶ ἐν τοῖς ὑποκριθεῖσι καὶ ἐν τοῖς ἀποκρινομένοις.

13. οὐ κεχώρισται ἀλλήλων τὰ ἐν τῷ ἑνὶ κόσμῳ οὐδὲ ἀποκέκοπται πελέκει οὔτε τὸ θερμὸν ἀπὸ τοῦ ψυχροῦ οὔτε τὸ ψυχρὸν ἀπὸ τοῦ θερμοῦ.

15. οὔτε γὰρ τοῦ σμικροῦ ἐστι τό γε ἐλάχιστον, ἀλλ' ἔλασσον ἀεί. τὸ γὰρ ἐὸν οὐκ ἔστι τὸ μὴ οὐκ εἶναι.

---

7. Simpl. *Phys.* 66 r; 300, 31. 33. *DE* καὶ, aF omit.

8. Simpl. *Phys.* 38 r; 179, 3. Cf. *Dox.* 562, 3.

   4. 179, 4 Diels would supply τὸ before διερὸν and ψυχρὸν. 5. From *Dox.* 562 add ἡ γῆ . . . τὸ λαμπρόν.

9. Simpl. *Phys.* 38 r 179, 8. In part 33 r 155, 21. Cf. 106 v 460, 13-14. 155, 22. λίθοι συμπήγνυνται.

12. Simpl. *Phys.* 33 r 157, 7. Simpl. ὅσα ἐστί τε, corr. Diels : πολλὰ περιέχοντι, corr. Diels; cf. p. 155, 31 : προσκριθεῖσι . . . ἀποκρινομένοις, corr. Diels ; cf. 156, 28.

13. Simpl. *Phys.* 37 r 175, 12 beginning with οὐδέ. Το πελέκει, 38 v 176, 29.

15. Simpl. *Phys.* 35 v 164, 17. Cf. 35 r 166, 15.

   164, 17. MS. τὸ μή, Zeller, *Phil. Gr.* i.⁴, 884 n. 3 τομῇ. After in whatever object there are the most, each single object is and was most distinctly these things.[1]

7. And when mind began to set things in motion, there was separation from everything that was in motion, and however much mind set in motion, all this was made distinct. The rotation of the things that were moved and made distinct caused them to be yet more distinct.

8. The dense, the moist, the cold, the dark, collected there where now is the earth; the rare, the warm, the dry, the bright, departed toward the farther part of the aether.

9. Earth is condensed out of these things that are separated. For water is separated from the clouds, and earth from the water; and from the earth stones are condensed by cold; and these are separated farther from water.[2]

12. But mind, as it always has been, especially now also is where all other things are, in the surrounding mass, and in the things that were separated, and in the things that are being separated.

13. Things in the one universe are not divided from each other, nor yet are they cut off with an axe, neither hot from cold, nor cold from hot.

15. For neither is there a least of what is small, but there is always a less. For being is not non-being.

---

[1] I.e things are called after the element or elements (homoeon.eries) which predominate in their make-up.

[2] Cf. Herakleitos, Fr. 68.

ἀλλὰ καὶ τοῦ μεγάλου ἀεί ἐστι μεῖζον. καὶ ἴσον ἐστὶ τῷ
σμικρῷ πλῆθος, πρὸς ἑαυτὸ δὲ ἕκαστόν ἐστι καὶ μέγα καὶ
σμικρόν.

16. καὶ ὅτε δὲ ἴσαι μοῖραί εἰσι τοῦ τε μεγάλου καὶ τοῦ
σμικροῦ πλῆθος, καὶ οὕτως ἂν εἴη ἐν παντὶ πάντα. οὐδὲ
χωρὶς ἔστιν εἶναι, ἀλλὰ πάντα παντὸς μοῖραν μετέχει.
ὅτε τοὐλάχιστον μὴ ἔστιν εἶναι, οὐκ ἂν δύναιτο χωρι-
σθῆναι, οὐδ' ἂν ἐφ' ἑαυτοῦ γενέσθαι· ἀλλ' ὅπωσπερ ἀρχὴν
εἶναι καὶ νῦν, πάντα ὁμοῦ. ἐν πᾶσι δὲ πολλὰ ἔνεστι, καὶ
τῶν ἀποκρινομένων ἴσα πλῆθος ἐν τοῖς μείζοσί τε καὶ
ἐλάσσοσι.

17. τὸ δὲ γίνεσθαι καὶ ἀπύλλυσθαι οὐκ ὀρθῶς νομί-
ζουσιν οἱ Ἕλληνες· οὐδὲν γὰρ χρῆμα γίνεται οὐδὲ ἀπόλλυται, ἀλλ' ἀπὸ ἐόντων χρημάτων συμμίσγεταί τε καὶ
διακρίνεται. καὶ οὕτως ἂν ὀρθῶς καλοῖεν τό τε γίνεσθαι
συμμίσγεσθαι καὶ τὸ ἀπόλλυσθαι διακρίνεσθαι.

(18.) πῶς γὰρ ἂν ἐκ μὴ τριχὸς γίνοιτο θρὶξ καὶ σὰρξ
ἐκ μὴ σαρκός;

εἶναι Schorn inserts οὔτε τὸ μέγιστον, comparing previous line
and 166, 16.

16. Simpl. *Phys.* 35 v 164, 24.
17. Simpl. *Phys.* 34 v 163, 20.
18. Schol. in Gregor. Naz. Migne 36, 911. (Cf. *Hermes* xiii. 4, Diels.)

But there is always a greater than what is great. And it is equal to the small in number; but with reference to itself each thing is both small and great.

16. And since the portions of the great and the small are equal in number, thus also all things would be in everything. Nor yet is it possible for them to exist apart, but all things include a portion of everything. Since it is not possible for the least to exist, nothing could be separated, nor yet could it come into being of itself, but as they were in the beginning so they are now, all things together. And there are many things in all things, and of those that are separated there are things equal in number in the greater and the lesser.

17. The Greeks do not rightly use the terms 'coming into being' and 'perishing.' For nothing comes into being nor yet does anything perish, but there is mixture and separation of things that are. So they would do right in calling the coming into being ' mixture,' and the perishing ' separation.'

(18.) For how could hair come from what is not hair? Or flesh from what is not flesh?

PASSAGES FROM PLATO REFERRING TO ANAXAGORAS.

Apol. 26 D. He asserts that I say the sun is a stone and the moon is earth. Do you think of accusing Anaxagoras, Meletos, and have you so low an opinion of these men and think them so unskilled in letters as not to know that the books of Anaxagoras of Klazomenae are full of these doctrines? And forsooth the young men are learning these matters from me, which sometimes they can buy from the orchestra for a drachma at the most, and laugh at Sokrates if he pretends that they are his—particularly seeing they are so strange.

Phaedo 72 c.   And if all things were composite and were not separated, speedily the statement of Anaxagoras would become true, ' All things were together.'

97 c.   I heard a man reading from a book of one Anaxagoras (he said), to the effect that it is mind which arranges all things and is the cause of all things.

98 B.   Reading the book, I see that the man does not make any use of mind, nor does he assign any causes for the arrangement of things, but he treats air and aether and water as causes, and many other strange things.

Lysis 214 B.   The writings of the wisest men say . . . that it is necessary for the like always to be loved by the unlike.

Hipp. Mai. 283 A.   They say you had an experience opposite to that of Anaxagoras ; for though he inherited much property he lost it all by his carelessness ; so he practised a senseless wisdom.

Kratyl. 400 A.   And do you not believe Anaxagoras that the nature of all other things is mind, and that it is soul which arranges and controls them ? (cf. *Phaedo* 72 c).

409 A.   It looks as though the opinion Anaxagoras recently expressed was a more ancient matter, that the moon has its light from the sun.

413 c.   Anaxagoras is right in saying that this is mind, for he says that mind exercising absolute power and mingled with nothing disposes all things, running through all.

Rival. 132 A.   But the youths seemed to be quarrelling about Anaxagoras or Oenopedos, for they were evidently drawing circles and imitating certain inclinations by the slope of their hands with great earnestness.

Phil. 28 c.   All the wise men agree that mind is king of heaven and earth for us.

30 D. Some long ago declared that always mind rules the all.

Legg. 967 B. And some had the daring to conjecture this very thing, saying that it is mind which disposes all things in the heavens. And the same men again, being in error as to the nature of soul, in that it is older than bodies, while they regarded it as younger, to put it in a word, turned all things upside down, and themselves most of all. For indeed all things before their eyes—the things moving in the heavens—appeared to them to be full of stones and earth and many other soulless bodies, which dispose the causes of all the universe.

Phaedr. 270 A. All the arts that are great require subtlety and the higher kind of philosophy of nature; so such loftiness and complete effectiveness seem to come from this source. This Perikles acquired in addition to being a man of genius; for as the result, I think, of his acquaintance with such a man as Anaxagoras he became imbued with high philosophy, and arrived at the nature of intelligence [νοῦς] and its opposite, concerning which Anaxagoras often discoursed, so that he brought to the art of speaking what was advantageous to him.

PASSAGES IN ARISTOTLE REFERRING TO ANAXAGORAS.

Phys. i. 4; 187 a 20. And others say that the opposites existing in the one are separated out of it, as Anaximandros says, and as many as say that things are one and many, as Empedokles and Anaxagoras; for these separate other things out of the mixture. . . And Anaxagoras seems to have thought (the elements) infinite because he assumed the common opinion of the physicists to be true, that nothing arises out of non-being; for this is why they say, as they do, that all things were together, and he established the fact that such 'arising' was change of form.

Phys. i. 4 ; 187 a 36. They thought that (what arose) arose necessarily out of things that are and their attributes, and, because the masses were so small, out of what we cannot perceive. Wherefore they say that everything was mixed in everything because they saw everything arising out of everything ; and different things appeared and were called different from each other according to what is present in greater number in the mixture of the infinites ; for the whole is not purely white or black or sweet or flesh or bone, but the nature of the thing seems to be that of which it has the most.

Phys. iii. 4 ; 203 a 19. And as many as make the elements infinite, as Anaxagoras and Demokritos, the former out of homoeomeries. . . .

Phys. iii. 5 ; 205 b 1. Anaxagoras speaks strangely about the permanence of the infinite ; for he says that the infinite itself establishes itself—that is, it is in itself; for nothing else surrounds it, so that wherever anything may be, it is there in virtue of its origin.

Phys. iv. 6 ; 213 a 22. Some who try to show that the void does not exist, do not prove this of what men are wont to call a void, but they make the mistake Anaxagoras did and those who attempted to prove it after this manner. For they show that air is something, blowing skins up tight, and showing how strong air is, and shutting it up in clepsydrae.

Phys. viii. 1 ; 250 b 24. For Anaxagoras says that when all things were together and had been at rest for an infinite time, mind introduced motion and caused separation.[1]

Phys. viii. 5 ; 256 b 24. So Anaxagoras is right in

[1] Cf. 263 b 22.

saying that mind is not affected by other things and is unmixed, since he makes it the first principle of motion. For thus only, being unmoved, it might move, and being unmixed, it might rule.[1]

De caelo i. 3 ; 270 b 24. Anaxagoras does not use this word [αἰθήρ] rightly, for he uses the word aether instead of fire.

De caelo iii. 2 ; 301 a 12. Anaxagoras starts to construct the universe out of non-moving bodies.

De caelo iii. 3 ; 302 a 31. Anaxagoras says the opposite to Empedokles, for he calls the homoeomeries elements (I mean such as flesh and bone and each of those things), and air and fire he calls mixtures of these and of all the other ' seeds ; ' for each of these things is made of the invisible homoeomeries all heaped together. Wherefore all things arise out of these things ; for he calls fire and aether the same. And since there is a peculiar motion of every material body, and some motions are simple and some complex, and the complex motions are those of complex bodies and the simple motions of simple bodies, it is evident that there will be simple bodies. For there are also simple motions. So it is evident what elements are, and why they are.

De caelo iv. 2 ; 309 a 20. Some of those who deny that there is a void say nothing definite concerning lightness and weight, for instance Anaxagoras and Empedokles.

Gen. corr. i. 1 ; 314 a 11. Others assert that matter is more than one, as Empedokles and Leukippos and Anaxagoras, but there is a difference between these. And Anaxagoras even ignores his own word, for he says that he has shown genesis and destruction to be the same as change, but like the others, he says there are many elements. . . . Anaxagoras et al. say there

[1] Cf. *Met.* 989 b 15.

are an infinite number of elements. For he regards the homoeomeries as elements, such as bone and flesh and marrow, and other things of which the part (μέρος) has the same name as the whole.

De anima i. 2; 404 a 25. In like manner Anaxagoras says that soul is the moving power, and if any one else has said that mind moved the all, no one said it absolutely as did Demokritos.

De anima i. 2; 404 b 1. Anaxagoras speaks less clearly about these things; for many times he rightly and truly says that mind is the cause, while at other times he says it is soul; for (he says) it is in all animals, both great and small, both honoured and dishonoured. But it is not apparent that what is intelligently called mind is present in all animals alike, nor even in all men.

De anima i. 2; 405 a 13. Anaxagoras seems to say that soul and mind are different, as we said before, but he treats both as one in nature, except that he regards mind especially as the first principle of all things; for he says that this alone of all things is simple and un-mixed and pure. And he assigns both to the same first principle, both knowledge and motion, saying that mind moves the all.[1]

De anima i. 19; 405 b 19. Anaxagoras alone says that mind does not suffer change, and has nothing in common with any of the other things.

De anima iii. 4; 429 a 18. It is necessary then that it be unmixed since it knows [νοεῖ] all things, as Anaxagoras says, in order that it may rule, that is, that it may know [γνωρίζη].

De part. anim. iv. 10; 687 a 7. Anaxagoras says that man is the most intelligent of animals because he has hands.

[1] Cf. iii. 4; 429 b 24.

De plant. i.; 815 a 16. Anaxagoras said that plants are animals and feel pleasure and pain, inferring this because they shed their leaves and let them grow again.

De plant. i.; 816 b 26. Anaxagoras said that plants have these (motion and sensation) and breathing.

De plant. i.; 817 a 26. Anaxagoras said that their moisture is from the earth, and on this account he said to Lechineos that the earth is mother of plants, and the sun father.

De X. Z. G. ii.; 976 b 20. Anaxagoras busying himself on this point, was satisfied with saying that the void does not exist, nevertheless he says beings move, though there is no void.

Meta. i. 3; 984 a 11. Anaxagoras of Klazomenae, who preceded him (Empedokles) in point of age and followed him in his works, says that the first principles are infinite in number; for nearly all things being made up of like parts (homoeomeries), as for instance fire and water, he says arise and perish only by composition and separation, and there is no other arising and perishing, but they abide eternal.

Meta. i. 3; 984 b 8. Besides these and similar causes, inasmuch as they are not such as to generate the nature of things, they (again compelled, as we said, by the truth itself) sought the first principle which lay nearest. For perhaps neither fire nor earth nor any other such thing should fittingly be or be thought a cause why some things exist and others arise; nor is it well to assign any such matter to its voluntary motion or to chance. Moreover one who said that as mind exists in animals, so it exists in nature as the cause of the universe and of all order, appeared as a sober man in contrast with those before who spoke rashly.

Meta. i. 4; 985 a 18. Anaxagoras uses mind as a device by which to construct the universe, and when he is

at a loss for the cause why anything necessarily is, then
he drags this in, but in other cases he assigns any other
cause rather than mind for what comes into being.

Meta. i. 8 ; 989 a 30. And if any one were to assume
that Anaxagoras said the elements were two, he certainly
would assume it according to a principle which that one
did not describe distinctly ; nevertheless he would follow
along a necessary path those who guided him. For
though it is strange particularly that he said all things
had been mixed together at first, and that they must
first have existed unmixed because they came together,
and because chance had not in its nature to be mingled
with chance ; and in addition to this it is strange that he
should separate qualities and accidental characteristics
from essences (for there is mixture and separation of
these), nevertheless if any one should follow him and try
to put together what he wanted to say, perhaps he would
seem to speak in a very novel manner. For when nothing
was separated, clearly it was not possible to say anything
true of that essence, I mean to say that anything was
white or black or grey or any other colour, but everything was necessarily colourless ; for it might have any
of these colours.   In like manner it is tasteless, nor
according to the same line of argument could it
have any other of the like qualities ; for it could not
have any quality, or quantity, or anything. For then
one of what are sometimes called forms would exist for
it, and this is impossible when all things are mixed
together ; for it would have been already separated,
and he says that all things are mixed together except
mind, and this alone is unmixed and pure.   It results
from these views that he says the first principles are unity
(for this is simple and unmixed), and what is different
from unity, such as we suppose the undefined to be
before it was defined and partook of any form. So he

does not speak rightly or clearly, still he means something like those who spoke later and with greater clearness.

Meta. iii. 5 ; 1009 b 25. And he called to mind the saying of Anaxagoras that just such things as men assume will be real for them.

Meta. iii. 7 ; 1012 a 26. The thought of Anaxagoras . . . that some things exist between contradictory propositions, so that all things are false; for when they are mixed together, the mixture is neither good nor not-good, so that there is nothing true to be said.[1]

Meta. x. 6 ; 1063 b 25. According to the position of Herakleitos, or of Anaxagoras, it is not possible to speak the truth.

Ethic. vi. 5 ; 1141 b 3. Wherefore they say that Thales and Anaxagoras and such wise men are lacking in intelligence, when they see them ignorant in things that are for their own advantage, and they say they know things extraordinary and wonderful and dreadful and divine, but these are of no use, because they do not seek human good.

Ethic. x. 9 ; 1179 a 13. And Anaxagoras did not seem to regard the rich man nor yet the powerful man as the happy one when he said he would not be surprised if any one appeared strange to the many ; for these judge by what is outside, for that is all they can see.

PASSAGES IN THE DOXOGRAPHISTS REFERRING TO ANAXAGORAS.

Aet. Plac. i. 3 ; *Dox.* 279. Anaxagoras of Klazomenae declared that homoeomeries are the first principles of things. For he thought it most difficult to

[1] Cf. iv. 4 ; 1007 b 25.

254 THE FIRST PHILOSOPHERS OF GREECE

understand how anything should arise out of not-being,
or perish into not-being. Certainly we take simple food
of one kind, such as the bread of Demeter, and we drink
water ; and from this nourishment there are nurtured
hair, veins, arteries, sinews, bones, and the other
parts. Since these arise we must acknowledge that
in the nourishment that is taken are present all
realities, and from them everything will grow. And
in that nourishment there are parts productive of
blood and of sinews and bones and the rest ; these
are the parts that may be discovered by contemplation. For it is not necessary to perceive everything
by sense, how that bread and water give rise to these
things, but the parts may be discovered in them by
contemplation. From the fact that parts exist in the
nourishment like the things that are generated, he called
them homoeomeries, and declared that they are the first
principles of things ; and he called the homoeomeries
matter, but the active cause that arranges all things is
mind. And he began thus : All things were together
and mind arranged and disposed them. So we must
assert that he associated an artificer with matter.
i. 7 ; 299. Anaxagoras says that bodies are established
according to first principles, and the mind of God
arranged them and caused the generations of all things.
i. 7 ; 302. The mind that made the universe is God.
i. 14; 312. Anaxagoras : The homoeomeries are of many
shapes. i. 17 ; 315. Anaxagoras and Demokritos : The
elements are mixed by juxtaposition. i. 24 ; 320. (See
p. 241. i. 29 ; 326.) Anaxagoras and the Stoics : Cause
is not evident to human reason ; for some things happen
by necessity, and others by fate, and others by purpose,
and others by chance, and others of their own accord.
i. 30 ; 326. Anaxagoras : Origination is at the same
time composition and separation, that is, genesis and
destruction.

Aet. *Plac.* ii. 1 ; 327. The universe is one. ii. 4 ; 331. The universe is perishable. ii. 8 ; 337. Diogenes and Anaxagoras: After the universe arose and the animals were brought forth out of the earth, it tipped somehow of its own accord towards its south part, perhaps intentionally, in order that some parts of the universe might be inhabited and others uninhabited according as they are cold, or hot, or temperate. ii. 13 ; 341. Anaxagoras: The surrounding aether is of a fiery nature, and catching up stones from the earth by the power of its rotation and setting them on fire it has made them into stars. ii. 16 ; 345. Anaxagoras et al.: All the stars move from east to west. ii. 21 ; 351. Anaxagoras: The sun is many times as large as the Peloponnesos. ii. 23 ; 352. Anaxagoras: The solstices are due to a repulsion of the air towards the south, for the sun compressed it and by condensation made it strong. ii. 25 ; 356. Anaxagoras and Demokritos: The moon is a fiery solid body having in itself plains and mountains and valleys. ii. 29 ; 360. Anaxagoras, as Theophrastos says, attributed eclipses to bodies below the moon which sometimes come in front of it.[1] ii. 30 ; 361. Anaxagoras says that the unevenness of the composition (the surface of the moon) is due to the mixture of earthy matter with cold, since the moon has some high places and some low hollows. And the dark stuff is mingled with the fiery, the result of which is the shadowy appearance; whence it is called a false-shining star.

Aet. *Plac.* iii. 1 ; 365. Anaxagoras: The shadow of the earth falls along this part of the heaven (the milky way), when the sun is beneath the earth and does not shed light on all things. iii. 2 ; 366. Anaxagoras and Demokritos: (Comets etc.) are due to the conjunction of two or more stars, and the combination of their rays. 367.

[1] Cf. Theophr. *Phys. op.* Frag. 19; *Dox.* 493.

The so-called shooting stars come darting down from the
aether like sparks, and so they are immediately extinguished. iii. 3; 368. Anaxagoras: When the hot falls
on the cold (that is, aether on air), it produces thunder
by the noise it makes, and lightning by the colour on the
black of the cloud, and the thunderbolt by the mass and
amount of the light, and the typhoon by the more material
fire, and the fiery whirlwind by the fire mixed with cloud.
iii. 4; 371. Anaxagoras: Clouds and snow are formed
in somewhat the same manner; and hail is formed
when, already cooled by its descent earthwards, it is thrust
forth from frozen clouds; and it is made round. iii. 5;
373. Anaxagoras: (The rainbow) is a reflection of the
sun's brightness from thick cloud, and it is always set opposite the star which gives rise to the reflection. And in
a similar way he accounts for the so-called parhelia, which
take place along the Pontos. iii. 15; 379. Anaxagoras:
(Earthquakes take place) when the air falls on the thickness of the earth's surface in a sheltered place, and it
shakes the surrounding medium and makes it tremble,
because it is unable to effect a separation. iii. 16; 381.
Anaxagoras: When the moisture which was at first
gathered in pools was burned all around by the revolution
of the sun, and the fresh water was evaporated into
saltness and bitterness, the rest (of the sea) remained.

Aet. *Plac.* iv. 1; 385. Anaxagoras: The Nile comes
from the snow in Ethiopia which melts in summer and
freezes in winter. iv. 3; 387. Anaxagoras et al.: The
soul is of the nature of air. iv. 5, 392. The intelligence
is gathered in the breast. The soul is imperishable.
iv. 9; 396. Anaxagoras et al.: Sensations are deceptive. 397. Sensations arise part by part according to
the symmetry of the pores, each particular object of
sense corresponding to a particular sense (organ).
iv. 19; 409. Anaxagoras: Sound arises when wind falls

on solid air, and by the return of the blow which is dealt to the ear; so that what is called an echo takes place.

Aet. *Plac.* v. 7; 420. Anaxagoras, Parmenides: Males are conceived when seed from the right side enters the right side of the womb, or seed from the left side the left side of the womb; but if its course is changed females are born. v. 19; 430. As Anaxagoras and Euripides say: Nothing of what is born dies, but one thing separated from one part and added to another produces different forms. v. 20; 432. Anaxagoras: All animals have reason that shows itself in activity, but they do not have a sort of intelligence that receives impressions, which may be called the interpreter of intelligence. v. 25; 437. Anaxagoras: Sleep is due to a weariness of the body's energy; for it is an experience of the body, not of the soul; and death is the separation of the soul from the body.

Theophr. *Phys. opin.* Fr. 4; *Dox.* 479. Theophrastos says that the teaching of Anaxagoras is much like that of Anaximandros; for Anaxagoras says that in the separation of the infinite, things that are akin come together, and whatever gold there is in the all becomes gold, and whatever earth becomes earth, and in like manner each of the other things, not as though they came into being, but as though they were existing before. And Anaxagoras postulated intelligence (νοῦν) as the cause of motion and of coming into being, and when this caused separation worlds were produced and other objects sprang forth. He might seem, he says, to make the material causes of things taking place thus infinite, but the cause of motion and of coming into being one. But if one were to assume that the mixture of all things were one nature undefined in form and in amount, which he seems to mean, it follows that he

s

speaks of two first principles, the nature of the infinite and intelligence, so that he appears to treat all the material elements in much the same manner as Anaximandros.

Phys. op. Fr. 19 ; *Dox.* 493.   See Aet. ii. 29 ; *Dox.* 360, translated above, p. 255.

Phys. opin. Fr. 28 ; *Dox.* 495.   And the third opinion about the sea is that the water which filters and strains through the earth becomes salt because the earth has such flavours in it ; and they point out as a proof of this that salt and saltpetre are dug up out of the earth, and there are bitter flavours at many places in the earth.   Anaxagoras and Metrodoros came to be of this opinion.

Theophr. *de sens.* 27 ; *Dox.* 507.   Anaxagoras held that sensation takes place by opposite qualities ; for like is not affected by like.   And he attempts to enumerate things one by one.   For seeing is a reflection in the pupil, and objects are not reflected in the like, but in the opposite.   And for many creatures there is a difference of colour in the daytime, and for others at night, so that at that time they are sharpsighted.   But in general the night is more of the same colour as the eyes.   And the reflection takes place in the daytime, since light is the cause of reflection ; but that colour which prevails the more is reflected in its opposite.   In the same manner both touch and taste discern ; for what is equally warm or equally cold does not produce warm or cold when it approaches its like, nor yet do men recognise sweet or bitter by these qualities in themselves, but they perceive the cold by the warm, the drinkable water by the salt, the sweet by the bitter, according as each quality is absent ; for all things are existing in us.   So also smell and hearing take place, the one in connection with breathing, the other by the penetration of sound into

the brain ; for the surrounding bone against which the
sound strikes is hollow.   And every sensation is attended
with pain, which would seem to follow from the fundamental thesis ; for every unlike thing by touching produces distress.   And this is evident both in the duration
and in the excessive intensity of the sensations.   For
both bright colours and very loud sounds occasion
pain, and men are not able to bear them for any long
time.   And the larger animals have the more acute
sensations, for sensation is simply a matter of size.   For
animals that have large, pure, and bright eyes see large
things afar off, but of those that have small eyes the
opposite is true.   And the same holds true of hearing.
For large ears hear large sounds afar off, smaller ones
escape their notice, and small ears hear small sounds
near at hand.   And the same is true of smell ; for the
thin air has the stronger odour, since warm and rarefied
air has an odour.   And when a large animal breathes, it
draws in the thick with the rarefied, but the small animal
only the rarefied, so that large animals have a better
sense of smell.   For an odour near at hand is stronger
than one far off, because that is thicker, and what is
scattered is weakened.   It comes about to this, large
animals do not perceive the thin air, and small animals
do not perceive the thick air.

Cic. *de Nat. Deor.* i. 11 ; *Dox.* 532.   Whence Anaxagoras, who was a pupil of Anaximenes, first taught that
the separation and character of all things were determined and arranged by the power and reason of infinite
mind ; but in this he fails to see that no motion can be
connected with and contiguous to infinite sensation, and
that no sensation at all can exist, by which nature as a
whole can feel a shock.   Wherefore if he meant that
mind is as it were some sort of living being, there will
be something inside of it from which that living being

is determined.   But what could be inside of mind ?   So
the living being would be joined with an external body.
But since this is not satisfactory, and mind is 'open
and simple,' joined with nothing by means of which
it can feel, he seems to go beyond the scope of our
intelligence.

Hipp. *Phil.* 8 ; *Dox.* 561.   After him came Anaxagoras of Klazomenae, son of Hegesiboulos.   He said
that the first principle of the all is mind and matter,
mind the active first principle, and matter the passive.
For when all things were together, mind entered and
disposed them.   The material first principles are infinite,
and the smaller ones of these he calls infinite.   And all
things partake of motion when they are moved by mind
and like things come together.   And objects in the
heavens have been ordered by their circular motion.
The dense and the moist and the dark and the cold and
all heavy things come together into the midst, and the
earth consists of these when they are solidified ; but the
opposite to these, the warm, the bright, the dry, and the
light move out beyond the aether.   The earth is flat in
form, and keeps its place in the heavens because of its
size and because there is no void ; and on this account
the air by its strength holds up the earth, which rides
on the air.   And the sea arose from the moisture on
the earth, both of the waters which have fallen after
being evaporated, and of the rivers that flow down into
it.[1]   And the rivers get their substance from the clouds
and from the waters that are in the earth.   For the
earth is hollow and has water in the hollow places.   And
the Nile increases in summer because waters flow down
into it from snows †at the north.†[2]

Sun and moon and all the stars are fiery stones that

[1] I translate the suggestion of Diels in his notes.
[2] Cf. Aet. iv. 1, *supra*, p. 256.

are borne about by the revolution of the aether. And sun and moon and certain other bodies moving with them, but invisible to us, are below the stars. Men do not feel the warmth of the stars, because they are so far away from the earth; and they are not warm in the same way that the sun is, because they are in a colder region. The moon is below the sun and nearer us. The sun is larger than the Peloponnesos. The moon does not have its own light, but light from the sun. The revolution of the stars takes them beneath the earth. The moon is eclipsed when the earth goes in front of it, and sometimes when the bodies beneath the moon go in front of it; and the sun is eclipsed when the new moon goes in front of it. And the solstices are occasioned because the sun and the moon are thrust aside by the air. And the moon changes its course frequently because it is not able to master the cold. He first determined the matter of the moon's phases. He said the moon is made of earth and has plains and valleys in it. The milky way is a reflection of the light of the stars which do not get their light from the sun. The stars which move across the heavens, darting down like sparks, are due to the motion of the sphere.

And winds arise when the air is rarefied by the sun, and when objects are set on fire and moving towards the sphere are borne away. Thunders and lightnings arise from heat striking the clouds. Earthquakes arise from the air above striking that which is beneath the earth; for when this is set in motion, the earth which rides on it is tossed about by it. And animals arose in the first place from moisture, and afterwards one from another; and males arise when the seed that is separated from the right side becomes attached to the right side of the womb, and females when the opposite is the case. He was in his prime in the first year of the eighty-eighth Olympiad, at the time when it is said Plato was born. They say that he became endowed with knowledge of the future.

Herm. *I. G. P.* 6; *Dox.* 652. Anaxagoras takes me aside and instructs me as follows :—Mind is the first principle of all things, and it is the cause and master of all, and it provides arrangement for what is disarranged, and separation for what has been mixed, and an orderly universe for what was disorderly.

APPENDIX

THE SOURCES OF THE FRAGMENTS.

THE value of a quotation depends on two things, (1) the habit of accuracy in the person who quotes it, and (2) whether it is quoted from the original or from some intermediate source. Consequently the careful student of the early Greek philosophers, who depends wholly on quotations for his direct knowledge of these thinkers, cannot neglect the consideration of these two questions. Closely connected with the accuracy of quotations is the question as to the accuracy of later writers in the opinions which they have attributed to these thinkers. These topics I propose to consider very briefly, that the student may have at least some clue to guide him in his studies.

I.

§1. We find in Plato[1] scarcely any quotations, since the literary character of the dialogue excludes anything that might seem pedantic. There are allusions to certain phrases of Herakleitos which had already become all but proverbs :—the Herakleitean sun, the harmony of opposites, 'all in motion' with the example of the river ; and the comparison 'god : man :: man : ape' is also given as the teaching of Herakleitos.[2] Similarly phrases of Anaxagoras are brought into the dialogues—'all things were together,' 'νοῦς disposed all things,'[3] but they hardly deserve the name of quotations. Other allusions to his

---

[1] Cf. the consideration of this topic by Zeller in the *Archiv f. d. Gesch. d. Philos.* Bd. V. (1892) p. 165 f.

[2] See I. Index of Sources, 'Plato.' Cf. *Krat.* 401 D, 402 A, 412 D, 439 B, 440 C, *Theaet.* 152 D.

[3] *Phaed.* 97 B, *Gorg.* 465 C, *Phaed.* 72 C, *Legg.* 595 A.

theory do not even suggest a quotation.   The only real quotations are from Parmenides,[1] and in two of these passages the
text as read by Simplicius was corrupt and unmetrical.   Simplicius quotes the same passage at one time from Plato, at another
time apparently from the original,[2] so that he enables us to
correct the form of the quotation which he (or the writer from
whom he drew) read in his MS. of Plato.   Plato's writings
betray no particular interest in any of the pre-Sokratic thinkers
except Parmenides and the Pythagorean school, nor do they
convey any hint as to the value of the work of the other early
thinkers.   So it need not surprise us that he alludes to
popular phrases and seems rather to avoid exact quotation.

§ 2. Beyond these allusions we get comparatively little light
from Plato as to the teachings of his predecessors. Xenophanes is once spoken of as the founder of the Eleatic school
and of its doctrine of unity. Parmenides is a far more interesting character to Plato, and the highest regard is expressed
for him.[3] When his position as to the unity of being and the
non-existence of not-being is discussed, there is no reason to
think that his opinions are not correctly given; but when
Parmenides is introduced as a speaker, we are not to believe
that he states the opinions of the real Parmenides any more
than the Platonic Sokrates states the positions of the real
Sokrates. Of Zeno we learn that he was skilled in the
art of dialectic.[4] Zeno's statement of the occasion and
purpose of his book[5] is of course Plato's deduction from the
book itself. The speculations of Anaxagoras are several times
mentioned.[6] The statement that he regarded the heavenly
bodies as 'λίθοι' is a welcome addition to our knowledge of
his doctrines; and Plato's criticism of Anaxagoras' use of his
fundamental principle is most important. Of Empedokles we
hear but little; the statement of his doctrine of sense-perception is a happy exception to the rule. The accuracy of Plato's
statements where they can be tested gives an added importance

[1] Parm. 52, 53 ap. *Soph.* 237 A, 258 D; 98 ap. *Theaet.* 180 E; 103–105 ap. *Soph.* 244 E; 132 ap. *Symp.* 178 B.
[2] Cf. Simpl. *Phys.* 7 r 29, 42 and 19 87, 1.
[3] *Theaet.* 183 E, *Soph.* 237 A.
[4] *Phaedr.* 261 D.   [5] *Parm* 128 B.
[6] *Apol.* 26 D, *Krat.* 400 A, 409 A, 413 A, *Legg.* 967 B.

to what he says about the Pythagoreans.[1] In a word all the data which we have from Plato are valuable, but these data are much fewer than we might expect.

§ 3. Both the citations from earlier philosophers and the statement of their opinions are much more frequent in the writings of Aristotle. Two of his references to the sayings of Herakleitos are not new to the reader of Plato ; indeed Fr. 41 *ap.* Meta. 1010a 13 is cited with direct reference to the passage where it is cited in Plato. Fr. 37, if we may accept the conjecture of Patin,[2] is a sarcastic phrase of Herakleitos which Aristotle has introduced seriously into a theory of sense-perception. Fr. 46 and 57 are summary phrases stating the fundamental positions of Herakleitos ; Fr. 51 and 55 proverbial sayings attributed to him ; Fr. 59 alone has the form of a genuine quotation.[3] It is evident that summary phrases give the philosopher's impression, just as proverbial sayings may come through the medium of popular thought, so that neither have quite the value of direct quotation.

From Xenophanes Aristotle gives two *mots*, which were attributed naturally enough to the poet-skeptic. There is no proof that Xenophanes was the original author of either of them.

From Parmenides four passages are quoted ; strangely enough three of them are passages that had been quoted by Plato. Lines 52–53 in our texts of Aristotle repeat the same error that appears in our texts of Plato ; ll. 103–105 are not so near to what seems to be the original (judged by the quotation in Simplicius) as is the Platonic version. Unless our MSS. are greatly at fault, two of the four passages were very carelessly reproduced, and we have reason to believe that they were drawn from Plato. The fourth passage, given by Aristotle and Theophrastos, has the appearance of careful quotation, though one verb has an unmetrical form in our Aristotle (where Theophrastos gives a correct form). Aristotle does not quote directly from either Zeno or Melissos.

Coming now to Empedokles, we find two extended passages which can only be regarded as genuine quotations, namely

---

[1] See *supra*, p. 133 f.; also *Phileb.* 16 c, 23 c, *Pol.* 530 D, 600 A.
[2] *Die Einheitslehre Heraklits*, p. 17 f.
[3] See I. Index of Sources, under 'Aristotle.'

ll. 287-311 and 316-325. On the other hand several phrases (ll. 208, 326, 443) give only a general idea of the language of Empedokles. Most of the quotations consist of from one to four lines preserving their metrical form, so that they deserve the name of quotations; but their accuracy is doubtful in matters of detail. This is most clearly seen by an examination of the ten cases where the same passage is quoted twice by Aristotle, namely : lines 36-39, 104-107, 146-148, 167, 208, 244, 270-271, 330-332, 333-335. In only three of these instances (38-39, 270-271, 333-335) is the quotation identical ; in the other cases there is some slight difference in the text, although commonly both versions scan correctly. An examination of the lines quoted only once in Aristotle shows very frequent deviation from the same lines as quoted by others. In two instances a line is omitted from the context (37 and 99); a case is changed, a connecting particle changed or omitted entirely, a common word is substituted for a rarer one (236-237) or an Aristotelian word for the word required by the full context (e.g. *Meta.* 1015 a 1), or finally only the substance of the line is given (e.g. lines 91, 92). These variations are so numerous as to justify the conclusion that the text furnished by Simplicius or by Sextus Empiricus deserves quite as much weight as that furnished by Aristotle, since the latter cares only for the thought and not at all for the exact language in which the thought had been clothed.

§ 4. In addition to these quotations we find in the writings of Aristotle a comparatively full statement of the opinions of the pre-Sokratic philosophers. Aristotle was interested in the work of his predecessors, since he rightly regarded his own system as the crowning result of partial views that had been set forth before. All that is valuable in their work he would give its place in his own philosophy, and their false or partial opinions he would controvert. Accordingly his ordinary method is to commence the discussion of a theme by stating the opinions of his predecessors and criticising them; and it is natural that the early thinkers who first set forth characteristic views with force and vigour should receive the fullest consideration, for indeed this position is still due to them in the history of philosophy.

Inasmuch as Aristotle set the fashion for later philosophic writers in collecting and criticising the opinions of earlier thinkers, it is important to form a clear conception of both the excellence and the defects of his method.

On a first examination of his statements of these opinions the student is struck by their fullness and comparative accuracy. Emminger [1] has collected and discussed these data, and arrives at the conclusion in every instance that Aristotle's statement is based on a use of the best materials at his command, and that it reproduces correctly the view of the philosopher in question. It is true that Emminger takes the position of an apologist. There is no doubt, however, that Aristotle was very familiar with the poems of Empedokles, the arguments of Zeno, the system of the Pythagoreans ; when he cannot verify his opinions, as in the case of Thales, they are commonly introduced with a λέγεται of caution ; and where the views of earlier thinkers seem to be distorted, it is generally due to one of several simple causes which we can estimate with considerable accuracy.

My own conclusion is that the data given by Aristotle are of the greatest value for the study of his predecessors, though they are to be used with caution.

Turning to the defects of the Aristotelian method, I would point out that there is apparently no little difference in the care with which Aristotle had studied the writings of his predecessors. His general attitude towards the Eleatic school is well known, and there is no evidence that he was really familiar with the works of Xenophanes or Parmenides or Melissos. The fact that three of the four quotations from Parmenides were at least suggested by Plato's writings should not receive undue weight, yet it is certainly suggestive. Several *sayings* are quoted from Herakleitos, and his logic is severely criticised ; we do not, however, obtain from Aristotle any conception of the real importance of Herakleitos. In fact, Aristotle does not seem at all to have understood the meaning of Herakleitos' work, whether we are to attribute it to his inability to put himself in sympathy with so different a

---

[1] Emminger, *Die vorsokratische Philosophie der Griechen nach den Berichten des Aristoteles.* Würzburg 1878.

thinker, or to his failure to study his writings. If we had only the data from Aristotle, we should really know more of the significant work of Anaximandros than of Herakleitos.

The conception of the earlier Greek thinkers which we obtain from Aristotle's writings is distorted along four lines.

1. Whether or not it was due to his failure to study certain of these thinkers, Aristotle's comparative estimate of them is not one with which we can agree. As for Herakleitos, we can say that Aristotle assigns him a very important place in early thought, even though he gives us but little clue to what his work really was. Perhaps he overestimates the work of Anaximandros and Anaximenes because he finds in them so clear an anticipation of his own thought. Certainly he does not give due weight to the Eleatic school as a whole, and in particular to Melissos. Melissos was not a great original thinker along entirely new lines, but his work in systematising Eleatic thought was very important. Perhaps because he resembled Aristotle in what he sought to do, although from so very different premisses, he is handled with the greater disdain.

2. We may get from Aristotle a slightly distorted view of the earlier thinkers because he stated their views in the terms of his own philosophic system. The commonest philosophical terms, such as ἄπειρον, ἕν, φύσις, κενόν, τὰ ὄντα, στοιχεῖον, σῶμα, οὐσία, πάθη, slightly changed their meanings as they gradually took their place in a definite philosophical terminology. ἀρχή is regularly used by Aristotle to denote the original principle of all things which the early thinkers sought, εἶδος is used in the statement of Herakleitos' position [1] and of the Pythagorean philosophy [2] : the latter a word introduced into philosophy by Plato, the former probably not used in this sense before Aristotle himself.

3. This tendency, however, is not limited to the use of philosophical terms. Aristotle states the general position of earlier thinkers from the standpoint of his own developed system. The arguments of Zeno and Melissos are thrown into logical form that he may the better criticise them. Herakleitean teachings also are stated in Aristotelian logic, and thereby lose the truth they might have had. Aristotle

---

[1] *Meta.* 1078 b 12.   [2] *Meta.* 1036 b 18.

finds his own theory of indeterminate potential matter in Anaximandros, and it is no easy task to discern what is due to Aristotle and what to Anaximandros in the Aristotelian account. Again in the case of Parmenides we may well question the statement [1] that his two principles were heat=fire =*being*, and cold=earth=*not-being*.

4. Finally Aristotle may be said to give a false impression of his predecessors when he assigns the probable causes for their opinions. Cf. *Meta.* 983 b 18, supra p. 2 ; *Phys.* 204 b 26, supra p. 10 ' in order that other things may not be blotted out by the infinite ;' *de anima* 405 a 25, supra p. 58.

The mere statement of these lines, along which Aristotle may be said slightly to distort the views of his predecessors, is sufficient to put the reader on his guard; and it is comparatively easy to make allowance for them.

§ 5. The fragments of Theophrastos that remain are sufficient only to show that he studied the work of the pre-Sokratic thinkers even more carefully than Aristotle ; to make any exact inferences as to his method of making quotations, however, is impossible on the basis of these fragments. Four of his quotations are also cited by Aristotle,[2] and it is interesting to notice that in the second and the fourth of this list Theophrastos gives a text that is probably more correct than that found in our MSS. of Aristotle. The remaining quotations found in Theophrastos [3] show a familiarity only with Empedokles. Only one of these scans correctly, and that by the change of one word, which probably was erroneously copied. Ll. 191–192 have lost some words, and ll. 423–424 are quite rewritten in prose. Apparently Theophrastos was even more careless of the form of his quotations than Aristotle, though he knows the early thinkers at first hand and can correct Aristotle's quotations. The statement of the *opinions* of these thinkers by Theophrastos will be considered later in connection with the doxographic tradition.

§ 6. From the time of Aristotle to Plutarch we know comparatively little of the works of the early philosophers, or of the habit of quoting from them. There is abundant evidence,

---

[1] *Meta.* 987 a 1.
[2] Herakl. 46 ; Parm. 146–149 ; Emped. 182–183, 219.
[3] Herakl. 84 ; Emped. 191–192, 314–315, 336–337, 423–421.

however, that they were studied ; the positions and sayings of
Herakleitos especially seem to have attracted much attention.
The works extant under the name of Hippokrates are
attributed by some writers to a period even before Aristotle.
In these works there are allusions to the positions of Empedokles and Anaxagoras, and Book I of the treatise περὶ διαιτῆς
contains much Herakleitean material.   There is scarcely one
direct quotation (cf. Fr. 60), and Bernays cannot be said to be
successful in reconstructing phrases of Herakleitos from this
source.   The book, however, is a comparatively early witness
to the work of Herakleitos, and doubly important because it
is independent of that Stoic study to which is due most of our
knowledge of him.

§ 7. More than the other schools that succeeded Aristotle
the Stoics devoted themselves to the history of philosophy,
and they were interested in Herakleitos for the same reason
that Aristotle had been interested in Anaximandros, because
they regarded him as a precursor in their own line of thought.
Herakleitean phrases occur already in the hymn of Kleanthes
to Zeus, thus showing that they had already been adopted into
the Stoic phraseology.[1]   Philodemos (vii. 81) quotes Chrysippos also as giving a quotation from Herakleitos.

It is only from later writers, however, that we can ascertain how much Herakleitos was studied in this period.   Apparently collections were made of his sayings, which soon
displaced the more complete form of his writings.   Indeed, it
is hard to prove that his book existed at all in later times,
although Sextus Empiricus quotes a passage of some
length which is considered to be the beginning of the work.
Further, the works of at least some Stoic writers must
have abounded in quotations from Herakleitos.   In the
writings of Philo there are numerous allusions to sayings of
Herakleitos ; and the Stoic context, the connection with Stoic
ethics, as well as Philo's general interest in the Stoic school,
make it probable that he finds his Herakleitos in his Stoic
sources.   But while Philo is thus an important witness to the
study of Herakleitos among the Stoics, he is of little value in
reconstructing the text of the Ephesian philosopher.   The

[1] See Index of Sources under ' Kleanthes.'

carelessness of his method of quotation is shown by the form in which he gives three lines of Empedokles (48–49, 386). To seven fragments of Herakleitos (1, 22, 24, 46, 56, 64, 70) Philo makes a mere allusion; in another series of instances (10, 67, 69, 79, 80, 82) a phrase, often a single word, of Herakleitos is worked into the context. Fr. 68 and 85 are quoted very carelessly, and 76 and 89 have assumed a form very different from that which they originally had. Commonly the name of the author (Herakleitos) is not given.

Cicero quotes Herakleitos 113 in Greek without the author's name, and translates 114 carefully; Bywater, p. x, suggests that he found the latter in somebody's *de exilio commentatio.* Returning to the Stoic school, we find in Seneca an accurate translation of Herakleitos 77 and 81, so that we are inclined to trust his version of 120. What seems to be Herakleitos 113, however, is assigned to Demokritos in an expanded form. The epistles attributed to Herakleitos belong to approximately this period, and are interesting only as additional evidence to the study of Herakleitos by Stoic philosophers Stobaeos quotes several Herakleitean phrases from Musonius. Fr. 20 and 69 are given only in substance, a phrase from 114 is worked into the context, and 75 is quoted in a later form. Fr. 75 as well as 27 and 67 is found in the second and third books of Clement's *Paedagogos,* books which draw largely from Musonius. The use of Herakleitean material by Lucian, especially in his *Vitarum auctio,* ch. xiv., is doubtless based on a Stoic source, as is indicated by the work ἐκπύρωσις. We may conclude this survey of Stoic writers with Marcus Aurelius. In his writings we find bare allusion to Herakleitos 2, 5, 20, 73, and perhaps to 97; a word or two of 34, 81, and 98 are worked into the text; while 25, 69, 90, 93, 94 are half quoted in the text. Apparently all are allusions to, or abbreviated citations of, sentences with which the reader was supposed to be familiar. It is wholly improbable that citations made in this manner were drawn from the book itself; rather they seem to point to a collection of 'sayings' of Herakleitos which must have been quite generally known. Unless such a collection is assumed, they must be regarded as phrases which were familiar to all because they were so often quoted. The former hypothesis seems to me the more tenable.

§ 8. We find in Plutarch one of the principal sources of
our fragments. Nearly fifty fragments of Herakleitos are
quoted more or less fully in his writings. Many of these
quotations consist of a single phrase containing perhaps only
a word or two of the original writer, so that they are not of
much value for purposes of reconstruction. Sometimes the
citation is given in Plutarch's own words ;[1] sometimes there
is only a careless allusion, as to Fr. 41, 43, and 120. Even
when we seem to have a real quotation, it may be expanded,
as in the case of Fr. 108 ap. *Moral.* 143 D compared with *Moral.*
644 F, or Fr. 31 ap. *Moral.* 98 D as compared with *Moral.* 957 A.
So I am inclined to regard Fr. 11, 22, and 44 as having been
expanded by Plutarch. We cannot therefore place much
reliance on the form of Plutarch's quotations from Herakleitos.
As to the source of these quotations we should notice that
two of them (Fr. 41 and 45) had been mentioned by Plato,
and others (38, 41, 43, and 105) by Aristotle ; it is probable
that Plutarch quotes these because they were familiar to the
readers of Plato and Aristotle. Fr. 20, 22, 24, 25, 34, 44, 75,
and 85 occur in Stoic writers, and Plutarch himself refers 91
to the Stoics. Fr. 45–56 are made Stoic in Plutarch by the
addition of the word κόσμου (defining ἁρμονίη) which does not
appear e.g. in Plato ; and Fr. 19, 20, 74, 75, and 87 have a
decided Stoic colouring. Thus we may suspect that about
half the quotations from Herakleitos were drawn from Stoic
sources. On the other hand 78 with its context seems to be
based on a considerable passage of Herakleitos, and 11, 12,
and 127 have the appearance of careful quotation.

Plutarch's method in handling quotations from philosophers who wrote in poetry is more satisfactory. It is only
rarely that the thought is put in his own words,[2] or that the
quotation consists of less than a full line. Sometimes lines
are grouped which do not belong together, as ap. *Moral.* 607 C
and 618 B. In some instances the text itself seems to be at
fault.[3] In general, however, the poetic form protected such
quotations from change, and the poetic form was naturally

---

[1] E.g. 78 ap. *Moral.* 106 E; 95 ap. 166 C.
[2] E.g. Emped. 272 ap. *Moral.* 917 C; 369 ap. *Moral.* 996 B.
[3] Emped. 232 ap. *Moral.* 745 C; 154–155 ap. *Moral.* 925 B;
Parmen. 29–30 ap. *Moral.* 1114 D.

retained in quotations for the purpose of embellishment. I may add that Plutarch rarely neglects to give the name of the author from whom he quotes. As to the source of these poetic quotations, we cannot doubt that Plutarch sometimes quotes Empedokles from the original. A literary man could hardly fail to be acquainted with his poems, and it is by no means likely that the quotations *Moral.* 607 c, 1111 F, 1113 are taken from an intermediate source. Five of the quotations from Parmenides, on the other hand, were not new to the readers of Plato and Aristotle, and the two remaining ones, together with some of the lines from Empedokles, as I have tried to show elsewhere,[1] were probably drawn from a collection of passages on the moon. There is no evidence that Plutarch knew Parmenides at first hand. Many passages of Empedokles also had become common property in the time of Plutarch, and in some instances Plutarch no doubt found collections of quotations suitable for his purpose, so that we cannot attribute all the single lines quoted from Empedokles to Plutarch's own study of his poems.

§ 9. Judged by the Herakleitos fragments which they yield, the works of Clement and Hippolytos are hardly second in importance to Plutarch for the student of early Greek philosophy. In the *Protreptikos* of Clement there is an interesting series of passages from Herakleitos on popular worship; in the *Paedagogos* and the first and fourth books of the *Stromata* there are scattered quotations most of which bear clear marks of their secondary origin; book II contains several quotations from the introduction to Herakleitos' works; while the third and fifth books of the *Stromata* contain a much larger collection of passages from Herakleitos, Xenophanes, Parmenides, and Empedokles. A casual glance at the whole series of quotations shows that Clement's method was by no means uniform, and that he was often contented with a secondary source for his quotations, not taking the trouble to look them up in the original. In the first book of the *Stromata* the first quotation from Herakleitos is a proverb familiar in Greek literature, the second passage a bare allusion to a sentence quoted by Plutarch, and the two remaining ones refer to two quotations also

---

[1] *Transactions of American Philol. Assoc.* XXVIII. pp. 82-83.

given by Diogenes.   That Clement used the βίοι which were
the basis of the work of Diogenes Laertios is probable from
his quotation of Parmenides 28–30 and Empedokles 26–28,
383–384.   It is also highly probable that Clement found much
of his material in Stoic sources.   It is generally agreed that in
Paedagogos ii. and iii. he freely used Musonius.   Hera. 122 *ap.*
Clement 188 ' what men do not expect at death ' is interpreted
by Clement as referring to Stoic fire, and Clement 649 (Hera.
123) also attributes to Herakleitos and the Stoics an idea be-
longing to the latter only.   Hera. 77 is alluded to by Seneca as
familiar to his Stoic readers, and other fragments cited by
Clement were apparently found by Philo in his Stoic sources.
Hera. 69 *ap.* Clement 718 looks like another form of Hera. 19
which Plutarch quotes from a Stoic source, and perhaps we may
regard 20 also as from the Stoic source from which Plutarch
drew.   Hera. 31 *ap.* Clement 87 includes an added phrase (as to
the stars) which appears also in *one* of the two passages in Plutarch where it is quoted.   One of the lines of Parmenides and six
of the single lines of Empedokles given by Clement are also
found in Plutarch.   Consequently I regard it as not improbable that Clement drew quotations from Plutarch, and as all
but certain that he drew from the Stoic sources of Plutarch.
The wrong interpretation of Hera. 116 (*ap.* Clement 699), 122
(*ap.* 18), 67 (*ap.* 251), 79 (*ap.* 111), and perhaps 27 (*ap.* 229)
is additional proof that Clement was entirely unfamiliar with
the context in which these passages originally stood, and
therefore probably did not draw from the original.   While we
are quite unable to trust Clement's interpretation of his quotations, it should be remarked that he is exceedingly careful to give
the correct form (e.g. Hera. 101 *ap.* Clement 586 as compared
with the same fragment in Hippolytos ; in this quotation he
gives the dialect forms with his usual fidelity).

It remains to consider several series of passages, and to ask
whether these were quoted at first hand.   In the *Protreptikos*
we find Herakleitos fragments 122, 124, 125 together, and a
little farther on 126–127 (cf. 122 *ap.* Clement 630, and 123
ap. 649) on the topic of popular worship.   These are clearly
quoted from a connected passage, and not phrases that have
been passed on as proverbs.   Moreover 124–127 are somewhat

closely connected with each other (perhaps 122 belongs with them). It is evident that Clement (or possibly the immediate source of Clement) drew them from a somewhat extended passage in the original. Another series of passages from Herakleitos and Empedokles (*ap.* Clement 516 and 520) are quoted as illustrating the misery of human life. They occur together in a long series of quotations on this topic, and at least one line, Empedokles 404, is not quite pertinent; its lack of fitness in this connection may mean that Clement is adapting a collection of passages made (wholly or in part) by another hand for a slightly different purpose. Again, a considerable number of fragments, especially in books ii. and v. of the *Stromata*, are pithy proverbial statements of the fundamental attitude of Herakleitos toward other men (cf. Herakl. 5–8, 104, 2–3, 49, 111b with its addition from Demosthenes *de corona* p. 324). These are all marked by their proverbial form, and are many of them quoted by other writers. It is most natural to think that they were drawn from a collection of Herakleitean sayings such as is presupposed by the allusions of Marcus Aurelius and perhaps by the parody of Lucian.

As to the poetic citations in the fifth book of the *Stromata* it seems to me wholly likely that the verses of Xenophanes, and Parmenides 133–139, are quoted from the original poems. Empedokles lines 74 and 165 are repeated as proverbs; lines 33, 74, 104 (quoted with Herakleitos 68) are often-quoted verses on the favourite topic of the elements; lines 342–343 are quoted with Herakleitos 49, lines 16–17 with Parmenides 28–30 and Herakleitos 111, and it is quite probable that Clement found the topical groups of quotations ready to his hand. Empedokles 26 f., 55 f., 81, 130 f., are all *introductory* lines, and these too may have been collected by some earlier writer. We may conclude, then, that many of the citations in Clement were not taken from the original works, but that some may have been; the most important fact is that Clement transcribes his quotations with great faithfulness.

§ 10. The citations given in the works of Sextus Empiricus are important because they are in a measure independent of the Stoic line of tradition; we may even say with confidence that some of them are cited from the original works. For

Herakleitos there is only one important series of fragments, namely that found in *adv. Math.* vii. §§ 126-134. Fragments 52 and 54 of Herakleitos are indeed mentioned in a series of epigrams with no name attached to them (*Pyrrh.* i. 55), and a little later (*Pyrrh.* iii. 115 and 230) there is an allusion to the well-known Fr. 42 and a statement of Herakleitos' opinion as to life and death (cf. Fr. 78). The discussion *adv. Math.* vii. §§ 126-134 is a statement of the doctrine of sense-perception which Sextus attributes to Herakleitos. Diels has given good reasons (*Dox.* 209-211) for believing that this passage is based on Aenesidemus, a skeptic philosopher with strong Herakleitean leanings of the first century B.C. In it are contained the full form of Fr. 2 (cited in part by other writers) and Fr. 4 and 92 (with comment based on a longer passage); there is also a phrase reminding the reader of Fr. 77 in § 130. This is the fullest extant material for reconstructing the introduction to Herakleitos' book, and was evidently based on the text of Herakleitos. While it is cited quite accurately, it is probable that Sextus took the citation from the same source as the rest of the discussion; still, when we remember Sextus' fondness for citing procemiums, we cannot say definitely that he did not take it himself from the work of Herakleitos.

Xenophanes is cited in passages varying in length from one to four lines. Most of these passages are not known from other writers or known only from late Homeric commentators. Where the same passage is cited twice, there is no variation except in the arrangement of the lines. Fr. vii. is given in part twice—once lines 3-4, and again lines 1, 2, and 4 (see *supra* p. 66).—From Parmenides (in addition to the line 132 given by Plato and Aristotle) Sextus gives the procemium of his work. Although earlier editors have extensively rearranged this passage, I believe it is substantially correct in Sextus, and I see no reason to doubt that it was taken from the work itself. The citation of other lines before 53 by Plato and by Simplicius confirms the suspicion, however, that Sextus had omitted something at this point. From Empedokles' main philosophical work Sextus gives a portion of the procemium (lines 2-23), as well as four lines from the introduction to the καθάρματα. It is reasonable to believe that

these lines with 428-435 were cited from the original poem ;
the only errors are copyists' blunders. Sextus also cites
Empedokles 33-35 and 78-80. These are much copied lines,
and the form in Sextus includes some obvious errors, e.g. ἀήρ
for αἰθήρ (l. 78) and φιλία for φιλότης (l. 80), (cf. ἧττον l. 79)—
errors which very likely were found in the source from which
Sextus drew the lines.[1] We may conclude that Sextus cited
sometimes from the original, sometimes at second hand ; and
that his citations reproduce his source accurately except that
he sometimes omits verses from their connection.

§ 11. The quotations in the *Refutatio omnium hæresium*,
which is now attributed to Hippolytos, include some that are
very accurate and others of which the text is hopeless, an
anomaly that is very difficult to explain. In the fifth book
one phrase reminds the reader of Herakleitos 71, while Herakleitos 68a is quoted with the author's name, and 101 without
it. In the sixth book there is an allusion to two forms of
fire (Hera. 21), and Herakleitos 29 combined with 95 is quoted
under the name of Pythagoras. Most of the quotations from
Herakleitos, however, are closely grouped in ix. ch. 9-10. Some
of these are phrases familiar in earlier writers (e.g. Hera. 3, 17,
and 69) ; 2, 44, 45, and 35 are passages of some length which
Hippolytos gives in accurate form ; 24 is accompanied by a
Stoic explanation, and probably the phraseology of 28 and 36
is Stoic ; in most of the citations in this group the text is very
carefully given, even to the connecting particles, but besides
the fragments in Stoic form just mentioned, the text of 123 is
corrupted beyond possibility of restoration, and 58 is almost as
bad. These fragments are consistently interpreted as antici-
pating the views of a Christian sect, and it is possible that the
κρινέει of 26 is due to this influence rather than to the Stoics.
Bywater (p. ix) suggests that Hippolytos drew his quotations
directly from the work of Herakleitos ; but it is not easy to
regard the difference in accuracy as wholly a difference in the
accuracy of one man's copying.

The quotations from Empedokles, as indeed from other
poets, show that Hippolytos was often very careless. The

[1] Simplicius copies the same error in line 78, probably finding it in
his copy of Empedokles.

omission of a word (e.g. lines 334, 335 *ap.* Hipp. 165, l. 34 *ap.*
246) is too common to be attributed wholly to the carelessness
of copyists, nor would the rest of the text of Hippolytos
justify this supposition.   Lines 33-35 are quoted twice (p. 246
and p. 313), and the last line differs in the two cases;
such a change as from τέγγει to σπόνδε (p. 313) is not one
that a copyist would be very likely to make.   On the other
hand, it is hardly conceivable that the errors in ll. 110 f. *ap.*
p. 247, 222 f. *ap.* p. 251, 338 f. *ap.* p. 254 existed in any text
that Hippolytos copied.   The only possible explanation for
this phenomenon is that sometimes Hippolytos quoted from
memory, paying no attention either to metre or to phraseology,
and sometimes (as in his quotations from Herakleitos generally) from either the original or a source that was very close
to the original.   Since so many of the Empedoklean passages
are not cited by any other writer, we may suppose that
Hippolytos drew them from the original.

§ 12. Of the quotations in Diogenes Laertios from Herakleitos, Bywater says (p. x) : ' Laertium . . . libro pervetusto
usum esse nemo jam adfirmaverit.'   We do find four sentences
of some length from Herakleitos, the genuineness of which is
not questioned (Fr. 16, 17, 112, 114) ; it is noticeable that
these fragments, together with the allusions to Fr. 33 and
119, all refer to particular men, and so possessed a special
interest for the biographical writers, who were Diogenes' main
source.   Three other fragments of more than two words are
given by Diogenes (71, 100, and 103), and these are not
found in any other Greek writer.   The remaining fragments
consist of only one or two words (22, 48, 62, 69, 80, 113), or
are now regarded as spurious (131, 132),   There is no reason
to think that the fragments of Herakleitos contained in this
work are not copied with reasonable accuracy ; on the other
hand, we may assume from what we know of Diogenes'
method of work that they were not drawn directly from the
writings of Herakleitos.

Diogenes quotes Xenophanes xiv. 1-2, and Empedokles
l. 6, in a series of passages on skepticism, Xen. xviii. in a
series on Pythagoreanism ; Fr. xxiv., the only one not found
elsewhere, relates to the life of Xenophanes. From Parmenides

are quoted lines 28-30 and 54-56. The last passage does not really illustrate the point for which it is quoted (the senses inexact), and our text of Diogenes contains two blunders from some copyist. Portions of the proœmium of Empedokles' main work on philosophy (1, 24-32, *ap.* viii. 60 and 59) are mentioned in connection with the name of Satyros. It is pretty clear (*ap.* viii. 62) that a ' Herakleitos ' is the source from which lines 352-363 are taken ; if so, the statement viii. 54 that this is the beginning of the καθάρματα comes from the same writer. Lines 384-385 are quoted much in the form in which they appear in Athenaeos, though with one copyist's error ; from the same work of Empedokles we have also lines 355, 415, 417 in passages where Diogenes had just mentioned Timaeos. The familiar lines 35 and 67-68 are found here— line 35 in a very confused form. In general these lines from poetic writers show numerous small errors, which may be due to the state of our manuscripts. Both the fragments from Herakleitos and those in poetic form are of great value, though we are in the dark as to their immediate source.

§ 13. The works of neo-Platonic writers frequently mention the earlier philosophers, but yield few fragments of value. Plotinos refers to ten fragments of Herakleitos. Four of these (80, 82, 83, 85) have the form of quotations, and in two instances the name of Herakleitos is mentioned ; they are, however, very short, and give no clue to their source. Sometimes Plotinos plays on words that were evidently known as Herakleitean, e.g. Fr. (47 ?), 54, 69, 80 ; or again an Herakleitean idea is stated in his own words, Fr. 32, 83, 99, 130. The manner in which these quotations and allusions are made shows that the phrases were very familiar, either in earlier writers or possibly in some collection of sayings. Line 81 b of Parmenides is quoted with no name ; line 40 b is quoted with the author's name, and is followed by an account of the context which shows that it was drawn from a passage of some length. From Empedokles we find only two phrases, taken from lines 381 and 382, that are worked into the text of Plotinos.

Porphyry quotes from Herakleitos only familiar phrases, and these in the briefest form (74 ap. *de antr. nym.* xi. and

72 ap. *de antr. nym.* x.). The phrases were so familiar that
it was only necessary to suggest the idea (e.g. 56 ap. *de antr.
nym.* xxix.) without mentioning the name of the philosopher.
Parmenides is not so well known ; Greeks and Egyptians, we
read, say that he mentioned the two gates in his *Physika* (*de
antr. nym.* xxiii.). Only the καθάρματα of Empedokles is quoted,
but here Porphyry knows the subjects treated in the work (*de
abst.* II. xxi.), and sometimes the full context of the passage
he quotes (e.g. *de antr. nym.* viii.).   In the case of lines
415–420 we are not sure that Porphyry was right in applying
the verses to Parmenides ; still, the quotations would seem
to be taken directly from the καθάρματα and copied with fair
accuracy.

Iamblichos draws a few quotations from his predecessors
in the neo-Platonic school (Empedokles, lines 415–420 from
Porphyry ; and Herakleitos, Fr. 69, 82, 83 from Plotinos, if
Stobaeos is correct in attributing this group of fragments to
Iamblichos).   Most of the allusions to fragments of Herakleitos, however, cannot be traced to this source.   The combination of Herakleitos 29 and 95, which Hippolytos had
attributed to Pythagoras, Iamblichos also attributes to the
same thinker ; his language, however, differs in detail from
that used by Hippolytos.   Two words of Herakleitos 114
(which had been cited by the Stoics and by Diogenes) are
given, with the additional statement that Herakleitos gave
laws to the Ephesians.   Bywater's number 128 is an allusion
probably including a single word from Herakleitos, as does
129 also.   Two words each from Fr. 11 and 12 (both found
in Plutarch) are worked into the text of Iamblichos—in the
former instance with the name of Herakleitos.   Finally 105,
which also appears in Plutarch, is given here in more accurate
form.   These references to Herakleitos, like those of the
earlier neo-Platonists, are all made to fragments assumed to
be familiar because they had been quoted often by earlier
writers.

The writings of his predecessors in this same school are
frequently mentioned by Proklos, but his quotations from pre-
Sokratic thinkers seem not to be derived from them.   In the
commentary on Parmenides several scattered lines are quoted

from the works of the original Parmenides. The quotations
are very brief; they include in all only parts of six or seven
lines, and sometimes these are cited more than once. It is
therefore quite unlikely that Proklos drew them directly
from the poem of Parmenides. In his commentary on the
Timaeos Proklos uses the form of quotation from Herakleitos
six times (alluding to Fr. 16, 32, 44, 68, 79, 80), but only 32
and 44 can be called quotations, while even these are very
brief. On p. 106 E we find part of what Diogenes gives in
connection with Fragment 80, but no part of 80 itself; 79 was
cited by the early Christian writers, and Proklos interpreted
it in the same manner that they had done; 68 also had been
paraphrased in the source from which Proklos drew it. So
far as Herakleitos is concerned, we see how far from their
origin the tradition of the fragments had gone, but we get no
new light on their original form.

A few lines of Parmenides we know only from Proklos.
Verses 29–30 had been given by Diogenes and Clement, but
some of the verses 33–40 are new. In these instances, as is
usually the case with the quotations in Proklos, the text of
the quotations is in a condition almost hopeless. Indeed, at
p. 160 D a line and a half of Parmenides are filled out with
half a line from Empedokles under the name of the former
writer. From Empedokles only single lines (once two lines
together) are given, and they aid but little in the reconstruction of the text. Proklos, like Plutarch, is very careful to
cite the name of his authorities; but the text of the quotations is so carelessly reproduced that they are of little value.

§ 14. The commentators on Aristotle early began to illustrate his statements about earlier thinkers by passages copied
from their works. Alexander of Aphrodisias and Joh.
Philoponos seldom add fragments not contained in the works
of Aristotle himself; but Simplicius copies long extracts, so
that, except for Herakleitos, his commentaries are the most
important source for our knowledge of the writings of the
pre-Sokratic philosophers. There can be no doubt that most
of these quotations—at least in his commentary on the
Physics of Aristotle—were drawn from the original works.
The most careful scrutiny of the passages from Zeno, Melissos,

and Anaxagoras fails to reveal any reason for questioning their character as genuine quotations, except in the case of some of the fragments of Melissos. Pabst (and independently Burnet) has shown that the so-called Fragments 1–5 of Melissos, though given in the form of quotations, are in reality an epitome covering more briefly the same ground that is covered by the following fragments, and adding almost nothing to our knowledge of Melissos. It is wholly unlikely that Simplicius made this epitome himself, for that would be at variance with his ordinary method of work, and with his custom later in dealing with Melissos. So we are driven to assume either that he drew them from some epitome of Melissos to which he had access, or, what seems to me more probable, that he copied them from an earlier commentator, whose habit it was to condense his quotations rather than to copy them at full length. If now we examine the quotations in Simplicius' commentary on the *de caelo* (Melissos Fr. 17 and numerous lines from Parmenides and Empedokles), it is noticeable that a considerable number of them occur also in the scholia to Aristotle. It is possible that as they appear in our scholia they all come from Simplicius. One long quotation (Melissos Fr. 17) is, however, taken by Eusebios from Aristokles, a much earlier commentator on Aristotle. This fact of course confirms the belief that earlier commentators on Aristotle accessible to Simplicius already contained quotations from the philosophers in question;[1] and the presence in our scholia of so many fragments quoted by Simplicius on the *de caelo* would at least suggest an investigation of the question whether our scholia drew them from an earlier source than Simplicius—in other words, whether Simplicius did not in all probability take them from the commentaries of his predecessors. So when we find Parmenides line 78 *ap.* Simplicius, *Physica* 29, 18 in the form that Plato had quoted it,[2] when we find line 60 *ap.* 120, 23 quoted from an indirect source (cf. p. 145, 4, where it is quoted in context), we may conclude that Simplicius took

---

[1] Diels, *Doxographi Graeci*, p. 112, shows that Simplicius used the work of Alexander of Aphrodisias.

[2] Cf. the correct form Simp. *Phys.* 159, 15; it is not unlikely that lines 52, 53 *ap.* 135, 21, and 122 *ap.* 39, 18 were also taken from Plato.

those quotations from Parmenides at second hand, and not improbably from earlier commentators on Aristotle. The quotations from Herakleitos are all of them in a late form, and show that Simplicius was not familiar with any work under the name of Herakleitos.[1] Nor did Simplicius know Xenophanes at first hand. The two quotations from his poem occur in the discussion of a passage from Theophrastos, and are probably taken from him. The quotations show, however, that Simplicius knew at first hand the works of Zeno, Melissos, Anaxagoras, Parmenides, and Empedokles, and it remains to examine the numerous quotations from the last two thinkers in order to form some idea as to the probable accuracy of Simplicius' method of quotation.

Stein in his attempt to restore the text of Parmenides finds numerous misarrangements of the lines and breaks where one or more lines have dropped out. Certainly there is evidence that Simplicius omitted four or more lines between 89 and 94, nor does he indicate the break in any way. Several times a phrase of his own is inserted in the middle of a line (e.g. *Phys.* 39, 28 ; 143, 22), and once a line is filled out metrically, according to our manuscripts, by a phrase which is generally regarded as a comment from Simplicius (*Phys.* 145, 16). The text itself of these fragments is often very dubious in our manuscripts (e.g. lines 96, 98, 100), but Simplicius may not be responsible for this. In our manuscripts also we read sometimes ωὑτός, sometimes αὑτός, and when either ὤν or ἐών (ὄντα or ἐόντα) is metrically possible, the shorter is usual ; here again we cannot with any confidence hold that Simplicius is responsible.

The quotations from Empedokles shed more light on the method of Simplicius. Not infrequently lines are omitted in sequence, as two lines between 68 and 70 (*Phys.* 158, 1 f.), and again in the same quotation one line between 90 and 92, and two lines between 93 and 94. According to Bergk the line between 174 and 176 should be omitted (it is identical with 184) ; and Schneidewin inserts here line 175 (of Stein)

---

[1] Four out of the six quotations from Herakleitos are given either in Plato or Aristotle, or both ; Frag. 20 comes directly or indirectly from a Stoic source.

from Stobaeos; the passage occurs twice in the same form in
Simplicius, however (and once in the scholia to Aristotle), so
that this error probably existed in the text from which Simplicius copied. On p. 33, 19 of the *Physica* two passages from
different parts of the poem of Empedokles are joined without
break, and the end of line 95 (Stein 115) is modified to
make the connection between the two passages. In two
instances I believe that Simplicius (or some copyist) has
repeated in a quotation some lines from the last previous
quotation. On p. 159 of the *Physica* the end of the first
quotation is repeated as the end of the second, except that a
summary phrase is substituted for the last half-line; again
on p. 160 (lines 6-8) we find three lines which had occurred
in the last previous quotation, and which are inserted here
with the change of a connecting word. Sometimes we can
point out an error that probably existed in the text from which
Simplicius copied, as in the case of line 175 mentioned above.
Thus ἐδεῖτο in line 99, κῆρυξ in 93, βεβλάστηκε at 105, and
probably ἤερος in 78 appear in repetitions of the same
quotation at different points, and so may be assigned to the
source of Simplicius. In other instances we may say that
Simplicius copied carelessly, as in the case of line 89, which
is corrected in the prose paraphrase, and possibly 138, where
the curious text in the *Physica* may be corrected from the *de
caelo*. The state of our manuscripts of Simplicius, however, is
probably responsible for most of the numerous errors in the
forms of words.

From this survey of the sources I have omitted the names
of many writers who furnish some little addition to our knowledge of the fragments, for their method of quotation is
relatively unimportant, nor have I thought it necessary to
consider later writers who throw light only on the later
history of the fragments. Accordingly I have not spoken of
Eusebios, who repeats quotations from Plutarch and from
Clement, or of Theodoret, who drew from Clement, or of
Julian, who drew from Plutarch. Again, I have not spoken
of Stobaeos, or Eustathios, or the scholia generally, as
sources, for we are not at present able to determine the
line of tradition for these fragments. I have, however,

examined the more important sources of fragments, in order
that the student may be able to estimate the relative value
of the sources, both as to text and as to directness of trans-
mission, in his own study of them.

II.

§ 15. Turning now to the doxographic tradition, we may
state the problem as follows :—In the *Placita philosophorum*
attributed to Plutarch, in the *Eclogae physicae* of Stobaeos, in
fragments from Arius Didymos, in Hippolytos, and in other
writers, we find copious statements as to the *opinions* of the
early philosophers. These opinions shed light on many points
not mentioned in the fragments of their writings now remaining, and so they have great importance for the student of their
systems. At the same time they are often confused and unre-
liable. The problem is to determine the relation of these
writers to each other, as well as to the source of the whole
series, in order that we may estimate their relative value.
This work has been most successfully accomplished in the
Prolegomena to Diels' *Doxographi Graeci*, a work that is
absolutely indispensable to the student of this subject. There
is no occasion to reopen here a question that Diels has so successfully solved, but I propose to state briefly a few of the
conclusions which the reader will find substantiated in the work
of Diels.

The most obvious fact to one who takes up the study of
the doxographic writers is that the *Placita* attributed to Plutarch, and the *Eclogae physicae*, which was originally a part of
the *Florilegium* of Stobaeos, are intimately related ; and when
the two are printed side by side, as the reader finds them in
the text of Diels, the likeness of the two is most striking. At
the same time the two books are not identical, and each gives
much material that the other omits. Stobaeos cannot have
copied from the work attributed to Plutarch, for even in passages that occur in the *Placita* Stobaeos not infrequently
gives the fuller form ; nor can the writer of the *Placita* have
copied from Stobaeos, for his work can be traced back nearly
three centuries before the time of Stobaeos. It was used by

Athenagoras in his defence of the Christians 177 A.D. (*Dox.* p. 4) ; it was mentioned by Theodoret (*Dox.* p. 47) ; and important corrections of the text are made by Diels on the authority of Eusebios, Cyril, and the pseudo-Galen, all of whom had used it.   Theodoret (*Therap.* IV. 31, *Dox.* 47) mentions the epitome by Plutarch, but only after he has mentioned the *Placita* of Aetios, Ἀετίου τὴν περὶ ἀρεσκόντων συναγωγήν, and it is this work of Aetios which Diels vindicates as the source both of Plutarch and of Stobaeos, while Theodoret also quotes from it occasionally.   A careful study of these three writers and their methods enables Diels to reconstruct a large part of the work of Aetios ; and it is the sections of this work bearing on the earlier philosophers which I have translated (see III. English Index under 'Aetios').   Of Aetios himself almost nothing is known ; the work assigned to him must have been written between the age of Augustus and the age of the Antonines (*Dox.* 100).   It was in four books, divided into chapters by topics, and in each chapter the opinions of the philosophers were given not by schools but by affinity of their opinions.

§ 16. Fortunately we are in a position to say what was the beginning of that style of composition of which the work of Aetios is an example.   Aristotle, as we have seen, paid considerable attention to the earlier thinkers and often stated their opinions as the introduction to his own position.   A list of the works of his pupil and successor Theophrastos is given by Diogenes Laertios (v. 46, 48), and in the list there is mentioned a book in eighteen chapters περὶ τῶν φυσικῶν, and a little later another book in sixteen chapters of φυσικῶν δόξων.   We have a long fragment *de sensibus* which Diels has edited in connection with the later doxographists (*Dox.* pp. 499 f.), and from this we can learn something of his method. In this fragment he discusses the opinions of his predecessors as to sense-perception, grouping them by affinity, and not chronologically or by schools.   The work is done conscientiously, and is based on a study of the original writings of the thinkers he treats (*v. supra*, pp. 230 f.).   Other fragments from the first book have been pointed out by Brandis and Usener (*Analecta Theophrastea*) in Simplicius' Commentary on

Aristotle's *Physics*; while we have also several pages preserved in Philo *de incorrupt. mundi*. In the first book, to judge from the fragments in Simplicius, Theophrastos arranged the earlier thinkers by schools and accompanied his statements with brief biographical notices (e.g. pp. 11, 257 *supra*). Such a work was of the greatest convenience to later writers, and especially to the compilers who were so numerous in the age of the decadence. In fact the whole doxographic tradition may be traced back to this work of Theophrastos.

In the last centuries of the pre-Christian era there was an unusual interest in the biographies of famous men. Apocryphal anecdotes were gathered from popular gossip, deduced from the works of these writers, or made up with no foundation at all. In the second century several writers of the peripatetic school wrote the lives of the philosophers after this fashion. We hear of βίοι by Hermippos and by Satyros, and of the διαδοχαὶ τῶν φιλοσόφων of Satyros; and we are told that Herakleides of Lembos worked over what his immediate predecessors had collected. Phanias of Eresos is one of the 'authorities' of this school. Much of this material has come down to us in the work of Diogenes Laertios.

On the book of Theophrastos, and on the 'Lives' or the 'Successions of the philosophers,' as they were often called, the later doxographic writers based their work. Even in Diogenes Laertios there is material from both sources, and we can define some fragments almost in Theophrastos' own words. In the *Philosophumena* of Hippolytos the two sources are pretty clearly distinguished: chapters 1–4 and 10 (on Thales, Pythagoras, Empedokles, Herakleitos and Parmenides, see III. English Index under 'Hippolytos') are made up of personal anecdotes such as writers of the lives were eager to collect and to repeat; chapters 6–8 and 11 (on Anaximandros, Anaximenes, Anaxagoras, and Xenophanes) come indirectly from the work of Theophrastos. The *Stromateis* attributed by Eusebios to Plutarch (see III. English Index under 'Plutarch,' and *Dox.* pp. 579 f.) are like the last-mentioned chapters of Hippolytos, though the language is often more careless.

A comparison of Aetios with Hippolytos, the *Stromateis*, and the doxographic material in Cicero and Censorinus (from

Varro) makes it clear that the *Placita* of Aetios are not based directly on the work of Theophrastos. Indeed (*Dox.* p. 100, and pp. 178 f.) it is evident from an examination of the work of Aetios by itself that much of his material is drawn from Stoic and Epicurean sources. As the main source for what remains after Stoic and Epicurean passages have been cut out, Diels postulates an earlier *Placita* (*Vetusta placita*, pp. 215 f.). He finds traces of this in the work of Varro as used by Censorinus, in Cicero's *Tusculan Disputations*, and in some later writers.

§ 17. Résumé. The doxographic tradition starts with the work of Theophrastos on the opinions of his predecessors. On this work is based immediately the *Vetusta placita*; on the *Vetusta placita* is based the *Placita* of Aetios, and there are traces of its use by later writers; the *Placita* of Aetios may be partially reconstructed from Plutarch's *Placita* and Stobaeos' *Eclogae*. Again, using Theophrastos and gathering anecdotes from every side, writers of the second century B.C. wrote the lives of the philosophers. A line of tradition probably independent of the *Placita* just considered appears in the work of Hippolytos, who used now the work of Theophrastos, now the lives; in Diogenes Laertios, where material from most various sources is indiscriminately mixed; and in the *Stromateis* attributed to Plutarch by Eusebios, which are related to the better material of Hippolytos. Simplicius used Theophrastos directly. Finally in the fragments of Philodemos and the related material in Cicero's *Lucullus* and *De natura deorum* we find traces of a use of Theophrastos either by Philodemos himself, or in a common source of both Cicero and Philodemos—probably a Stoic epitome of Theophrastos made by the Phaedros whom Cicero mentions.

INDEXES

I. INDEX OF SOURCES

II. *GREEK INDEX*

Parmenides (P.) and Empedokles (E.) are referred to by lines ; Anaximandros (Ad.), Herakleitos (H.), Xenophanes (X.), Zeno (Z.), Melissos (M.), and Anaxagoras (A.), by the number of the fragment in which the word occurs. Occasional references to pages are indicated by p.

III. ENGLISH INDEX

The references are to pages ; a star * indicates the important reference in a series.